THE ULTIMATE CLASSIC CAR BOOK

THE ULTIMATE CLASSIC CAR BOOK

Quentin Willson
with David Selby

A DORLING KINDERSLEY BOOK

PROJECT EDITOR
PHIL HUNT

ART EDITOR
KEVIN RYAN

US EDITOR
JOHN HEILIG

PHOTOGRAPHY
ANDY CRAWFORD, MATTHEW WARD

DESIGNERS
WENDY BARTLET, LUISE ROBERTS

MANAGING EDITOR
KRYSTYNA MAYER

MANAGING ART EDITOR
DEREK COOMBES

DTP DESIGNER
CRESSIDA JOYCE

PRODUCTION CONTROLLER
ADRIAN GATHERCOLE

•

First American Edition, 1995
First American paperback edition, 2006

06 07 08 09 9 8 7 6 5 4 3 2 1

Published in the United States by
DK Publishing, Inc.
375 Hudson Street
New York, New York 10014

First published in Great Britain in 1995
by Dorling Kindersley Limited,
A Penguin Company
80 Strand, London, WC2R ORL

Library of Congress Cataloguing-in-Publication Data

Willson, Quentin.
    The ultimate classic car book / by Quentin Willson. – 1st American ed.
      p. cm.
    Includes index.
    ISBN 0-7566-1885-1
    1. Automobiles – Pictorial works. 2. Antique and classic cars –
Collectors and collecting. I. Title.
TL7.A1W48 1995
629.222'022'2–dc20
                                                      95–11903
                                                      CIP

Color reproduced by Colourscan, Singapore
Printed and bound by L.Rex Printing Company Limited, China

•

NOTE ON SPECIFICATION BOXES
Every effort has been made to ensure that the information
supplied in the specification boxes is accurate. As a rule,
engine capacity is measured in cubic inches (cid) for American cars and
cubic centimeters (cc) for all other cars. Power output is expressed as horsepower
(hp) for American cars and brake horsepower (bhp) for all other cars.
A.F.C. is an abbreviation for average fuel consumption.

CONTENTS

AUTHOR'S FOREWORD 7

INTRODUCTION

WHY CLASSIC? 8
THE CLASSIC CAR PHENOMENON 10
HOW TO BUY A CLASSIC CAR 16

THE CLASSIC CAR GALLERY

Author's Foreword

BETWEEN THESE COVERS you'll find ninety of what are loosely termed classic cars – a catholic collection of some of the most fascinating motoring confections spanning four decades. There's no particular order or hierarchy, no attempt at a definitive roll of honor. This is a selection of curious cars, products of another age that remind us of the way we were. The biggest problem I've had in compiling this book is deciding which cars should go in and which shouldn't. Not an easy job. Only a fool would argue that a Facel Vega HK500 is a better car than an Mk II Jaguar. It isn't. But the Facel, with its gloriously eccentric Gallic styling, is the more interesting of the two. And that's why it's here and the Jag isn't. Degas once said that people should be full of those charming little idiosyncrasies without which there is no life. I think it's the same with cars. We prefer them to be interesting, diverting, beguiling even. Classic cars didn't exist before we invented them – a knee-jerk reaction to all that soulless modern metal that looks like it's been carved from a solid block of tungsten. In today's car, efficiency has supplanted aesthetics and technology has displaced charm. Our affair with old cars is purely emotional, fiercely partisan, terminally subjective, and completely without logic or order. And that's why nobody can define exactly what a classic car is. We've been trying for twenty years and still no one has even come close. The best I can do is to say that a classic car makes you smile when you look at it, grin when you drive it, and feel warm approval for the era it evokes. Old cars are awfully good fun.

QUENTIN WILLSON

Why Classic ?

CLASSIC CARS are simply nostalgia triggers. They're a reminder of how we used to be. Of all the material symbols in society that define our worth and position, the automobile is the most powerful. It's tangible, mobile, and a currency everybody understands. Many of us have an uneasiness with modernity that makes us retrospective creatures. We're drawn back to those decades of change and excitement – hence our love affair with all things of the '50s and '60s. From tall, round-shouldered Frigidaires, neon diner signs, and flamboyant Wurlitzer jukeboxes to sunglasses, clothes, and music, they all appeal to us as talismans of what we remember as golden years.

VEHICLES FOR NOSTALGIA
Classic cars like this AC Ace are not simply quaint mechanical objects, but social monuments that remind us of the way we were.

surely a need to re-create fond memories. We grew up with old cars, went on vacation in them, were taken to and from school in them, saw them in movies and on TV, and idolized our role models who drove them. They're as much a part of our consciousness as Elvis Presley, miniskirts, Kennedy, Lee Harvey Oswald, Korea, Vietnam, Woodstock, and Jimi Hendrix. It's not surprising that '60s classics are proving the most popular of all. We take one look at an Edsel or a Chevy Impala and realize that the world will never be the same again. Apart from being able to drive them every day (and keep up with modern traffic) they were the cars many of us promised ourselves as children, nose stuck to the showroom window thinking, "some day, some way."

Part of our Past

And what better transport of delight than the period automobile? The act of buying an old car demonstrates a subliminal desire to revisit our youth. We may say we've bought a beautiful inanimate object in need of restoration, rejuvenation, and preservation, but one of the prime motivations is

Decades of Change

And we're doing it again with the '80s, another decade of upheaval. Cars like the Mk I Golf GTi, Saab Turbo, Audi Quattro, Jaguar XJS, and Lancia Delta Integrale are already being hailed as emergent classics. We feel the growing urge to cherish them as social sculptures, monuments to a faded lifestyle. Previous generations initiated the preservation of buildings, music, paintings, and literature. As New Age technological sophisticates, we are now choosing to cherish fine examples of the manufactured objects that have become such a dominant feature of our twentieth century past – the automobile. Perhaps this love affair is all about a need for simplicity, a suppression of reality. Modern life can be unromantic, and modern automobiles are mostly clinical, complex things. Who with a soul could not be moved by the wholesome innocence of an MGA or a Bugeye Sprite? With their

1959 EDSEL

POSTWAR STYLING
Cars like the flamboyant Edsel are empirical proof that post-war America really was like Hollywood told us. Their baroque styling shows everything that was right, or indeed wrong, with the swansong years of the most powerful nation on earth.

quaint buttons and
switches, dainty gauges,
spoked wheels, and
hectic styling, they exude
an eccentric charm that
has no modern-day equivalent.

THE RETRO LOOK
The modern Mazda MX-5
looks like the 1960s Lotus
Elan; it trades heavily on our
fascination for retro styling.

If you want to know exactly how deeply classic cars
have penetrated the suburban psyche, look at a new
movement evolving from the car designer's drawing
board. For years, car manufacturers thought we
wanted the last word in sanitized efficiency. They tried
to banish every sensation of noise and movement,
sought to purge the automobile of every tremor and
vibration. Yet our worship of yesterday's technology,
the fact that we actually like an engine that sounds like
someone tearing sheets, that we want our instruments
to look like instruments and not LCD computer
readouts, means that really, if we're honest, we don't
want perfection. We want our cars to have personality.
When Mazda designed its MX-5 Miata sports car it
spent months trying to reproduce the authentic rasping
exhaust note of a '60s sports car. It wanted to re-create
the past with modern engineering.

Consumer Durables

There's already a detectable movement away from the
efficiency and order of modern metal. Most people,
if they had the choice, would really prefer something
more separate. Our punishment for buying all those
blameless zero-defect cars is a plague of bland models
with all the passion of a dishwasher. Our obsession
with control has made cars look and feel like
consumer durables, labor-saving devices to be parked
a short step away from the microwave. Mass produced
for mass appeal, they lack sexuality, emotion, and
excitement. But some car
manufacturers have

recognized the fashion for old cars for what it is – a
consumer's cry of protest. They've realized that so
much retrospective admiration has a point – people
prefer cars to look like cars. Jaguar has made its new
models look so much like its old ones, because it
knows that the Sir William Lyons tradition of
swooping curves and chrome grins is actually what
people want, and to lose that stylistic blood line
would turn its products into pale facsimiles.

The retro look, they say, is back. Witness the latest
crop of sports cars with hooded headlights, rakish
lines, white dials, and badges in flowing chrome
script. Bristling with antique styling features, they're
all part of a new wave of cars deliberately sculpted to
tap into the vogue for nostalgia. And the classic effect
has even touched the occasional mainstream car.
Major manufacturers are considering it necessary to
add occasional flourishes of Old World dignity with
wood and leather interiors and chrome radiator grilles.
For all its self-indulgent enthusiasm, the old car
movement has had a greater effect than you might
think and has influenced the way
multinational car makers style their
products. It has taken two decades,
but now the car mandarins have
heard the message. If a large body of
people, faced with buying a shiny
new sedan or an elderly Austin-
Healey, choose the Healey, then it
means that classic cars are here to stay.

CLASSIC GLAMOR
Jaguar boss Sir William Lyons hands over
an XK120 to Clark Gable. With period
visions like this dripping with '50s glamor,
how could classic cars fail to capture the
popular imagination?

The Classic Car Phenomenon

THIRTY YEARS AGO, the classic car hadn't been invented. There were "old cars," which were the province of the lunatic fringe, feted and adored by characters with twigs in their beards and oil under their fingernails. Before this, during the '50s, vintage and veteran cars had been quietly preened and polished by an insular group of car buffs. In England, clubs like the Vintage Sports Car Club and the Historic Sports Car Club laid down the ground rules. Pre-1919 cars were Edwardian, pre-1931 were Vintage, and a handful of models produced up to the beginning of World War II were loosely named Post-Vintage Thoroughbreds. The icons then were machines like the Bugatti Type 35, Eight Liter Bentley, Duesenberg, Auburn, and Hispano Suiza. These were the Chippendales and Sheratons of an arcane catalog of motorized antiques.

1960s Sports Cars

Then came the 1960s, when Britain invaded the rest of the world with a new secret weapon – the sports car. These were the heady days of the E-Type, MGB, Austin-Healey, and Triumph TR. Roads without speed limits opened up a whole new fantasy world of power, sexuality, and image. Mass production brought beauty and hard-charging performance to the ordinary driver. America came up with the

VETERAN VERSUS CLASSIC
Veteran and vintage cars have never had the mass appeal of '50s and '60s boomer classics. These dignified Edwardians are expensive, need constant tinkering, and can be a liability in modern traffic. More importantly, they are too old to be part of most people's childhood memories and are just museum pieces.

EYE OF THE BEHOLDER
This 1935 Lagonda Rapide might look a million dollars, but most old car fanciers get more excited over a '60s Jaguar E-Type.

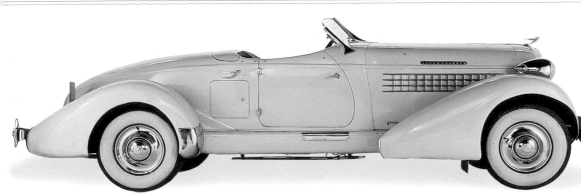

"muscle car" – Mustangs, Corvettes, Chargers, 'Cudas and Firebirds. It was driving's most exciting decade, when a generation let its motoring imagination run riot. But one day the humorless legislators slapped on mandatory speed limits, and choked engine power outputs with sweeping emission regulations. The automobile, they insisted, was getting too big for its boots.

1970s Kitsch

Their legacy was the car-history of the 1970s, a decade of kitsch that spawned machines like the gawky Triumph TR7, the rubber-bumpered MGB, the emasculated Mustangs, the potbellied V-12 E-Type, the truncated Cadillac Seville, and the unlovely Rolls-Royce Camargue. Mainstream cars were even worse. Who will ever forget the Edsel, DeSoto, Studebaker Lark, Chrysler 180, Datsun Skyline, Volkswagen K70, or AMC Pacer? They were truly awful cars, painted in violent hues, laden with safety devices, and strangled by emission pipery. In desperation, enthusiasts looked backward and found that there was a cornucopia of interesting secondhand vehicles that could be bought for a fraction of the price of new ones. XK Jaguars, MG TFs, Aston Martins, and '60s Maseratis and Ferraris could be bought for the price of a two-year-old Ford. $6,000 was all it took to buy a Ferrari Lusso, $7,000 bought a Dino 246, and forking out $10,000 meant you drove home a genuine AC Cobra.

Cars with Attitude

In October 1973 a British magazine appeared called *Classic Cars*, its alliterative title coining a badly needed generic term. From then on, these old cars with attitude became affectionately known as classics, giving a new name to a hobby that in just ten years would mushroom into a multibillion dollar industry. By 1982 interest in old cars had increased dramatically and the price of an E-Type had risen from $2,000 to around $10,000, Dinos sold for $20,000, and Ferrari Lusso ads were followed by the ominous phrase – Price on Application. Classic cars had become fashion accessories.

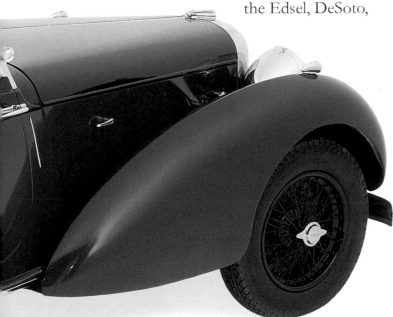

SIXTIES CLASSIC
This Ferrari Lusso is the most admired car on the page because it's neat, modern-looking, easy to drive, and summons up the glamorous '60s.

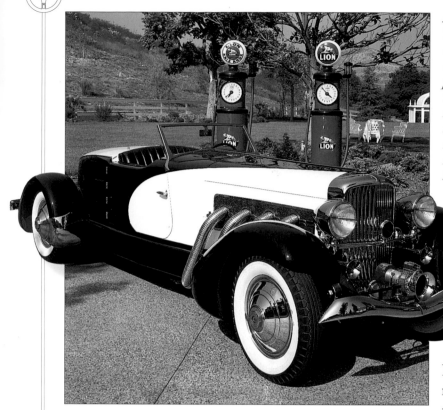

ANOTHER WORLD

This 1933 Duesenberg SJ Speedster is serious collector's stuff and so far removed from most people's sphere of reference that it has assumed the status, not to mention the price tag, of fine art. Cars like this have become the province of the very wealthy — mothballed in heated garages or exhibited as rarefied automotive antiques.

MAGAZINE COVERAGE

Classic Cars, *the magazine that really started it all, first appeared in October 1973, and kick-started an automotive revolution – giving voice to a growing disenchantment with modern cars.*

ENGLISH TOURER

This 1934 Bentley 3-liter may be the quintessential prewar English touring car, but, given the choice of a weekend with the Bentley or the Ferrari Testarossa, which would you choose?

Greatness was suddenly thrust upon old cars. Demand for classics was so huge that values exploded. The real price rises began in 1983 when Ronald Reagan gave the American public tax cuts. Within months, Americans came to England, lavishing their newfound affluence on "collectible" cars, accelerating an unbelievable price spiral in the process. In England, interest rates had fallen, house values soared, and corporate profits were up. The taxman hadn't even dreamed about taxing the capital gain on classic cars, so opportunist speculators moved in. The smart money poured out of the world's stock markets into "investment cars," graphs of appreciation were plotted, and syndicates laid down old cars like fine wine.

In 1984, the first of many banner headlines proclaimed the highest price ever paid for a classic. Sotheby's sold the ex-Woolf Bernato "Blue Train" Speed Six Bentley for a jaw-dropping

FERRARI TESTAROSSA
The Testarossa is exciting because it comes from an exciting decade – the 1980s. Many of the world's most admired classics reflect times of social change and upheaval.

$450,000 – awesome at the time but a fraction of the amounts that were to be bandied about in the next four years. Dealers, some of whom had quietly become large and very profitable corporations, crammed the pages of the classic car press with "gilt-edged investments" and "appreciating assets." Restoration firms and parts suppliers flourished, owners clubs grew, and historic racing boomed. Messing about with old cars had become big business.

Market Mayhem

By 1986, things started to go berserk. Prices went up by the month, propelled by a seemingly insatiable demand tearing away at a dwindling supply. Auction records were made and broken in the same month. An American Duesenberg sold for the magic sum of $1 million, becoming the new highest amount paid for a car at auction. Within eight months a Bugatti Royale sold for $6.5 million, changing hands again only three months later for a staggering $8.1 million. The press fanned the flames with more hype and headlines, and in 1987 the sale of a Bugatti Royale Kellner took the market's breath away by selling at Christie's for an absurd $9.4 million. With the vintage greats out of reach for all but multimillionaires, other lesser cars were suddenly catapulted to stardom. Investors cast around for other sources of capital gain, and word spread that Ferraris had what it took, so up went their value. The Daytona that might have sold for $8,000 in 1973 had an asking price of $325,000 by 1988. GTOs and 250 Testarossas hit the $1.6 million mark and rumors were rife of a 330 P4 selling privately for

over $8 million. Even the modern Ferrari Testarossa – a brand new car with a list price of $134,000 – was being advertised at $340,000. Then the value of Aston Martins exploded with DB5s and DB6s soaring from $20,400 in 1987 to a peak of $120,000 by 1989. The domino effect dragged up Maserati values, which in turn invigorated E-Type prices, and so it went on. By the peak in 1989, the once $2,000 3.8 E-Type was homing in on $67,000.

As the supply of cheap classics in England evaporated, the classic car trade turned to America, South Africa, and New Zealand as a rich vein of rust-free '60s sports cars. Thousands of left-hand drive MGs, TRs, and Jaguars filtered onto the world's markets – some of them not so rust-free. The small ads were crammed with cars advertised by owners and dealers out to turn a profit. Classic car auctions were held every week and more and more classic car magazines lined the newsstands. But suddenly the market started to creak. In 1989, there was a worldwide recession. Interest rates rose, and borrowing money became expensive. There was a retail slowdown, cash was tight and the old car market spluttered and stopped. Demand died almost overnight and cars weren't selling.

BUGATTI LEGEND
Bugatti is still one of the world's most evocative and romantic car badges, but unfortunately accessible only to the privileged few.

CAR AUCTIONS
The first classic car auctions, like this one held in England by Sotheby's in 1982, were rather charming, ingenuous affairs. These days, old car sales are hi-tech, with satellite link-ups, multinational bidders, and glossy four-color magazines.

Prices fell, slowly at first, but by 1990, grass roots enthusiasts who had jumped on the bandwagon too late unloaded their cars in desperation to the highest bidder. Distress sales were common and prices hit the floor. The value of an Aston Martin DB6 that had pole-vaulted to $120,000 plunged to $42,000. The $68,000 E-Type Roadster swallow-dived to $34,000, and the Ferrari F40 that was hyped to nearly $1.6 million in '88 languished unsold with a price tag of $340,000. In the late '80s, speculators jammed Jaguar's phone lines, desperate to put down deposits on the new XJ220 at a whopping $685,000. They were sure it would double in value overnight, that it was the king of classics. They couldn't have been more wrong. When they took delivery — and many tried not to — it was too late. The market had crashed like a milk bottle falling on a stone doorstep. XJ220s wouldn't even return their list price, let alone make a profit. One desperate owner put a low mileage example through an English auction house only to watch it struggle to make $250,000 for a net loss of $435,000. For a while, classic cars had fired the world's imagination as recreational money-makers. Prices had been inflated by market stimulation and, if we're honest, by pure greed. Owners of classics had seen similar cars advertised at crazier and crazier prices and priced theirs accordingly. The less scrupulous auctioneers had invented nonexistent high bids to further boost values and dealers had done what they always do — slapped on a couple of thousand more for profit.

The Emperor's New Clothes

Was it all just sound and fury signifying nothing, a momentary derangement of the mass imagination, or were classic cars really "investments" that would have gone on increasing in value but for a badly timed recession? Certainly there was an awful lot of trash talk spiked with naive enthusiasm and dubious authority. Here the classic press must shoulder some of the blame for deifying old cars indiscriminately. What started as an innocent and enthusiastic hobby went totally out of control. No enthusiast would deny that a Ferrari Daytona is worthy of

JAGUAR E-TYPE
The most romantic E-Type, the 3.8 Roadster, is probably one of the most lusted-after classics of all. Its appeal functions on many levels, but primarily as a direct link to the swinging '60s. Most of today's E-Type buyers vividly remember its launch day in March 1961, just as they recall the day JFK was assassinated.

preservation, but a Datsun Bluebird ? Surely not. Toward the end of the boom the earnest amateurs and dilettante buyers arrived and proceeded to hail some of the most appalling pieces of scrap ever to disgrace asphalt as desirable properties. Cars that should have been allowed to go the way of all flesh were often just cosmetically resurrected and unloaded on adoring fools as collectors' items.

A Good Return?

As for the notion that an old car is a "good investment," there must be scores of old car buyers who now regret the day that they were taken in by the idea. Some cars have indeed appreciated above the rate of inflation and shown their owners handsome gains. But they're usually the rare, very expensive, and highly desirable models rather than the less substantial mass-produced machines, which represent the bulk of the market. You could have bought a Jaguar 3.8 E-Type for $2,000 back in 1970. Today that car, in superlative condition, is worth around $40,000.

A considerable profit you might say – but don't forget inflation. Remember that $2,000 had quite a bit of purchasing power in 1970. Then consider that you'd have to add the cost of storing, insuring, and keeping the thing immaculate for 25 years, and that's only if it never turned a wheel. Enjoy your investment and drive it around and you'll have to throw in fuel, oil, tires, body restoration, servicing, and more, by which time your paper profit turns into an actual loss. Shrewd and strict accounting says that you'd have been better sticking your money in a bank for 25 years and forgetting all about the Jag.

It is a sad but inescapable fact of life that to popularize is to debase. The concept of the classic car was adulterated beyond recognition by greed, ignorance, and misrepresentation. Profit overtook pleasure, misty-eyed idealists were duped into handing over handsome amounts for indifferent cars, and, as with all mass markets, the lure of easy money attracted the less than upright. Chassis numbers were doctored, origin was falsified, and authenticity manufactured. Too many people jumped on the boat and it began to take on water. Glossy ads appeared from finance companies, banks, insurers, auctioneers, and car brokers, all hungry for a piece of the action. They spoiled an innocent pastime by creating a bull market that wasn't mature enough to support itself.

The Wheel Turns Full Circle

Those knowledgeable car buffs who stood back and shook their heads now breathe a deep sigh of relief. The market mayhem is over and most old cars are no longer being talked of as investments or designer accessories. The cautious and learned enthusiast, who drew the world's attention to classic cars in the first place, has supplanted the opportunist speculator and now represents the only market force. Prices are down to affordable levels and cars are once more being bought for enjoyment. The classic car boom was undoubtedly a bad thing for everybody, but out of it has come some good. Many cars were lavishly restored and saved for posterity, we've all learned a lasting lesson, and the huge losses suffered must serve as an awful warning that such anarchy should never happen again.

Those Were the Days
'50s and '60s sports cars radiate nostalgic messages. This Triumph TR2 sales brochure evokes laurel wreaths, checkered flags, and bravado – a glamorous, innocent world when men were men, cars were cars, and the girl in the passenger seat always wore a headscarf and pearls.

How to Buy a Classic Car

ONLY THE BRAVE SAY they can accurately and honestly evaluate a classic car. The old car market got the jitters because there was no established, thorough guide to the delicate business of accurate evaluation. The pricing structure that exists is based on opinion and exaggeration. Traditional methods of collating historical auction prices, along with publicly advertised prices, all too often ignore the vital factor of condition. It isn't enough to take an auction figure and accept that price as a benchmark for similar models. And you can't base values on advertised prices where descriptions of condition are imprecise and prices optimistic. The classic car in question will have been subjected to many years of wear and deterioration. Age alone doesn't give it any value – it's the condition in which it has survived the ravages of time that really matters. So no two cars can ever be assumed to be in the same condition and command the same price.

Buyer Beware

All used cars are by definition flawed and defy accurate evaluation. Modern cars are priced with the help of data from daily auctions, leasing companies, franchised dealers, used car dealers, and fleet operators. Even with so much regular information available, values of modern cars are still unpredictable. So what hope is there for classic car values? The used car is a unique product – only a third is actually visible. The rest lies

behind a cosmetic skin, hidden from view unless dismantled. This is why documentation like service history, number of previous owners, and accuracy of mileage are vital to help make an informed guess about a car's previous existence. With old cars, the job is ten times more difficult. Most classics have had many owners and many restorations and have covered hundreds of thousands of miles. Buyers have been conditioned to accept that documentation is not always necessary or available because it's been lost or obscured in the mists of time. Without documentary help you're left to judge a car's mechanical and bodily state by eye. Unless you're very experienced or psychic, you can make expensive mistakes.

Only recently have old cars caught the public's imagination, so the market is young and foolish. Demand propelled by emotion accelerated values, ignoring more down-to-earth considerations. The desire to own, at any price, sometimes obscures reason. Buyers entered the market without questioning the intrinsic value and condition of the cars they were buying. Only now has it become clear that the prices they paid were based, in most cases, on nothing more than hot air.

For enthusiasts to buy and enjoy old cars, the pivot on which the market hinges, they must be affordable and realistically priced. The market is loaded with bad cars dressed up as good, whether restored at exorbitant cost or not, which places a considerable premium on well kept, genuine, and properly documented examples.

Classic Caveats

Honest, well-maintained, and unrestored cars are worth more than recent restorations. And don't ignore mileage or take it on trust. Find a car that has documentary evidence. Ignore statements like "mileage believed genuine." Make sure the mileage is warranted in writing. Recognize the value of

MANUFACTURED BY
DELOREAN MOTOR CARS LTD.
MONTH AND YEAR
OF MANUFACTURE   OCT, 81
  GROSS VEHICLE WEIGHT RATING 3180 LBS
  GROSS AXLE WEIGHT RATING FRONT 1244 LBS
                            REAR 1936 LBS
THIS VEHICLE CONFORMS TO ALL
APPLICABLE FEDERAL MOTOR VEHICLE
SAFETY AND BUMPER STANDARDS IN
EFFECT ON THE DATE OF MANUFACTURE
SHOWN ABOVE.
V.I.N. SCEDT2GT1BD004579
PASSENGER CAR.   105196

CHASSIS CHECK
This DeLorean chassis plate can help establish the exact date of manufacture and the name of the first owner. Avoid cars with missing chassis plates.

previous servicing bills and invoices. Choose a classic with a history file. Remember that originality is all. Carefully evaluate cars with color changes, nonstandard plastic instead of leather, or replacement engines. Watch out for chassis and engine numbers that don't match, and go for a car with as few owners as possible.

Be fussy about detail. Don't tolerate anything that looks like it's just been spruced up. While you may not be bothered about originality and sources, the next person who buys your car almost certainly will. Don't assume all classic car sellers and dealers are nice people. Rough cars and rough people sometimes go together, classic or not. If you're in any doubt about mechanical and bodily condition, have your potential purchase inspected by a qualified independent examiner.

The Desirability Factor

Old car values rely on desirability, which depends on their image and how much nostalgia they evoke. Some cars, even though identical in body shape, can be miles apart in value. A '68 Jaguar 240 is the least valuable and desirable Jaguar Mk II. Why? The 240 has the smallest engine of the range and cheaper trim. 240s had slimline bumpers and plastic upholstery, which aren't as nostalgic as the broad-bladed bumpers and leather seats of the pre-'67 models.

Why is a 2 + 2 E-Type worth considerably less than a Series I 3.8 E ? The 2 + 2 was designed as a four-seater and looks ungainly with a higher roof line and steeper windshield. It's slower, too. The earliest 3.8s are romantic because they were the lightest, fastest, and purest E-Types of them all, so they're the most sought after. The same is true of Series II E-Types.

PANHARD PL17
Garish mock tiger skin door inserts might offend the untrained eye, but they are completely original and exactly the way they left the factory – making this PL17 a prince among Panhards. Unusual period weirdness is highly desirable.

These had open headlights and bulky rear light clusters spoiling the smooth lines. Sounds silly – it's still an E-Type – but a mint Series II will always be worth less than a mint Series I. Why is a Bugeye Sprite worth more than a Mk II Sprite? Even though the later car has more creature comforts, is faster, and has a trunk that opens, the Bugeye is the most loved. Nostalgia wins again. The Bugeye looks saucy and is the oldest and purest Sprite, so it has become a cult car.

And so it goes, illogically and irrationally. It's not always age that's the deciding factor either. The last of the Jensen Interceptors, the Series III, is worth more than the first Series I models simply because the later car is faster, better built, and more refined. Unless you know which models have a fashionable image, and high market profile, you can easily overvalue a car. Some cars have added value because of special coachbuilt or limited edition bodywork. A Harrington Sunbeam Alpine is worth 30 percent more than a standard Alpine because of its rarity. Rolls-Royces and Bentleys are other examples. Hand-built and specialist coachwork conversions such as Hooper, James Young, and Mulliner Park Ward are more coveted and therefore more valuable than standard steel cars.

CLASSIC WITHIN A CLASSIC
Not every Jaguar Mk II is worth a mint. This one, a 240, might have wire wheels, but it also has slimline bumpers and plastic upholstery. Pre-'67 Mk IIs had much more nostalgic broad-bladed bumpers and leather trim, and are worth more. The market prefers its old cars as traditional as possible.

Factory-listed options can enhance an old car's value, whereas nonoriginal aftermarket accessories can actually detract from the value. Power steering on Bentley S-Series and Rolls-Royce Silver Clouds is considered essential to their value. Cars without it should be penalized by as much as 20 percent. An automatic transmission on an MGB or a Sunbeam Alpine, although a factory option, reduces the car's value because it spoils the sporting character and performance. Wire wheels are a period accessory and highly sought after. On an MGC they're essential, even though they are an option. On a '70s Mercedes 350 SL, leather interior and air conditioning will boost the car's value by 30 percent. But things like modern fender mirrors, spotlights, glass sunroofs and nonstandard aluminum wheels ruin a car's originality and its period attraction.

Classic Car Auctions

Over the last few years the classic car auction has dominated the old car market as the most convenient way of buying a classic. Auctions, whether for old or modern cars, are dangerous places. You can't drive the car, have it inspected on ramps or speak to the seller. Sometimes you can't even hear the engine running. So the risk of buying something that is not what it seems is huge. Many believe that the classic car auction is the best place to

CAUTION REQUIRED
Classic car auctions are dangerous and expensive places where you cannot inspect or test-drive properly. Emotion and money make unhappy bedfellows and it's easy to get carried away in the heat of the moment.

buy old cars – in fact it's the worst. Buying anything in a competitive and emotional environment without the time or opportunity to make a rational decision is courting disaster. Add to this such dubious practices as unrealistic reserves, invented bids, and a system that conceals the seller from the buyer, and you begin to question the popularity of auctions. Often it's much wiser and cheaper to buy privately or from a dealer, where you have the time to ask questions, make a thorough inspection, and drive the car at operating temperature. It's no coincidence that some of the highest prices achieved for classic cars have been at auction. The most important thing to remember is that unless the car is sold with a warranty, which is rarely the case, your rights at auction are few.

The Bottom Line

Buying a classic requires a steady hand. Reason, not emotion, must be your constant companion. Go at it blind, giddy with dewy-eyed sentimentality, and you'll regret the day you ever went near an old car. Practice a little temporary detachment, negotiate ruthlessly, and you'll buy a winner. And there's no better feeling than being a successful player in that sepia-tinted fantasy we call classic cars. They're a unique, innocent, and disarming form of amusement – fashionable, separate, and involving. Old cars have class.

Classic Car
GALLERY

·

Here are 90 of the world's most beguiling old automobiles. From the quaint and charming to the stridently flamboyant, they're just a small foretaste of the magic called classic cars.

AC *Ace-Bristol*

AGONIZINGLY PRETTY, the AC Ace catapulted the homespun Thames Ditton company into the automobile limelight, instantly earning it a reputation of a maker of svelte sports cars for the tweedy English middle classes. Timelessly elegant, swift, poised, and mechanically uncomplicated, the Ace went on to form the platform for the legendary AC Cobra *(see pages 24–25).* Clothed in a light aluminum body and powered by a choice of AC's own delicate UMB 2.0 unit, the hardier 2.0 Bristol 100D2 engine, or the lusty 2.6 Ford Zephyr unit, the Ace drove as well as it looked.

Its shape has guaranteed the Ace a place in automobile annals. Chaste, uncluttered, and simple, it makes a Ferrari look top-heavy and clumsy. Purists argue that the Bristol-powered version is the real thoroughbred Ace, closest to its original inspiration, the Bristol-powered Tojeiro prototype of 1953.

ENGINE
Shared by the BMW 328, the hemi-head 125 bhp 2.0 Bristol engine was offered as a performance conversion for the Ace. With triple Solex carburetors, pushrod overhead valve gear, a light aluminum head, and cast iron crankcase, the Ace was a club racer's dream.

STEERING WHEEL SHARED WITH THE AUSTIN-HEALEY (SEE PAGES 36–39) AND THE DAIMLER SP DART (SEE PAGES 78–81)

INTERIOR
In pure British tradition, the Ace's cockpit was stark, with gauges and switches haphazardly scattered across the dash.

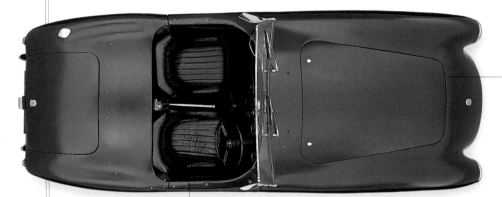

HANDLING
Production cars used Bishop cam-and-gear steering, which gave a turning circle of 36 ft (11 m), and required just two deft turns of the steering wheel lock-to-lock.

PROPORTION
Simplicity itself – a box for the engine, a box for the people, and a box for the luggage.

OTHER MODELS

Founded in 1902, AC was one of the longest established English car makers, nicknamed "the Savile Row of motordom."

AC ACECA
A coupe version of the Ace, the Aceca was sold until mid-1955.

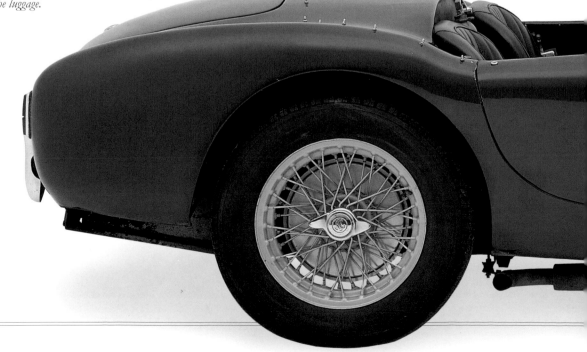

COOLING
The Ace's wide, toothy grin fed air into the large radiator that was shared by the two-liter sedan.

REAR VIEW
Later Aces had a revised rear deck, with square tail-lights and a bigger trunk.

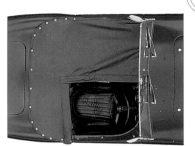

FOOT WARMER
For diehards who always drove with the hood down, the tonneau cover kept your feet warm while your face froze.

AC ACE-BRISTOL

The handsomest British roadster of its day, and as lovely as an Alfa Romeo Giulietta Sprint, the Ace had an Italianate simplicity. Proof of the dictum that less is more, the Ace's gently sweeping profile is a triumph of form over function. Known as *Superleggera* construction, a network of steel tubes was covered by aluminum panels, based on the outline of the 1949 Ferrari 122. Engines were placed well back and gave an 18 percent rearward bias to the weight distribution.

SIDESCREENS
Folding plastic sidescreens helped to prevent turbulence in the cockpit at speed.

OWNER DRIVING
An Ace-Bristol recorded an average of 97 mph (156 km/h) over 2,350 miles (3,781 km) at the 1957 Le Mans 24 Hours (a record for a Bristol-engined car).

HOOD CATCHES
Forward-hinged hood was locked by two chrome catches, opened by a small T-shaped key.

SPECIFICATIONS

MODEL AC Ace-Bristol (1956–61)
PRODUCTION 463
BODY STYLE Two-door, two-seater sports roadster.
CONSTRUCTION Space-frame chassis, light aluminum body.
ENGINE Six-cylinder pushrod 1971cc.
POWER OUTPUT 105 bhp at 5000 rpm (optional high performance tune 125 hp at 5750 rpm).
TRANSMISSION Four-speed manual Bristol gearbox (optional overdrive).
SUSPENSION Independent front and rear with transverse leaf spring and lower wishbones.
BRAKES Front and rear drums. Front discs from 1957.
MAXIMUM SPEED 117 mph (188 km/h)
0–60 MPH (0–96 KM/H) 9.1 sec
0–100 MPH (0–161 KM/H) 27.2 sec
A.F.C. 21.6 mpg

BRAKES
Front disc brakes, an option in 1957, were later standardized.

AC *Cobra 427*

AN UNLIKELY ALLIANCE BETWEEN AC Cars, a traditional British car maker, and Carroll Shelby, a charismatic Texan racer, produced the legendary AC Cobra. AC's sports car, the Ace *(see pages 20–21),* was turned into the Cobra by fitting a series of American Ford V-8s into the car, starting with 4.2-liter and 4.7-liter Mustang engines. In 1965 Shelby, always a man to take things to the limit, squeezed in a thunderous 7-liter Ford engine, in an attempt to realize his dream of winning Le Mans. Although the 427 was not fast enough to win and failed to sell in any quantity, it was soon known as one of the most aggressive and romantic cars ever built.

GTM 777F once held the record as The World's Fastest Accelerating Production Car. In 1967 it was driven by British journalist John Bolster to record such Olympian figures as an all-out maximum of 165 mph (265 km/h) and a 0–60 time of an unbelievable 4.2 seconds.

OTHER MODELS

AC Cars Limited began in 1922 and earned itself a reputation as a maker of good-looking, hand-built, luxury sports cars.

AC COBRA 289
Early Cobras had 260 engines. Later cars were fitted with Mustang 289 V-8s.

BODYWORK
The body was handrolled aluminum wrapped around a tubular steel frame, which proved to be very light yet extremely strong.

SPEEDY APPEAL
Even the "baby" 4.7 Cobras were good for 138 mph (222 km/h) and could squeal up to 60 mph (96 km/h) in under six seconds.

INTERIOR
The interior was kept stark and basic, with traditional 1960s British sports car features of black-on-white gauges, small bucket seats, and wood-rim steering wheel. 427 owners were not interested in creature comforts, only raw power, great brakes, and wonderful suspension.

TIRES
Cobra tires were always Goodyear since Shelby was a long-time dealer.

RADIATOR HEADER TANK KEPT THINGS COOL, HELPED BY TWIN ELECTRIC FANS

UNDER THE AIR CLEANER ARE TWO LARGE FOUR-BARREL CARBURETORS

ENGINE
The mighty 7-liter 427 block had years of NASCAR (National Association of Stock Car Automobile Racing) racing success and easily punched out power for hours. The street version output ranged from 300 to 425 bhp. Competition and semicompetition versions with tuned engines could exceed 500 bhp.

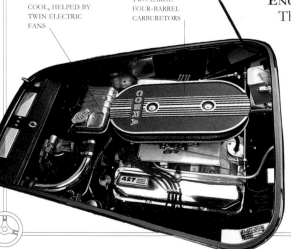

AC COBRA 427

The 427 looked fast standing still. Gone was the lithe beauty of the original Ace 289, replaced by bulbous front and rear arches, fat 7½-in (19-cm) wheels, and tires wide enough to roll a ball field. The chassis was virtually all new and three times stronger than the 289's, with computer-designed anti-dive and anti-squat characteristics. Amazingly, the 289's original Salisbury differential proved more than capable of handling the 427's massive wall of torque.

WHEELS
Initially pin-drive Halibrand magnesium alloy but changed for Starburst wheels (designed by Shelby employee Pete Brock) when supplies dried up.

SIDESCREENS
Small plastic side screens helped cut down cockpit-fender buffeting at speed.

COOLING
Fender vents helped reduce brake and engine temperatures.

FRAME
The windshield frame was handmade and polished.

BUMPERS
Bumpers were token chromed tubes with the emphasis on weight-saving. Racers took them off completely.

EXHAUSTS
Racing Cobras usually had side exhausts, which increased power and noise.

GTM 777F

GTM 777F

— SPECIFICATIONS —

MODEL 1965 AC Cobra 427 (1965–68)

PRODUCTION 316

BODY STYLE Light aluminum, two-door, two-seater, open sports.

CONSTRUCTION Separate tubular steel chassis with aluminum panels.

ENGINE V-8 6989cc

POWER OUTPUT 425 bhp at 6000 rpm.

TRANSMISSION Four-speed all-synchromesh.

SUSPENSION Four-wheel independent with coil springs.

BRAKES Four-wheel disc.

MAXIMUM SPEED 165 mph (265 km/h)

0–60 MPH (0–96 KM/H) 4.2 sec

0–100 MPH (0–161 KM/H) 10.3 sec

A.F.C. 15 mpg

AC 428

THE AC 428 NEEDS a new word of its very own – "brutiful" perhaps – for while its brute strength derives from its Cobra ancestor, the 428 has a sculpted, stately beauty. This refined bruiser was born of a thoroughbred crossbreed of British engineering, American power, and Italian design. The convertible 428 was first seen at the London Motor Show in October 1965; the first hardtop car – the so-called fastback – was ready in time for the Geneva Motor Show in March 1966.

But production was beset by problems from the start; first cars were not offered for sale until 1967, and as late as March 1969, only 50 had been built. Part of the problem was that the 428 was priced between the more expensive Italian Ferraris and Maseratis and the cheaper British Astons and Jensens. Small-scale production continued into the 1970s, but its days were numbered and it was finally done in by the fuel crisis of October 1973; the last 428 – the 80th – was built soon afterward and sold during 1974. But if you own one of them you have a rare thing – a refined muscle car, a macho GT with manners and breeding.

BADGING
The letters AC derive from Autocarrier, the company's name until it became known as AC Cars Ltd. in 1922.

SUSPENSION
Front suspension uses unequal-length wishbones with combined coilspring and telescopic-shock units.

ENGINE
Using the same 427 cubic inch (6998cc) V-8 engine as the Cobra, the car was known initially as the AC 427. In 1967, it gained the Ford Galaxie engine and an extra cubic inch. Both four-speed manual and three-speed automatic transmissions were available.

UNDER-HOOD HEAT MEANT THAT ON LONG, FAST RUNS THE ENGINE OIL COULD LITERALLY BOIL

TOP COVER
Early convertibles had a detachable metal tonneau to cover the top when folded, but this was soon abandoned.

SITTING COMFORTABLY
Interiors are lavishly furnished, with top-quality leather seats and extensive use of chrome-plated fittings.

SUBTLE FILLER
The 18-gallon (82-liter) fuel tank is filled through a flap on the rear deck.

DASHBOARD
Switches may be scattered around like confetti, but the instruments are grouped just in front of the driver. The speedometer *(far left)* reads to an optimistic 180 mph (290 km/h), the tachometer *(far right)* to 8000 rpm.

MAKING AN IMPACT
Slim, wraparound, chrome-plated bumpers accentuate the 428's length, but provide minimal impact protection.

BODY BEAUTIFUL
Like any Italian or Italian-bodied car of the period, the 428 suffers from corrosion due to poor quality steel.

SPECIFICATIONS

MODEL AC 428 (1966–73)
PRODUCTION 80 (51 convertibles, 29 fastbacks)
BODY STYLES Two-seat convertible or two-seat fastback coupe.
CONSTRUCTION Tubular steel backbone chassis/separate all steel body.
ENGINE Ford V-8, 6997cc or 7016cc.
POWER OUTPUT 345 bhp at 4600 rpm
TRANSMISSION Ford four-speed manual or three-speed automatic; Salisbury rear axle with limited slip differential.
SUSPENSION Double wishbones and combined coil spring/telescopic shock units front and rear.
BRAKES Power-assisted Girling discs front and rear.
MAXIMUM SPEED 139.3 mph (224 km/h) (auto)
0–60 MPH (0–96 KM/H) 5.9 sec (auto)
0–100 MPH (0–161 KM/H) 14.5 sec
A.F.C. 12–15 mpg

WEATHER BEATER
While the top has rather large rear quarter panels which can make the cockpit feel rather claustrophobic, the plastic rear window is generously proportioned.

SUSPENSION
Salisbury final drive, with limited slip differential, is bolted to the tubular chassis. Short external shafts drive the rear wheels.

AIR VENTS
In an effort to combat engine overheating, later cars have air vents behind the front wheels.

PARTS BIN
The 428 features parts from other manufacturers; rear lights came from Fiat.

AC 428

Styled by Pietro Frua in Turin, the AC 428 was available in both convertible and fastback form. It was based on an AC Cobra 427 chassis, virtually standard apart from a 6 in (15 cm) increase in wheelbase. The design contains subtle reminders of a number of contemporary cars, not least of which is the Maserati Mistral – which is hardly surprising really, since the Mistral was also designed by Frua.

THIN SKINNED
Early cars had aluminum doors and hood; later cars were all steel.

LIFTING THE LID
Like the Cobra, the 428's vast hood is hinged at the front.

DESIGN CREDIT
Frua is credited with a discreet "Creazione Frua" badge behind each front fender vent.

ALL LACED UP
Standard wheels were substantial wire-spoked affairs, secured by a three-eared nut.

ALFA ROMEO 1300 Junior Spider

DRIVEN BY DUSTIN HOFFMAN to the strains of Simon and Garfunkel in the film *The Graduate*, the Alfa Spider has become one of the most accessible cult Italian cars. This is hardly surprising when you consider the little Alfa's considerable virtues: a wonderfully responsive all-aluminum, twin-cam engine, accurate steering, sensitive brakes, a finely balanced chassis, and matinee idol looks. It has been called "the poor man's Ferrari."

First launched at the Geneva Motor Show in 1966, Alfa held a worldwide competition to find a name for its new baby. After considering 140,000 entries, with suggestions like Lollobrigida, Bardot, Nuvolari, and even Stalin, they settled on Duetto, which neatly summed up the car's "two's-company-three's-a-crowd" image. Despite having the same price tag as the much faster and more glamorous Jaguar E-Type *(see pages 140–143)*, the Spider sold over 100,000 units during its remarkable 26-year production run. Alfa purists favor the pre-1970 "boat-tailed" cars, with the 1600 Duetto and 1750 model among the most collectible. Because of their large production numbers and relatively expensive maintenance costs, not to mention a serious propensity for body decay, prices of Spiders are invitingly low, running at similar levels to MGBs, Triumph TR6s, and Bugeye Sprites.

OTHER MODELS

The Spider has to be one of Alfa's great postwar cars. Next to the Alfasud, GTV, and Giulia, it is perhaps one of its most romantic concoctions.

ALFA ROMEO GIULIETTA
The Spider's ancestor was the comely little Giulietta, available in convertible, two-door coupe, or four-door Berlina versions.

ALFA ROMEO MONTREAL
For six years the Montreal was the jewel in Alfa's crown. A race-bred 2.5 V-8 gave a top speed of 140 mph (225 km/h).

REAR VIEW
The "boat-tail" rear was shared by all Spiders up to 1970, replaced by a squared-off Kamm tail. "Duetto" correctly refers to 1600 Spiders only.

LOGO
The Spider was designed by Battista Pininfarina, founder of the Turin-based design house.

HOOD
The Spider's hood is beautifully effective. It can be raised with only one arm without leaving the driver's seat.

TRUNK
Spiders have huge trunks by sports car standards, with the spare wheel tucked neatly away under the trunk floor.

BODYWORK
The Spider's bodywork corrodes alarmingly quickly. Poor-quality steel, scant rustproofing, and inadequate drainage make rust a serious enemy.

ENGINE
Some of the mid-'70s Spiders imported to the US were overly restricted – the catalyzed 1750 could only manage 99 mph (159 km/h).

DASHBOARD
The dashboard was painted metal up to 1970. All Spiders had the Italian "apelike" (long arms, short legs) driving position. Minor controls were on fingertip stalks, while the wipers had an ingenious foot button on the floor.

ALFA ROMEO 1300 JUNIOR SPIDER

One of Pininfarina's last designs, the Spider's rounded front and rear and deep-channelled scallop running along the sides attracted plenty of criticism. One British motoring magazine dubbed it "compact and rather ugly." The 1300 Junior was the baby of the Spider family, introduced in 1968 to take advantage of Italian tax laws.

FLOOR MATS
Spiders came from the factory with austere rubber mats, now much prized by enthusiasts as they do not absorb water.

STYLISH GRILLE
This hides a twin-cam energy-efficient engine with hemispherical combustion chambers.

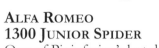

SPECIFICATIONS

MODEL Alfa Romeo 1300 Junior Spider (1968–78)
PRODUCTION 7,237
BODY STYLE All steel.
CONSTRUCTION All steel monocoque body.
ENGINE All-aluminum twin-cam 1290cc.
POWER OUTPUT 89 bhp at 6000 rpm.
TRANSMISSION Five-speed.
SUSPENSION *Front:* independent; *Rear:* live axle with coil springs.
BRAKES All disc.
MAXIMUM SPEED 106 mph (170 km/h)
0–60 MPH (0–96 KM/H) 11.2 sec
0–100 MPH (0–161 KM/H) 21.3 sec
A.Г.С. 29 mpg

HEADLIGHTS
Plastic headlight covers look good and raise the top speed slightly. They were banned in the United States and never fitted to 1300 Juniors.

NOSE SECTION
Disappearing nose is very vulnerable to parking dents. Many a Spider's snout contains more filler than it should.

ASTON MARTIN DB4

THE DEBUT OF THE DB4 in 1958 heralded the beginning of the Aston Martin glory years, ushering in the breed of classic six-cylinder DB Astons that propelled Aston Martin onto the world stage. Earlier postwar Astons were fine sporting enthusiasts' road cars, but with the DB4 Astons acquired a new grace, sophistication, and refinement that was, for many, the ultimate flowering of the grand tourer theme. Clothed in an Italian body by Carrozzeria Touring of Milan, it possessed a graceful yet powerful elegance. Under the aluminum shell was Tadek Marek's twin-cam straight-six engine, which evolved from Aston's racing program.

In short, the DB4 looked superb and went like the wind. The DB5, which followed, will always be remembered as the James Bond Aston. The final expression of the theme came with the bigger DB6. The cars were glorious, but the company was in trouble. David Brown, the millionaire industrialist owner of Aston Martin and the DB of the model name, had a dream. But, in the early '70s, with losses of $1.5 million a year, he bailed out of the company, leaving a legacy of machines that are still talked about with reverence as the David Brown Astons.

— OTHER MODELS —

Aston Martin's first postwar car was the short-lived DB1, a curious whale-shaped device replaced by the more shapely DB2 in 1950.

ASTON MARTIN DB2/4
With its WO Bentley engine, the DB2 evolved into the DB2/4, an occasional four-seater sports model.

UNHINGED
First-generation DB4s have a rear-hinged hood.

GAS FLAP
The single gas-tank is out of sight behind a discreet flap on the left-hand rear pillar.

SUSPENSION
Front suspension is double wishbones with coil springs and telescopic shocks.

1037 TE

LUXURIOUS LEATHER
While rear seats in the hardtop offer limited space, just look at the richness and quality of the leather.

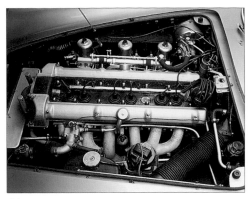

ENGINE
While looking very much like the contemporary Jaguar XK twin-cam straight-six, Tadek Marek's design is more powerful and more complicated. Triple SU carburetors show this to be a Vantage engine with an extra 20 bhp.

IT'S IN THE MIRROR
The dipping rear-view mirror is also found in many Jaguars of the period.

DASHBOARD
The dash is an unergonomic triumph of form over function; gauges are scattered all over an instrument panel deliberately similar to the car's grinning radiator grille.

SPECIFICATIONS
MODEL Aston Martin DB4 (1958–63)
PRODUCTION 1,040 (hardtop); 70 (convertible); 95 hardtop DB4 GTs.
BODY STYLES Hardtop coupe or convertible.
CONSTRUCTION Pressed-steel and tubular inner chassis frame, with aluminum-alloy outer panels.
ENGINE In-line six 3670cc/3749cc.
POWER OUTPUT 240 bhp at 5500 rpm.
TRANSMISSION Four-speed manual (with optional overdrive).
SUSPENSION *Front:* independent by wishbones, coil springs and telescopic shocks. *Rear:* live axle located by trailing arms and Watt linkage with coil springs and lever-arm shocks.
BRAKES Discs front and rear.
MAXIMUM SPEED 140+ mph (225+ km/h)
0–60 MPH (0–96 KM/H) 8 sec
0–100 MPH (0–161 KM/H) 20.1 sec
A.F.C. 14–22 mpg

BRITISH LIGHTWEIGHT
Superleggera, Italian for "super-lightweight," refers to the technique of body construction: aluminum panels rolled over a framework of steel tubes.

ASTON MARTIN DB4
There is no doubt that the DB4 has serious attitude. Its lines may be Italian, but it has none of the dainty delicacy of some contemporary Ferraris and Maseratis; the Aston's spirit is truly British. Its stance is solid and powerful, but not brutish – more British Boxer than lumbering Bulldog, aggressive yet refined – and is an ideal blueprint for a James Bond car.

1037 TE

ASTON SMILE
The vertical bars in this car's radiator grille show it to be a so-called Series 4 DB4, built between September, 1961 and October, 1962.

ASTON MARTIN V8

A NEAR TWO-TON GOLIATH powered by an outrageous hand-made 5.3-liter engine, the DBS V8 was meant to be Aston's bread winner for the 1970s. Based on the six-cylinder DBS of 1967, the V8 did not appear until April 1970. With a thundering 160 mph (257 km/h) top speed, Aston's new bulldog instantly earned a place on every millionaire's shopping list. The trouble was that it drove into a worldwide recession – in 1975 the Newport Pagnell factory produced just 19 cars.

Aston's bank managers were worried, but the company pulled through. The DBS became the Aston Martin V8 in 1972 and continued on until 1989, giving birth to the legendary 400 bhp Vantage and gorgeous Volante Convertible. Excessive, expensive, impractical, and impossibly thirsty, the DBS V8 and AM V8 are wonderful relics from a time when environmentalism was just a word in the dictionary.

— OTHER MODELS —

The DBS was sold alongside the DB6, here in convertible Volante form. David Brown Astons were the staple vehicle of well-heeled British aristocrats.

ASTON MARTIN DB6 VOLANTE
Cars with incredible presence, Astons were good enough for James Bond, King Hussein of Jordan, Peter Sellers, and even the Prince of Wales – who still owns a DB6 Volante he bought new.

RACING ENGINE
The aluminum V-8 was first seen in Lola sports-racing cars. The massive air-cleaner box covers a quartet of twin-choke Weber carburetors.

CLASSY INTERIOR
Over the years the DBS was skillfully updated, without losing its traditional ambience. Features included leather and wood trim, air conditioning, electric windows, and state-of-the-art Blaupunkt radio cassette. Nearly all V8s were ordered with Chrysler Torqueflite automatic.

ASTON LINES
Smooth tapering cockpit line is an Aston hallmark echoed in the current DB7.

SPOILER
Discreet rear spoiler is part of the gently sweeping fender line.

SUSPENSION
Rear suspension was semi-independent De Dion tube with double trailing links, Watts linkage, coil springs, and lever arm shocks.

TIRES
Tires were massive 7-in (18-cm) Avon Turbospeeds.

REAR VIEW
Prodigious rear overhang makes the rear aspect look cluttered.

TWIN PIPES
Hand-made bumpers cover huge twin exhausts – a gentle reminder of this Aston's epic V-8 grunt.

ASTON MARTIN V8

DBS was one of the first Astons with a chassis and departed from the traditional Superleggera tubular superstructure of the DB4, 5, and 6. Like Ferraris and Maseratis, Aston prices were ballyhooed up to stratospheric levels in the 1980s. The best examples changed hands for $100,000 plus. But now sobriety has returned to the market; you can buy a decent V-8 for the price of a new Nissan.

WHEELS
To handle 300-plus bhp, V8s wore cast aluminum wheels instead of wires.

BODYWORK
V8 aluminum body was hand-smoothed and lovingly finished.

B391 AJD

SPECIFICATIONS

MODEL Aston Martin V8 (1972–89)
PRODUCTION (including Volante and Vantage) 2,842
BODY STYLE Four-seater coupe.
CONSTRUCTION Aluminum body, steel platform chassis.
ENGINE Twin OHC 5340cc V-8.
POWER OUTPUT Never released but approx. 345 bhp (Vantage 400 bhp).
TRANSMISSION Three-speed automatic or five-speed manual.
SUSPENSION Independent front, De Dion rear.
BRAKES Four-wheel disc.
MAXIMUM SPEED 161 mph (259 km/h); Vantage 173 mph (278 km/h)
0–60 MPH (0–96 KM/H) 6.2 sec (Vantage 5.4 sec)
0–100 MPH (0–161 KM/H) 14.2 sec (Vantage 13 sec)
A.F.C. 13 mpg

BOND CAR
The 1984 AM V8 Volante from the film *The Living Daylights*, with James Bond actor Timothy Dalton. In 1964 a DB4 was the first Aston to star alongside James Bond, in the film *Goldfinger*.

HOOD BULGE
Massive hood power bulge is to clear four carburetors.

SPOILER
Chin spoiler and undertray help reduce front-end lift at speed.

FRONT END
Shapely "cliff-hanger" nose was always a DBS trademark.

ASTON MARTIN V8

AUDI *Quattro Sport*

THE MOST EXPENSIVE AND EXCLUSIVE Audi ever sold was the $100,000, 155 mph (250 km/h) Quattro Sport. With a short wheelbase, all-aluminum 300 bhp engine, and a body made of aluminum reinforced fiberglass and Kevlar, it has all the charisma, and nearly all the performance, of a Ferrari GTO. The Quattro changed the way we think about four-wheel drive. Before 1980, four-wheel drive systems had foundered through high cost, weight, and lousy road behavior. Everybody thought that if you bolted a four-wheel drive system onto a performance coupe it would have ugly handling, transmission whine, and an insatiable appetite for fuel. Audi's engineers proved that the accepted wisdom was cockeyed and, by 1982, they were World Champions. Four-wheel drive cars are now part of most large carmakers' model ranges and, along with airbags and anti-lock brakes, have played their bit toward safer driving. We must thank the car that started it all, the Audi Quattro – a technical trailblazer.

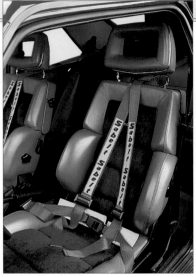

INTERIOR
The interior looks like it may accommodate four people, but in practice it is a two-seater only, unless a rear passenger is willing to travel in the lotus position! Ride is harder than in normal Quattros, but steering is quicker.

FOUR-WHEEL SWITCH
Center Torsen differential gives a 50/50 front-to-rear split. Rear differential lock disengages as soon as the car passes 15 mph (24 km/h).

DASHBOARD
While the dashboard layout is nothing special, everything is typically Germanic – clear, tidy, and easy to use. The only touch of luxury in the Quattro is half-leather trim.

BOX WHEELARCHES ARE A QUATTRO HALLMARK, ESSENTIAL TO COVER FAT 9JX15 WHEELS

INTER-AXLE QUATTRO DIFFERENTIAL WAS BORROWED FROM THE VW POLO

TURBO LAG WAS A BIG PROBLEM ON EARLY QUATTROS; FROM 20–60 MPH IN TOP GEAR IT WAS SLOWER THAN A 900CC VW POLO

POWER OUTPUT IS A MONSTER 304 BHP AT 6500 RPM – 0 TO 60 IN FOUR-AND-A-BIT SECONDS IS VERY QUICK

ENGINE

The five-cylinder 2133cc aluminum engine is 50 lb (22.7 kg) lighter than the stock item, with twin overhead cams, four valves per cylinder, a giant KKK-K27 turbocharger and Bosch LH-Jetronic injection.

karosserie BAUR

BAUER BADGING

Some body parts were made by German coachbuilder Bauer, who was also responsible for the early BMW 3-Series Convertible.

LONGER NOSE AND HOOD BULGE COVER INTERCOOLER FOR THE TURBO UNIT

REAR VIEW WAS LIMITED

┤ SPECIFICATIONS ├

MODEL Audi Quattro Sport (1983–87)
PRODUCTION 220 (all LHD)
BODY STYLE Two-seater, two-door coupe.
CONSTRUCTION Monocoque body from Kevlar, aluminum, fiberglass, and steel.
ENGINE 2133cc five-cylinder turbocharged.
POWER OUTPUT 304 bhp at 6500 rpm.
TRANSMISSION Five-speed manual, four-wheel drive.
SUSPENSION Independent all around.
BRAKES Four-wheel vented discs with switchable ABS.
MAXIMUM SPEED 155 mph (250 km/h)
0–60 MPH (0–96 KM/H) 4.8 sec
0–100 MPH (0–161 KM/H) 13.9 sec
A.F.C. 17 mpg

LIMITED EDITION

Of the 1,700 Audis produced each day in the mid-1980s, only 3 were Quattros, and of a year's output only a tiny amount were Sport Quattros.

DUE TO BOXY STYLING, QUATTRO AERODYNAMICS WERE POOR AT 0.43Cd

Audi Sport!

FOUR-WHEEL VENTILATED DISCS HAVE SELECTABLE ANTI-LOCK BRAKING SYSTEM (ABS). SINCE ABS IS NOT DESIRABLE IN ALL DRIVING CONDITIONS, SPORT DRIVERS CAN SWITCH IT ON AND OFF AT WILL

—QUATTRO RALLY SUCCESS—

In its day the Audi Quattro Sport had the latest four-wheel drive technology, married to the reliability and durability of Prussian engineering perfection.

THE SPORT'S capabilities make it not just a fast car, but a superfast supercar, more than able to rub noses with the best from Maranello and Stuttgart. Despite its passing resemblance to the more prosaic Audi GT Coupe, the Quattro Sport is one of the quickest, most surefooted cars in the world.

In 1984 Stig Blomqvist took Audi to the rank of world champion, with wins in Greece, New Zealand, and Argentina. But it was at the Ivory Coast event, the Sport's first true outing, that he showed just how competitive this incredible machine could be, trouncing all opposition in his wake. In competition trim, Audi's remarkable turbocharged engine was developing 400 bhp. By 1987, Audi was admitting to an Olympian 509 bhp at 8,000 rpm for the fearsome S1 Sport that took Walter Rohrl to victory at Pikes Peak. To meet Group B homologation requirements, only 220 examples of the Sport were built, all left-hand drive,

and only a few were destined for sale to some very lucky private owners.

In its first full competition season in 1985, the Sport took the laurels on the San Remo rally, as well as second place on the Monte Carlo, Swedish, and Acropolis rallies. The San Remo was to be the last Group B Quattro win in the World Rally Championship because the competition had come to

AUDI SPORT IN RALLY ACTION

AUDI
Quattro Sport

DARKENED REAR LIGHTS WERE INCLUDED ACROSS THE QUATTRO LINE IN 1984

HOT PROPERTY
From any angle the Sport is testosterone on wheels, with a bold and aggressive stance.

AUDI SPORT, 1983 EAST AFRICA SAFARI RALLY

STIG BLOMQVIST IN ICY CONDITIONS, 1985

grips with the Quattro phenomenon and was producing a growing number of four-wheel drive supercars, custom built for rallying events. Ultra-quick projectiles like the Metro 6R4, Ford RS 2000, Peugeot 205 T16, and Lancia

Delta S4 began to chew away at the Quattro's tail feathers. The reason for the Sport's short life was that all Group B supercars were outlawed after a number of terrible accidents. Audi withdrew from competition following the ill-fated 1986 Portugal

Rally that rewrote the rule book. From 1987 onward, the World Rally Championship would be contested by Group A cars in stock showroom specification, rendering the foreshortened Sport obsolete at a stroke. Gone but certainly not forgotten, the Quattro Sport is now a much admired collector's item, valued as high as three times its original price.

ROOF SECTIONS ARE OF ALUMINUM-BONDED FIBERGLASS

HAND-CRAFTED
Body shells were welded together at Ingolstadt, Germany, in small batches by a team of just 22 craftsmen.

AUSTIN-HEALEY *Sprite* MK1

Sprite

SOME AUTOMOTIVE THEORISTS believe all the best car designs have a recognizable face. If that is the case, few cars have a cuter face than this little fellow, with that ear-to-ear grinning grille and those wide-open, slightly astonished, eyes. Of course, it is those trademark bulging peepers that prompted the nickname "Bugeye," by which everyone now recognizes this engaging little character. It is a compliment of kinds that the recent retro fad has offered similar designs, like the Suzuki Capuccino and Honda Beat, in an attempt to recapture some of the charm of the original. But these modern charm-bracelet trinkets lack one thing – real character. So much of the Bugeye's character was born of necessity. The Donald Healey Motor Company and Austin had already teamed up with the Austin-Healey 100. In 1958, its little brother, the Sprite, was born, a spartan little sports car designed down to a price and based on the engine and running gear of the Austin A35 sedan, with a bit of Morris Minor, too. Yet the Bugeye really was a sports car and had a sweet raspberry exhaust note to prove it.

INTERIOR
The Bugeye fits like a glove. Everything is within reach – speedometer on the right, tach on the left, and a well-placed stubby gear lever.

THE BUG'S EYES
Gerry Coker's original design incorporated retracting headlights like the later Lotus Elan, but extra cost ruled these out; the protruding headlight pods created a car with a character all of its own.

ENGINE ACCESS
Front-hinged hood gives great engine access and makes the Bugeye a delight for DIY tinkerers.

ENGINE
The Austin-Morris A-series engine was a little gem. It first appeared in the Austin A35 sedan and went on to power several generations of Mini *(see pages 40–41)*. In the Bugeye it was modified internally with extra strong valve springs and equipped with twin SU carburetors to give a peppy 50 bhp gross (43 bhp net).

DUAL LIGHTS
Sidelights double as turn signals.

BUMPERS
The Bugeye was a budget sports car built down to a price. Bumpers with overrider were a sensible and popular extra that would set you back $10–15 in 1958.

GVS 668

GV

WHEELS
Drilled steel disc wheels with AH on plain hub.

AUSTIN-HEALEY SPRITE MK1

At just under 11 ft 5 in (3.5 m), the Bugeye is not quite as small as it seems. Its pert looks were only part of the car's cult appeal, for with its firm, even harsh, ride it had a traditional British sports car feel. A nimble performer, you could hustle it along a winding road, cornering flat and clicking through the gears on the gear lever.

CLEAN LINES
The design has a classic simplicity, free of needless chrome embellishment; there is no external door handle to interrupt the flowing flanks.

SPECIFICATIONS

MODEL Austin-Healey Sprite Mk1 (1958–61)
PRODUCTION 38,999
BODY STYLE Two-seater roadster.
CONSTRUCTION Unibody/chassis.
ENGINE BMC A-Series 948cc, four-cylinder, overhead valve.
POWER OUTPUT 43 bhp at 5200 rpm.
TRANSMISSION Four-speed manual, synchromesh on top three ratios.
SUSPENSION *Front:* Independent, coil springs and wishbones. *Rear:* Quarter-elliptic leaf springs, rigid axle.
BRAKES Hydraulic, drums all around.
MAXIMUM SPEED 84 mph (135 km/h)
0–60 MPH (0–96 KM/H) 20.5 sec
A.F.C. 35–45 mpg

ROUND RUMP
It is not so much a trunk, as it does not open; more a luggage locker with access behind the rear seats.

HOOD
The complex one-piece hood is made up of four main panels.

LOW DOWN
The Bugeye's low stance aids flat cornering. Ground clearance is better than it looks, just under 5 in (12.7 cm).

COMPETITION
With its tunable A-series engine, the Bugeye is still a popular club racer. Sprites also put up spirited performances at Le Mans and Sebring. Special-bodied Sebring Sprites are rare and prized.

AUSTIN-HEALEY 3000

THE HEALEY HUNDRED was a sensation at the 1952 Earl's Court Motor Show. Austin's Leonard Lord had already contracted to supply the engines, but when he noticed the sports car's impact, he decided he wanted to build it, too. It was transformed overnight into the Austin-Healey 100, with a new badge designed in the wee small hours. Donald Healey had spotted a gap in the American sports car market between the Jaguar XK120 *(see pages 134–35)* and the cheap and cheerful MG T series *(see pages 172–73)*. His hunch was right, for about 80 percent of all production went Stateside. Over the years this rugged bruiser became increasingly civilized. In 1956, it received a six-cylinder engine in place of the four, but in 1959 the 3000 was born. It became increasingly refined – with front disc brakes, then windup windows – and ever faster. Our featured car is the last of the generation, a 3000 MkIII. Although it edges into grand tourer territory, it is also the fastest of all Big Healeys and is still a true sports car.

ENGINE
Under the hood of the biggest of the so-called Big Healeys is the 2912cc straight six that was designated as the 3000. This is the most powerful of the big bangers, pumping out a hefty 150 bhp.

COUNTRY CLUB STYLE
Period advertisement emphasizes Austin-Healey's fine pedigree as a surefooted thoroughbred sports car.

WINDSHIELD
In 1962, the 3000 acquired a wraparound windshield and windup windows, as the once raw sports car adopted trappings of sophistication.

WHEELS
Wire wheels were options on some models, standard on others.

HOOD SCOOP
All six-cylinder Healeys featured a hood scoop; the longer engine pushed the radiator forward, the scoop cleared the underhood protrusion to aid airflow.

THE HEALEY GRIN
From the traditional Healey diamond grille, the mouth of the Austin-Healey developed into a wide grin, initially with horizontal bars and finally with vertical slats.

STOP AND GO
As the Healey 3000 became beefier throughout the 1960s, modern radial tires helped keep it on course.

SPECIFICATIONS

MODEL Austin-Healey 3000 (1959–68)
PRODUCTION 42,926 (all 3000 models)
BODY STYLES Two-seater roadster, 2+2 roadster, 2+2 convertible.
CONSTRUCTION Separate chassis/body.
ENGINE 2912cc overhead-valve, straight-six.
POWER OUTPUT 3000 MkI: 124 bhp at 4600 rpm. 3000 MkII: 132 bhp at 4750 rpm. 3000 MkIII: 150 bhp at 5250 rpm.
TRANSMISSION Four-speed manual with overdrive.
SUSPENSION *Front:* Independent coil springs and wishbones, antiroll bar. *Rear:* Semielliptic leaf springs. Lever-arm shocks all around.
BRAKES Front discs; rear drums.
MAXIMUM SPEED 110–120 mph (177–193 km/h)
0–60 MPH (0–96 KM/H) 9.5–10.8 sec
A.F.C. 17–34 mpg

AUSTIN-HEALEY 3000 MkIII

The Austin-Healey put on weight over the years. It became gradually more refined, too, but stayed true to its original sports car spirit. The two major influences on its changing faces were the all-important needs of the American market and the impositions of Austin, both as parts supplier and as frugal keeper of purse strings. But from the start, the styling was always a major asset and what you see here in the 3000 MkIII is the eventual culmination of those combined styling forces.

MORE POWER
In 1959, the 2639cc six cylinder of the Healey 100/6 was bored out to 2912cc and rounded up to give the model name 3000.

COMFORTS
Updated weather equipment is an improvement on earlier efforts, which took two jugglers 10 minutes to erect.

REFINED REAR
The first prototype rear end treatment featured fins that were replaced by a classic round rump.

INTERIOR
Once spartan, the cockpit of the Austin-Healey became increasingly luxurious, with a polished veneer dash and even a lockable glove box to complement the fine leather and rich carpet. One thing remained traditional — engine heat meant the cockpit was always a hot place to be.

AUSTIN *Mini Cooper*

THE MINI COOPER was one of Britain's great sports car legends, an inspired concoction that became the definitive rally car of the 1960s and 1970s. In the 1964 Monte Carlo Rally, with Paddy Hopkirk at the wheel, the Cooper produced a giant-killing performance, trouncing 4.7-liter Ford Fairlanes and coming in first, followed in fourth place by yet another Cooper driven by Timo Makinen. After that it never looked back, winning the 1962 and 1964 Tulip Rallies, the 1963 Alpine Rally, and the 1965 and 1967 Monte Carlo, as well as notching up more than 25 other prestigious competition wins.

Because of its size, maneuverability, and front-wheel drive, the Cooper could dance around bigger, more unwieldy cars and scuttle off to victory. Even driven to the absolute limit, it would still corner as if it were on rails long after rear-wheel drive cars were sliding sideways. The hot Mini was a perfect blend of precise steering, terrific handling balance, and a feeling that you could get away with almost anything. The Mini Cooper was originally the brainchild of racing car builder John Cooper, who received $4.00 royalty on every car. However, the Mini's designer, Alec Issigonis, thought it should be a "people's car" rather than a performance machine and did not approve of a tuned Mini. Fortunately BMC (British Motor Corporation) did, and agreed to a trial run of just 1,000 cars. One of BMC's better decisions.

ENGINE
The 1071cc A-series engine would rev to 7200 rpm, producing 72 bhp. Crankshaft, connecting rods, valves, and rockers were all toughened. The Cooper also had a bigger oil pump and beefed-up gearbox.

INTERIOR
The Cooper has typical rally-car features: wood-rim Moto-Lita wheel, fire extinguisher, Halda trip meter, tachometer, stopwatches, and map light. Only the center speedometer, heater, and switches are standard equipment.

THE RALLY CAR
Sir Peter Moon and John Davenport leave the start ramp in the 1964 Isle of Man Manx Trophy Rally in 24 PK. But, while leading the pack on the penultimate stage of the rally at Druidale, 24 PK was rolled and needed a complete rebodying. Many factory-built Coopers led a hard life, often rebuilt and rebodied several times.

SPEEDY CORNERING
With a low center of gravity and a wheel at each extreme corner, the Mini had the perfect credentials for race-car-like handling.

GRILLE
Front grille was quick-release to give access for emergency repairs.

COOPER S
The Cooper S, built between 1963–67, had wider wheels, radial tires, different badging, and a choice of 970 or 1071cc engines. The 970 S is the rarest of all Coopers, with only 964 made.

SPOTLIGHT
Roof-mounted spotlight could be rotated from inside the car.

WINDSHIELD
Windshield was glass but all other windows were made out of plastic to save weight.

BRAKES
Lockheed disc brakes and power assist provided the stopping power.

NUMBER PLATE
Competitions departments often changed number plates, bodyshells, and chassis numbers, making it hard to identify genuine ex-works Coopers.

AUSTIN MINI COOPER
24 PK wears the classic Mini rally uniform of straight-through exhaust, Minilite wheels, roll bar, twin fuel tanks, and lightweight stick-on number plates. British Motor Corporation had a proactive Competitions Department, preparing racing Minis with enthusiasm and precision. The Cooper's success in the 1960s is testament to the department's work.

SPECIFICATIONS
MODEL Austin Mini Cooper (1963–69)
PRODUCTION 145,000 (all models)
BODY STYLE Sedan.
CONSTRUCTION All steel two-door monocoque mounted on front and rear sub-frames.
ENGINE 4-cylinder 970cc/997cc/ 998cc/1071cc/1275cc.
POWER OUTPUT 65 bhp at 6500 rpm to 76 bhp at 5800 rpm.
TRANSMISSION Four-speed, no synchromesh on first.
SUSPENSION Independent front and rear suspension with rubber cones and wishbones (hydrolastic from late 1964).
BRAKES Lockheed front discs with rear drums.
MAXIMUM SPEED 100 mph (161 km/h)
0–60 MPH (0–96 KM/H) 12.9 sec
0–100 MPH (0–161 KM/H) 20 sec
A.F.C. 30 mpg

BENTLEY R-Type Continental

IN ITS DAY the Bentley Continental, launched in 1952, was the fastest production four-seater in the world and was acclaimed as "a modern magic carpet which annihilates distance." Some 43 years later, it is rightly considered one of the greatest cars of all time. Designed for the English country gentleman, it was understated, but had a lithe, sinewy beauty rarely seen in any other car of its era.

Rolls-Royce's plan was to create a fast touring car for wealthy customers, and to do that the company had to reduce both size and weight. Aluminum construction helped shed the weight, while wind tunnel testing created that slippery shape. Small fins at the back were not for decoration – they actually aided the car's directional stability. The result was a magnificent touring machine that could exceed 115 mph (185 km/h) and manage a 0–60 mph (96 km/h) time of just over 13 seconds. But such avant-garde development did not come cheap. In 1952, the R-Type Continental was the most expensive production car in the world at $18,000 – today's equivalent is about $750,000.

HALFWAY THROUGH THE CONTINENTAL'S PRODUCTION RUN, AUTOMATIC GEARBOXES WERE OFFERED AS AN OPTION AND ADDED TO NO LESS THAN 46 OF THE 208 CARS BUILT

DASHBOARD
Beautifully detailed dash mirrored the Continental's exterior elegance. The first R-Types had manual gearboxes with a right-hand floor-mounted lever, thus reflecting the car's sporting character.

PRODUCTION CARS HAD AN EVEN LOWER ROOFLINE THAN THE ORIGINAL PROTOTYPE

PROTOTYPE HAD SKIRTS COVERING THE REAR WHEELS TO AID AIR FLOW

BENTLEY S-SERIES CONVERTIBLE
The Bentley S-Series Convertible of the late 1950s and early 1960s may bear a passing family resemblance to the Continental, but it does not possess the same tense urgency of line.

THE CONTINENTAL'S AERODYNAMICS WERE DECADES AHEAD OF ITS TIME

BODY WEIGHT WAS KEPT TO A MINIMUM BECAUSE NO 1950s TIRES COULD COPE WITH SPEEDS OVER 120 MPH (193 KM/H)

GENTLY TAPERING
REAR FENDERS
FUNNEL AIR INTO
THE SLIPSTREAM

SMALL REAR
WINDOW WAS A
THROWBACK TO
PREWAR CARS

AERODYNAMIC TESTING

The Continental spent much time in the wind tunnel to reduce air drag during forward motion. Sweeping rear quarters directed the wind over the rear wheels.

ENGINE

Continentals used a 4-liter straight six engine of 4566cc—increased to 4887cc in May 1954, known as the big bore engine. Carburetion was by two SU HD8 units. Speeds ranged from 50 mph (80 km/h) in first to almost 120 mph (193 km/h) in top.

ALUMINUM CONSTRUCTION

The body, side window, and window frames were made from lightweight aluminum – courtesy of H.J. Mulliner & Co. Ltd. The prototype had heavy-duty aluminum bumpers; production cars had steel ones.

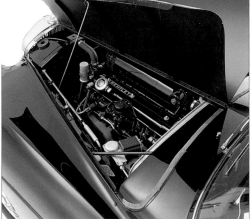

BENTLEY ORNAMENT

The Continental traded heavily on Bentley's prewar reputation for quick touring cars. Perhaps more than any other postwar Bentley, it remained loyal to that tradition of aristocratic speed.

DURING PROTOTYPE TESTING NORMAL SIX-PLY TIRES LASTED ONLY 20 MILES (32 KM)

—A POSTWAR CLASSIC—

Designed by Rolls-Royce stylist John Blatchley, the Continental bears an uncanny resemblance to a Pininfarina R-Type prototype shown at the 1948 Paris Salon.

BLATCHLEY INSISTED that he arrived at the Continental's unmistakable shape using only the then-new principles of aerodynamics. He reduced the radiator height to help air distribution and gave the front windshield a steep angle, joining it to the sides of the body to allow the air to spill away. Such dramatic lines were claimed not to be a product of artistic endeavor, but of scientific research. Such was the lure, and indeed the cost, of the Continental that it was first introduced on an export-only basis – 100 of the total production of 208 went abroad. Only 108 were left in the hands of UK owners. This forced the British motoring magazine *Autocar* to remark: "such a car as the Continental is bound to be costly, and the British, who make it, cannot own it: but it goes abroad as proof that a nation where the creators are constantly subjected to the debasement of their own living standards can still keep alive the idea of perfection for others to enjoy." Nothing, it would seem, has changed.

Another car that possibly pre-empted the Continental's lines is the late 1940s Cadillac. There is the vaguest hint of plagiarism by Bentley. British motoring historian Andrew White declared "the 1949 Cadillac was certainly an inspiration for the 1952 Bentley Continental." And he might be

1953 BENTLEY R-TYPE CONTINENTAL

BENTLEY
R-Type Continental

TRUNK WAS CONSIDERED LARGE ENOUGH TO CARRY LUGGAGE FOR TOURING

REAR FLANKS ARE LIKE THE TENSE HAUNCHES OF A SPRINTER

REPATRIATED CONTINENTALS
During the Classic Car boom of the eighties, many Continentals were exported to America and Japan. British collectors, anxious to preserve their disappearing heritage, are now actively repatriating as many as possible. A full list of the whereabouts of every Continental made is now being compiled.

GB

UKL 109

right. Both had sweeping tails, dorsal fins, and lean, smooth lines. American historian Richard Langworth asserts that, "the Cadillac was one of the industry's all-time design greats. Indeed, the grandly praised Bentley Continental, which appeared in '52, had body styling not unlike that of the '49 Caddy."

But that is where the similarity ends. The Bentley handled, the Cadillac did not. America's luxury car was happy wallowing along Sunset Boulevard. The Continental was more at home on a hectic run from London to St. Tropez. It was a car that begged you to depress its accelerator pedal to the floor and reassured you with its immensely powerful brakes and commendable body control, always exuding the poise and grace of a well-

1947 CADILLAC "62" COUPE

mannered thoroughbred.

Collectors seem to agree that the Continental stands alone as the finest postwar Bentley and one of the world's all-time great cars. Proof that it is a far better car than the Cadillac can be found in the current market values of each. The Cadillac is merely admired; the Bentley is revered, which is why you can buy ten 1949 Cadillacs for the price of a single R-Type Continental.

DOING THE CONTINENTAL

In 1952, with wartime austerity a fading memory, this was one of the flashiest and most rakish cars money could buy. Today, this exemplar of breeding and privilege stands as a resplendent memorial to the affluence and optimism of 1950s Britain.

DESPITE THE NEED TO KEEP WEIGHT DOWN, IT WAS UNTHINKABLE TO SKIMP ON THAT LAVISH INTERIOR

CLASSIC GOTHIC RADIATOR SHELL WAS CONSIDERED FAR MORE SPORTING THAN ROLLS-ROYCE'S DORIC EXAMPLE

FRONT FOG LIGHTS WERE KNOWN AS PASS LIGHTS FOR OVERTAKING

UKL 109

BENTLEY *Flying Spur*

ARGUABLY THE MOST BEAUTIFUL postwar Bentley, the Flying Spur was the first four-door Continental. Initially, Rolls-Royce would not allow coachbuilder H.J. Mulliner to use the name Continental, insisting it should only apply to two-door cars. After months of pressure from Mulliner, R-R relented and allowed the shapely coachbuilt car to be known as a proper Continental. More than worthy of the hallowed name, the Flying Spur was launched in 1957, using the standard S1 chassis. In 1959, it inherited R-R's 220 bhp, oversquare, aluminum V-8. By July 1962, the body was given the quad headlight treatment and upgraded into what some consider to be the best of the breed – the S3 Flying Spur. Subtle, understated, and elegant, Flying Spurs are rare. In their day they were among the most admired and refined machines in the world.

ENGINE
Rolls-Royce's long-serving 6.2-liter V-8, still in use today, has aluminum cylinder heads, block, and pistons. The hydraulic tappets were originally supplied by Chrysler, but since this was not good for R-R's image, they insisted they be made back in England.

CAM AND ROLLER POWER STEERING PROVIDES 50 PERCENT ASSISTANCE AT HIGH SPEED, 80 PERCENT WHEN PARKING

INTERIOR
The Interior is pure gentleman's club, with carefully detailed switches, the finest leather and walnut, and West of England cloth for the headlining. The large, spindly steering wheel was power-assisted, standard equipment in 1962. All S3s were automatic, although a few manual S1 Continentals were built.

FRONTAL ASPECT
The four-headlight nose was shared with the standard Steel Bentley S3, although the radiator and hood line were lowered. The body is hand-rolled aluminum.

FPG 74B

SUSPENSION
Rear suspension was by semielliptic leaf springs and radius arm and could be adjusted hydraulically between "firm" and "soft" settings.

BRAKES
Flying Spur has four-shoe drum brakes. Because Rolls-Royce brakes should never squeal, the company waited until 1965 to put disc brakes on its cars.

OPTIONAL UNIT
Optional air-conditioning unit hidden behind the front wheel.

S2 FLYING SPUR
Beautifully proportioned, many believe the Flying Spur to be more handsome than other R-Rs or Bentleys of the period.

S3 BENTLEY CONTINENTAL H.J. MULLINER FLYING SPUR
Coachbuilder H.J. Mulliner would receive the chassis from Rolls Royce and clothe it with a hand-built body. Although customers would often have to wait up to 18 months for their cars to be completed, the finished product was considered the epitome of good taste and refinement.

TIRES
Tires were 8.20x15 Dunlop tubeless cross plys.

SPECIFICATIONS

MODEL S3 Bentley Continental HJ Mulliner Flying Spur (1962–66)
PRODUCTION 291
BODY STYLE Four-door, five-seater.
CONSTRUCTION Aluminum body, separate steel cross-braced box section chassis.
ENGINE V-8, 6230cc.
POWER OUTPUT Never officially declared.
TRANSMISSION Four-speed automatic.
SUSPENSION *Front:* independent coil springs and wishbones. *Rear:* semielliptic leaf springs.
BRAKES Four-wheel Girling drums.
MAXIMUM SPEED 115 mph (185 km/h)
0–60 MPH (0–96 KM/H) 10.8 sec
0–100 MPH (0–161 KM/H) 34.2 sec
A.F.C. 13.8 mpg

WEIGHTY REAR
Rear view shows sheer bulk of the car, which weighed in at close to two tons. Yet the swooping roof line and tapering tail still manage to lend an air of performance.

BMW *507*

INSTRUMENT PANEL
CONSISTS OF A CLOCK
FLANKED BY A BIG
SPEEDOMETER AND A
6500 RPM TACHOMETER

WHOEVER WOULD have thought that in the mid-'50s BMW would have unveiled something as voluptuously beautiful as the 507. The company had a fine pre-World War II heritage that culminated in the crisp 328, but it did not resume car manufacturing until 1952, with the curvy, but slightly plump, six cylinder 501 sedan. Then, at the Frankfurt show of late 1955, BMW hit us with the 507, designed by Count Albrecht Goertz. The 507 was a fantasy made real; not flashy, but dramatic and with poise and presence. BMW hoped the 507 would solve its precarious finances, winning sales in the lucrative American market. But the BMW's exotic looks and performance were more than matched by its high price. Production, which had been largely by hand, ended in March 1959 after just 252 – some say 253 – had been built. In fact, the 507 took BMW to the brink of financial oblivion, yet if that had been the last BMW it would have been a beautiful way to die.

INTERIOR
There are gimmicky horn pulls behind the steering wheel, but other features foretold later innovations; some cars had internally adjusting door mirrors.

RAKISH BODY
The 507's body is an all-aluminum affair atop a simple tubular steel chassis.

TOP
You rarely see a 507 with its top raised, but it is simple to erect and remarkably handsome.

REAR BUMPER
The 507 features minimal chrome. Rear bumpers have no bulky overriders.

PIPE MUSIC
The BMW has a brisk, wholesome bark and the unmistakable creamy wuffle of a V-8.

WHEELS
Bolt-on steel wheels were fitted to many cars, but knock-off Rudge items like these remain the most sought-after option.

LUGGAGE
Inside, there is enough room for a reasonable amount of luggage.

DOOR HANDLES
Like the bumpers, the door handles are surprisingly discreet – if not particularly easy to use.

ROUNDELS
Eight BMW stylized propeller roundels, including those on wheel trims and wheel spinners, grace the 507, nine if you include the badge in the center of the steering wheel.

BRAKES
Most 507s were built with four-wheel Alfin drum brakes. Some later cars have more effective front disc brakes.

HANDLING
The 507 exhibited marked understeer; throttle response is so instant that the tail easily snaps out.

RADIATOR GRILLE
BMW's familiar kidney grilles become widely flared "nostrils."

TWIN ZENITH CARBURETORS ARE THE SAME AS THOSE OF CONTEMPORARY PORSCHES

— SPECIFICATIONS —

MODEL BMW 507 (1956–59)
PRODUCTION 252/3, most LHD
BODY STYLE Two seater roadster.
CONSTRUCTION Box section and tubular steel chassis; aluminum body.
ENGINE All-aluminum 3168cc V-8, two valves per cylinder.
POWER OUTPUT 150 bhp at 5000 rpm; some later cars 160 bhp at 5600 rpm.
TRANSMISSION Four-speed manual.
SUSPENSION *Front:* Unequal length wishbones, torsion bar springs and telescopic shocks.
Rear: Live axle, torsion bar springs.
BRAKES Drums front and rear; front discs and rear drums on later cars
MAXIMUM SPEED 125 mph (201 km/h); 135–140 mph (217–225 km/h) with optional 3.42:1 final drive.
0–60 MPH (0–96 KM/H) 9 sec
A.F.C. 18 mpg

BMW 507

Mounted on a tubular steel chassis cut down from sedans, Albrecht Goertz's aluminum body is reminiscent of the contemporary – and slightly cheaper – Mercedes-Benz 300SL roadster; from the front it resembles the later AC Aces and Cobra *(see pages 20–23)*. All 252 cars were built as convertibles; a detachable hardtop was available as an option.

HOOD VENT
The ornate chrome plated grilles in the front fenders cover functional engine bay air vents.

ENGINE
The 3.2-liter all-aluminum engine was light and powerful and tuned 160 bhp versions, when mated to an optional 3.42 – 1 final-drive ratio, were good for 140 mph (225 km/h).

TOOL KIT
Like all modern BMWs, the 507 has a tool kit – now rarely complete – to carry out minor repairs and adjustments.

BMW 3.0 CSL

ONE LITTLE LETTER CAN MAKE so much difference. In this case it is the L at the end of the name tag that makes the BMW 3.0CSL so special. The BMW CS pillarless coupes of the late 1960s and early 1970s were elegant and good-looking green house tourers. But add that L and you have a legend. The letter actually stands for "Leightmetall," and when tacked to the rump of the BMW it amounts to war paint, far more intimidating than today's impotent GTi acronyms. The original CSL of 1974 had a 2985cc engine developing 180 bhp, no front bumper, and a mixture of aluminum and thinner-than-standard steel body-panels. In August 1972, a cylinder-bore increase took the CSL's capacity to 3003cc with 200 bhp, and allowed it into Group 2 for competition purposes. But it is the wild-winged, so-called "Batmobile" homologation special that really boils the blood of boy racers. An ultimate road car and great racer, rare, short-lived and high-priced, this charismatic, pared-down Beemer has absolutely classic credentials.

ROAD-GOING RACER
The Batmobile's aerodynamic aids had to be homologated by fitting to at least 500 road cars. They were considered so outrageous that most were supplied as kits for owners to fit – or not – at their discretion.

FLYING MACHINE
The highly effective fenders and spoilers of the so-called Batmobile (left) were developed to keep the 3.2-liter racing 3.0CSLs firmly on the track at high speed.

DO-IT-YOURSELF
Road-going cars were only slightly lighter than the CS and CSi; they even had BMW's trademark toolkit, neatly hinged from the underside of the aluminum trunk lid.

STEERING WHEEL IS STRAIGHT OUT OF THE CS/CSi

RACING TRIM
Optional air guide for rear end of roof.

INTERIOR

British-spec CSLs, like this car, retained Scheel lightweight bucket seats, but had carpets, electric windows (front and rear), power steering, and a sliver of wood.

SPECIFICATIONS

MODEL BMW 3.0CSL (1971–74)

PRODUCTION 1,208 (all versions)

BODY STYLE Two-door pillarless coupe.

CONSTRUCTION Steel monocoque, steel and aluminum body.

ENGINE 2985cc, 3003cc, or 3153cc in-line six.

POWER OUTPUT 200 bhp at 5500 rpm (3003cc).

TRANSMISSION 4-speed manual.

SUSPENSION *Front:* MacPherson struts and anti-roll bar. *Rear:* Semi-trailing arms, coil springs, and anti-roll bar.

BRAKES Power assisted ventilated discs front and rear.

MAXIMUM SPEED 135 mph (217 km/h) (3003cc)

0–60 MPH 7.3 sec (3003cc)

0–100 MPH 21 sec (3003cc)

A.F.C. 22–25 mpg

KS·K 5405

CALLING CARD
The large script leaves no one in any doubt about what has just overtaken them.

KS·K 5405

BMW 3.0CSL

Mild rather than wild and winged, the CSL is certainly one of the best-looking cars of its generation. With its pillarless look, the cabin is light and airy, despite the black interior. But all that glass made it hot; air vents behind the BMW rear-pillar badge helped a little.

ENGINE

In genuine racing trim, the Batmobile's 3.2-liter straight-six engine gave nearly 400 bhp and, for 1976, nearly 500 bhp with turbocharging. But road cars like this British-spec 3003cc 3.0CSL gave around 200 bhp on fuel injection.

ORIGINAL 2985CC CAPACITY WAS INCREASED TO THIS 3003CC ENGINE FOR HOMOLOGATION PURPOSES

WHEELS
7-in (18-cm) light-aluminum wheels covered by delicate chrome-plated wheelarch extensions.

BUMPER TO BUMPER
German-market CSLs had no front bumper and a fiber-glass rear bumper; this car's metal items show it to be a British-spec model.

3.0 CSL

BMW M1

THE M1 – A SIMPLE NAME, a simple concept. M stood for Motorsport GmbH, BMW's separate competition division. And the number one? Well, this was going to be a first, because this time BMW was not just going to develop capable racers from its competent sedans and coupes. It was going to build a high-profile, beat-all racer, with roadgoing versions basking in the reflected glory of on-track success.

The first prototype ran in 1977, with the M1 entering production in 1978. By the end of production in 1980, a mere 457 racing and roadgoing M1s had been built, making it one of the rarest and most desirable of modern BMWs. Although its racing career was only briefly distinguished, it is as one of the all-time ultimate road cars that the M1 stands out, for it is not just a 277 bhp, 160 mph (257 km/h) "autobahnstormer." It is one of the least demanding supercars to drive, a testament to its fine engineering, and is in many ways as remarkable as the gorgeous 328 of the 1930s.

SPECTACLE ON THE TRACK
BMW teamed up with the FOCA (Formula One Constructors' Association) to create the spectacular Procar series – M1-only races planned primarily as supporting events for Grand Prix meetings in 1979 and 1980.

INTERIOR
The all-black interior is somber, but fixtures are all made to a high standard; unlike those of many supercars, the heating and ventilation systems actually work. The driving position is good, with an adjustable steering wheel and well-placed pedals in the narrow footwells.

ENGINE
The M1's 3453cc straight six engine uses essentially the same cast-iron cylinder block as BMW's 635CSi coupe, but with a forged-aluminum crankshaft and slightly longer connecting rods. The cylinder head is an aluminum casting, with two chain-driven overhead cams operating four valves per cylinder.

LEFT-HAND DRIVE
All BMW M1s are left-hand drive.

AIR DAM
Unlike many of today's high-performance sedan cars, the M1 has only a vestigial lip-type front air dam.

HEADLIGHTS
Retractable headlights are backed up by grille-mounted driving lights.

SLATTED COVER
Rearward visibility through the slatted, heavily buttressed engine cover is restricted.

BMW M1

The BMW M1 was not a strict in-house BMW product, but one with widespread international influences. From a concept car created in 1972 by Frenchman Paul Bracq, the final shape of the body was created in Turin, Italy, by Giorgio Giugiaro's ItalDesign. Lamborghini also contributed to the engineering. Yet somehow it all comes together in a unified shape and, with the double kidney grille, it is still unmistakably a BMW.

REAR LIGHTS
Large rear light clusters are the same as those of the BMW's 6-series coupe and 7-series sedan models.

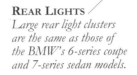

GAS CAP
Twin tanks are refilled via an orifice behind each door. Remarkably, fuel consumption can be as good as 30 mpg.

MIRROR
Big door mirrors — essential for maneuvering the M1 — are electrically adjustable.

AIR VENT
Strategically positioned air vents keep the powerful 3.5-liter engine cool.

SPECIFICATIONS

MODEL BMW M1 (1978–80)
PRODUCTION 457, all LHD
BODY STYLE Two seater mid-engined sports.
CONSTRUCTION Tubular steel space-frame with fiberglass body.
ENGINE Inline six, four valves per cylinder, dohc/3453cc.
POWER OUTPUT 277 bhp at 6500 rpm.
TRANSMISSION Combined ZF five-speed gearbox and limited slip differential.
SUSPENSION Coil springs, wishbones and Bilstein gas-pressure telescopic shocks front and rear.
BRAKES Power assisted ventilated discs all around.
MAXIMUM SPEED 162 mph (261 km/h)
0–60 MPH (0–96 KM/H) 5.4 sec
A.F.C. 24–30 mpg

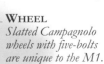

WHEEL
Slatted Campagnolo wheels with five-bolts are unique to the M1.

BUICK *Roadmaster*

V-8 HAD 10:1 COMPRESSION RATIO, WHICH MEANT 100 OCTANE FUEL

IN 1957 AMERICA WAS gearing up for the 1960s. Little Richard screamed his way to the top with "Lucille" and Elvis had nine hits in a row. Jack Kerouac penned his immortal novel *On the Road*, inspiring carloads of Americans to seek the adman's "Promised Land" along Eisenhower's new interstates. Fins and chrome were applied with a trowel and General Motors, whose styling had begun to lag behind the rest of Detroit's excesses, spent several hundred million dollars restyling its Buick model range. Despite celebrating the ninth million Buick built, 1957 sales were down 24 percent, ranking it fourth in the industry.

The Roadmaster of 1957 was low and mighty, a massive 17 ft 11 in (5.46 m) long and 6 ft (1.83 m) wide. Power was up to 300 hp, along with trendy dorsal fins, Sweepspear body moldings, and a trio of chrome chevrons on the rear fenders. Four Ventiports, a Buick trademark harking back to the original 1949 Roadmaster, still graced the sweeping front fenders. But America did not take to Buick's new look, especially some of the fashionable jet-age design motifs. The chrome bands separating the three-piece rear windows, for example, met with huge consumer resistance and were an option that could be deleted on the order form.

FAST BUICK
The 5.9-liter V-8 pushed out 300 hp, making it one of the hottest Buicks; it was capable of 112 mph (180 km/h) and a zero-to-60 in ten seconds. Dynaflow transmission had variable pitch blades, which changed their angle like those of an airplane propeller.

FICKLE FASHION
Wraparound windshields first emerged in 1954 and by 1957 were standard.

AMERICAN CLASSIC
The 1951 Roadmaster Convertible had become an American icon, the shape of things to come, and one of the first of the great American land yachts with some "get-up-and-go."

GRATUITOUS ORNAMENTATION
The Roadmaster's flattened Ventiports were useless vanities, suggesting fire-breathing power.

GAS CAP
The Roadmaster's rear bumper was home to a new centered gas cap.

STYLING EXCESS
Vast chrome rear bumper made for a prodigious overhang, with massive Dagmar-like overriders, razor-sharp taillights and fluted underpanel – a stylistic nightmare.

FIN FASHION
The Roadmaster showed that by 1957 tail fin fashion was rising to ridiculous heights.

SPECIFICATIONS	
MODEL	Buick Roadmaster (1957)
PRODUCTION	36,638
BODY STYLE	Two-door, five-seater hardtop coupe.
CONSTRUCTION	X-braced chassis with steel body.
ENGINE	V-8 364cid.
POWER OUTPUT	250 hp at 4400 rpm.
TRANSMISSION	Dynaflow two-speed automatic.
SUSPENSION	Independent coil springs.
BRAKES	Hydraulic power-assisted drums all around.
MAXIMUM SPEED	112 mph (180 km/h)
0–60 MPH (0–96 KM/H)	10.5 sec
0–100 MPH (0–161 KM/H)	21.2 sec
A.F.C.	12 mpg

GM BADGE INDICATES THAT BUICKS WERE BUILT AT GM'S FACTORY IN FLINT, MICHIGAN

DASHBOARD
Roadmaster standard special equipment included a Red Liner speedometer, glovebox light, trip odometer, and a color-coordinated dash panel.

BUICK ROADMASTER

Aircraft design exerted a major influence on automotive styling in the 1950s and the '57 Roadmaster was no exception. With wraparound windshield, cockpitlike roof area, and turbine-style wheel covers, a nation of Walter Mittys could imagine themselves vapor-trailing through the stratosphere.

PRESTIGE
The Roadmaster was one of Buick's most luxurious models and wore its hood ornament with pride.

JET AGE
Giant chrome protuberances suggested jet-turbine power.

CABIN OR COCKPIT?
Rakish swooping roof line borrows heavily from bubble cockpits of jet fighters.

CADILLAC *Eldorado Convertible*

FOR 1950s AMERICA, cars did not come much more glamorous than the 1953 Eldorado. "A car apart – even from other Cadillacs," assured the advertising copy. The first Caddy to bear the Eldo name, it was seen as the ultimate and most desirable American luxury car, good enough even for Marilyn Monroe and Dwight Eisenhower. Conceived as a limited edition, the '53 brought avant-garde styling cues from Harley Earl's Motorama Exhibitions. Earl was General Motors' inspired chief designer, while the Motoramas were yearly futuristic car shows where his whims of steel took on form. At a hefty $7,750, nearly twice as much as the Cadillac Convertible and five times as much as a Chevrolet, the '53 was special. In 1954, Cadillac cut the price by 50 percent and soon Eldorados were leaving showrooms like heat-seeking missiles. Today collectors regard the '53 as the one that started it all – the first and most fabulous of the Eldorados.

ULTIMATE CRUISER
As Cadillac's finest flagship, the Eldorado had image by the bucketful. The 331cid V-8 engine was the most powerful yet, and the bodyline was ultrasleek.

WINDSHIELD
The standard Cadillac wraparound windshield was first seen on the '53.

INTERIOR
Standard equipment on the Eldo convertible was Hydra-Matic transmission, hydraulic windows, leather and cloth upholstery, tinted glass, vanity and side mirrors, and a "search" radio.

CHROME STYLING
The missile-shaped protuberances on the bumpers were known as Dagmars after the lushly upholstered TV starlet of the day.

SPARE WHEEL
The trunk-mounted spare wheel was an after-market continental touring kit.

FUTURISTIC EXHAUST
The twin exhausts emerge from the rear bumper – the beginnings of "jet-age" styling themes that would culminate in the outrageous 42-in (107-cm) fins on the 1959 Cadillac Coupe de Ville (see pages 58–61).

CADILLAC ELDORADO CONVERTIBLE
At the time the '53 was America's most powerful car, with a cast-iron V-8, four-barrel carburetor and wedge cylinder head. With the standard convertible weighing 300 lb (136 kg) less, the Eldorado was actually the slowest of the Cadillacs. But despite air conditioning boosting the car's weight to 4,800 lb (2,177 kg), top speed was still a brisk 116 mph (187 km/h).

DOOR HANDLE
Low and sleek, the '53's bodyline made a dip near the door handle that imitated the cut-down doors of British sports cars.

SLICK DESIGN
The hood neatly disappeared below a steel panel, giving the Eldorado a much cleaner uninterrupted line than other convertibles.

HOOD MADE OF ORLON ACRYLIC

WHEELS
Flashy whitewall tires and chrome wire wheels were standard on the Eldorado convertible but a $373 option on all other Cadillacs.

— **SPECIFICATIONS** —

MODEL Cadillac Eldorado Convertible (1953)
PRODUCTION 532
BODY STYLE Five-seater convertible.
CONSTRUCTION Steel bodywork.
ENGINE 5424cc V-8.
POWER OUTPUT 210 hp at 4150 rpm.
TRANSMISSION Three-speed Hydra-Matic Dual-Range automatic.
SUSPENSION *Front:* independent MacPherson strut; *Rear:* live axle with leaf springs.
BRAKES Front and rear drums.
MAXIMUM SPEED 116 mph (187 km/h)
0–60 MPH (0–96 KM/H) 12.8 sec
0–100 MPH (0–161 KM/H) 20 sec
A.F.C. 14–20 mpg

TWO-WAY MIRROR
The heavily chromed, hand-operated swiveling spotlight doubled as a door mirror.

BODY COLOR
Colors available were Alpine White, Aztec Red, Azure Blue, and Artisan Ochre.

CALIFORNIA
DRM CARS

CADILLAC *Convertible*

NO CAR BETTER sums up America at its peak than the 1959 Cadillac – a rocket-styled starship for orbiting the galaxy of new freeways in the richest and most powerful country on earth. With 42-inch fins, the '59 Caddy marks the zenith of American car design. Two tons in weight, 20 ft (6.1 m) long, and 6 ft (1.83 m) wide, it oozed money, self-confidence, and unchallenged power. Under a hood almost the size of Texas nestled an engine almost as big as California, a 6.3-liter 390cid V-8 – welcome to the world of eight miles to the gallon. But while it might have looked like it was jet-powered, the '59 handled like the Exxon Valdés. That enormous girth meant you needed a nine-lane freeway to do a U-turn and two tons of metalwork gave it all the get-up-and-go of the Empire State Building.

But the '59 Caddy will always be remembered as a glorious monument to the final years of shameless American optimism. And for a brief, hysterical moment the '59 was the preeminent American car, the ultimate in crazed consumerism. It was not only a car, but a symbol of its time that says more about 1950s America than a trunk of history books. The '59 Caddy *was* the American dream.

OTHER MODELS

As well as the eight-seater Fleetwood limo, you could have a four-door sedan, convertible, or the cinematic Eldorado Biarritz convertible, which was the most valuable '59 Cadillac of all.

1959 COUPE DE VILLE
Anybody who was anybody in early 1960s America drove a '59 Caddy. It was the best American car money could buy, with the pillarless two-door Coupe de Ville its most popular incarnation.

STYLING
General Motors went crazy in 1959 and the Cadillac pushed car styling to a new peak of absurdity.

LOW PROFILE
The '59's outrageous fins are accentuated by its very low profile, 3 in (8 cm) lower than the '58 model's already modest elevation.

EGG-SHAPED RUBY TAILLIGHTS ARE PURE JET AGE

42-INCH FINS ARE THE HIGHEST OF ANY CAR IN THE WORLD

EXTRAVAGANT MOUNDS OF CHROME MIGHT LOOK LIKE TURBINES BUT CONCEAL BACKUP LIGHTS

WITH HOOD CLOSED, THE CADDY HAD AN UNINTERRUPTED, DARTLIKE PROFILE

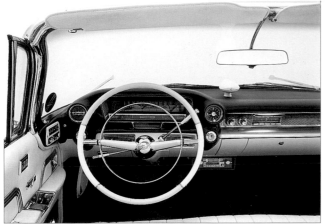

INTERIOR EXTRAS

Along with power brakes and steering, automatic transmission, central locking, and tinted glass, you could specify automatic headlight dimmers, and electrically operated seats, windows, and trunk.

ELECTRIC WINDOW PANEL

Four electric window controls and remote control for the side mirrors live in a neat panel on the driver's door. Detailing can only be described as Baroque, with large helpings of chrome all around.

CAR'S THE STAR

The '59 starred in many films. Here, in the aptly named movie *Pink Cadillac*, Clint Eastwood reclines on those dagger sharp fins.

AUTRONIC EYE WAS A GIMMICK THAT SOON DISAPPEARED FROM THE BROCHURES

AUTRONIC EYE

For $55, you could specify the Autronic Eye, which dimmed your headlights automatically when it sensed the lights of an oncoming car.

NOSE APPEAL

With a hood the size of an aircraft carrier, the '59 Caddy was perfect for a society where a car's importance was defined by the length of its nose.

SPECIFICATIONS

MODEL Cadillac Convertible (1959)
PRODUCTION 11,130
BODY STYLE Two-door, six-seater convertible.
CONSTRUCTION X-frame chassis, steel body.
ENGINE 6.3-liter 390cid V-8.
POWER OUTPUT 325/345 hp at 4800 rpm.
TRANSMISSION GM Hydra-Matic three-speed automatic.
SUSPENSION Coil springs all around with optional Freon-12 gas suspension.
BRAKES Four-wheel hydraulic power-assisted drums.
MAXIMUM SPEED 112 mph (180 km/h)
0–60 MPH (0–96 KM/H) 10.3 sec
0–100 MPH (0–161 KM/H) 2 3.1 sec
A.F.C. 8 mpg

ENGINE

The monster 6.3-liter V-8 engine had a cast-iron block, five main bearings, and hydraulic valve lifters, pushing out a not inconsiderable 325 hp at 4800 rpm.

CHROME DOOR QUARTERLIGHTS COULD BE SWIVELED FROM INSIDE THE CAR

STEEP, WRAP-AROUND WINDSHIELD COULD HAVE COME STRAIGHT OUT OF A FIGHTER PLANE

MASSIVE SLAB-SIDED DOORS GAVE EASY ENTRANCE AND EXIT

CHROME WAISTLINE STRIP GAVE BODY PANELS PROTECTION AGAINST JEALOUS CHEVROLETS

GLAMOROUS WHITE SIDEWALL TIRES WERE A CONVENIENCE OPTION AT $57

—FIN DE SIECLE CADILLAC—

Harley Earl, the man responsible for the '59, once said, "You can design a car so that every time you get into it, it's a relief – you have a little vacation for a while." His creations were not just a means of transportation but suggested an entire consumer culture and established a new set of national values.

AT THE END of the 1950s, the Russians had put the first Sputnik into orbit, Castro proclaimed a new government in Cuba, Khrushchev got cozy with China, and the gathering specter of nuclear war grew closer and closer. A year later, Kennedy would be elected to the White House and America would enter a new

decade of stylistic, social, and political change that would alter the fabric of its culture and lifestyle forever.

But the '59 Cadillac really did belong to the 1950s. With tail fins that rose a full 3½ ft (1.07 m) off the ground, it is an artifact, a talisman of its times. It was not just a car, but a styling icon, wonderfully representative of the

ONE OF HARLEY EARL'S FUTURISTIC DESIGNS

1920S CIGARETTE CARD SHOWING A "CAR OF THE FUTURE"

end of an era – the last years of American world supremacy and an obsession with rockets and space travel.

Harley Earl, directly responsible for the design of 50 million vehicles, completely changed the face of America and the way Americans perceived themselves. No single individual has had such a profound impact on the shape of man-made objects as Earl, and nobody since has been guilty of so many design excesses. On top of the space-

CADILLAC
Convertible

SEATS SIT 4 IN (10 CM) LOWER THAN THE '57 MODEL

EXTENSIVE INTERIOR
The interior is vast, and a true six-seater, with acres of leg, knee, head, and elbow room. Bucket seats were an optional extra on the Biarritz – only 99 out of 1,320 had them.

TRUNK IS CAVERNOUS AND CAN HOLD FIVE WHEELS AND TIRES

AUG PENNSYLVANIA
XSU-385

PONTIAC FIREBIRD PROTOTYPE

age theme, Earl grafted other images to his cars. Grilles had rows of chromium dentures, dashboards looked like flight decks with dozens of gratuitous switches, hoods sported phallic mascots, and bumpers sprouted enormous breast-shaped protrusions known as Dagmars. The grille was a subliminal form of threat display, while the sensuous bumpers were patently erotic. By the late 1950s, the American car was loaded with so many strange and sometimes contradictory symbols that the average American must have

felt as though he was in command of a four-wheeled, jet-powered bordello.

But the Caddy does not have a special place in the motoring history because it was an exceptional car. Far from it. '59s had a reputation as rust-raisers, front ends were notorious for

vibration, and the general quality was not up to what the market had come to expect from the premier American carmaker. In fact, commentators thought the '59 was too strident and garish. So did Cadillac, which lopped 6 in (15.5 cm) off the fins the next model year. Yet it is those fins which give the car such status in the annals of excess and have guaranteed its collectibility as a glorious piece of American 1950s kitsch.

SKETCH OF JET-POWERED TWO-SEATER DRAWN UP BY FORD'S ADVANCE STYLING SECTION

THE '59 HAD A BIG THIRST, WITH A 21-GALLON FUEL TANK, 23-PINT (US) TRANSMISSION, 12-PINT CRANKCASE, AND 10-PINT RADIATOR CAPACITY

DOUBLE HEADLIGHTS WERE A STYLING ESSENTIAL ON ALL 1960s AMERICAN CARS

STEERING ASSISTANCE

The featherlight power steering required only three-and-a-half turns lock-to-lock. The '59 could be hustled around with great panache, but you needed a 24-ft (7.3 m) turning radius.

2 FINNS
XSU-385

CHEVROLET *Corvette Sting Ray*

THE CHEVROLET CORVETTE is America's native sports car. The "plastic fantastic," born in 1953, is still plastic, and still fantastic more than 40 years later. Along the way, in 1992, it recorded its millionth sale and it is still hanging in there. Admittedly it has mutated over the years, but it has stayed true to its roots on every important aspect. Other US sports car contenders, like the Ford Thunderbird *(see pages 116–17)*, soon abandoned any sporting pretensions, adding weight and middle-aged girth, but not the Corvette. All Corvette fanciers have their favorite eras: for some it is the purity of the very first generation from 1953; others favor the glamorous 1956–62 models; but for many the Corvette came of age in 1963 with the birth of the Sting Ray.

ENGINE CHOICES
Sting Rays came in three engine sizes – naturally all V-8s – with power options from 250 hp to more than twice that. This featured car is a 1966 Sting Ray with "small block" 327cid V-8 and Holley four-barrel carburetor.

HIDDEN LIGHTS
Twin, pop-up headlights were hidden behind electrically operated covers; more than a gimmick, they aided aerodynamic efficiency.

"DUAL COCKPIT"
The Batmobile-style interior, with twin-hooped dash, is carried over from earlier Corvettes, but updated in the Sting Ray. The deep-dished, wood-effect wheel comes close to the chest. Power steering was an option.

— OTHER MODELS —
Until 1963, all Corvettes were open roadsters, but with the arrival of the Sting Ray, a hardtop coupe was now also available.

1963 SPLIT-SCREEN COUPE
The distinctive two-piece back window was used for 1963 only; consequently, this "design failing" is now the most sought after of Sting Ray coupes.

19 MICHIGAN 71
RMG·319
GREAT LAKE STATE

CHEVROLET CORVETTE STING RAY

The Sting Ray was a bold design breakthrough, giving concrete expression to many of the ideas of new GM styling chief Bill Mitchell. More than half of all production was in convertible roadsters, for which a hardtop was an option. From the rear, charismatic fastbacks could be a totally different car.

SIDE EXHAUST
Aluminum strip conceals side-mounted exhaust option; standard exhausts exited through bodywork below the rear bumper.

SPECIFICATIONS

MODEL Chevrolet Corvette Sting Ray (1963–67)

PRODUCTION 118,964

BODY STYLES Two-door sports convertible or fastback coupe.

CONSTRUCTION Fiberglass body; X-braced pressed-steel box-section chassis.

ENGINE OHV V-8, 327cid, 396cid, 427cid.

POWER OUTPUT 250–375 hp (327cid), 390–560 hp (427cid).

TRANSMISSION Four-speed, all-synchromesh manual, optional three-speed manual, or Powerglide automatic.

SUSPENSION Independent all around. *Front:* Unequal-length wishbones with coil springs; *Rear:* Transverse leaf.

BRAKES Drums to 1965, then four-wheel discs.

MAXIMUM SPEED 152 mph (245 km/h, 427 cid).

0–60 MPH (0–96 KM/H) 5.4 sec, 427 cid

0–100 MPH (0–161 KM/H) 13.1 sec

A.F.C. 9–16 mpg

SEATING
Seats are low and flat, rather than figure-hugging, but the view over the hood is great.

BRAKES
In 1965 the Sting Ray added four-wheel disc brakes in place of drums.

FLAG WAVING
The checkered flag denotes sporting lineage, the other flag bears the GM corporate "Bow Tie" and a Fleur de Lis — lest we forget that Louis Chevrolet was French.

NAME TRIVIA
Corvettes from 1963 to 1967 were Sting Rays; the restyled 1968 model became Stingray, one word.

HOOD
You can tell this is a "small block" engine – the hood power bulge was widened to accommodate the "big block" unit.

TRUNK SPACE
Fuel tank and spare tire took up most of the available trunk space, but at least the trunk opened; it did not on the fastback.

CHEVROLET *Impala*

THE CHEVY IMPALA was an evergreen best-seller and America's favorite family sedan. Chevrolet's product planners figured that America's middle classes would be a boom market in the early 1960s – and they were right. The Impala notched up nearly half a million sales in 1960. The fins, chrome, and mock vents meant it was bumper-to-bumper glitz, all at a sticker price of under $3,000.

With a wide range of engine sizes, transmission types, and body styles to choose from, the Impala had it all. And those crossed racing flags were not just empty chrome rhetoric. Enlightened buyers could specify the special Turbo-thrust V-8, making the Impala a "hot one" with a respectable 0–60 mph canter of just over nine seconds. Even though the styling was toned down for the 1960 model year, the finny Impala remains a perfect embodiment of 1960s American exuberance.

ENGINE
From a 235cid six-cylinder all the way up to a hot 348cid V-8, the Impala could be specified with some serious iron under its hood.

CHEVROLET BADGE
1959 marked a watershed for Chevrolet, moving out of the budget market to seduce aspirational suburbia with new styling themes.

ORIGINAL '58 IMPALA
1958 was the first year of the Impala, the flagship of the Chevy fleet and a calculated attempt to catch Ford and Plymouth, which had restyled their products the previous year. Styling was close to Cadillac's, and the Impala's new look rendered Buick and Oldsmobile dated. Some 181,500 Impalas were sold in 1958 – 15 percent of Chevy's production.

DASHBOARD
Aeronautical styling motifs abound, with gauges enclosed in flight-deck-type modules. Lower dash and glove compartment were covered in anodized aluminum for that high-tech look. Radio and electric clock were options.

LIGHT CLUSTER
Triple taillights and an aluminum rear panel were glorious pieces of gratuitous kitsch.

GLASS AREA
With the windows rolled down, the car is pillarless, with 90 percent all-around visibility.

TURN SIGNALS
Clear white lights nestling under the front bumper were not parking lights, but turn signals.

WHEEL COVERS
Deluxe wheel covers and whitewalls helped cut a mild suburban dash.

LABELING
Only crazy stylists would stoop to putting labels on the rear doors.

TAILPIPE
Single rear chrome exhaust exits impudently from behind the rear wheel.

CHEVROLET IMPALA FOUR-DOOR HARDTOP

Low, flashy, and beguiling, the Impala looked fast just standing still. Styling was a riot of streaking chrome. Quarter panel missile ornaments thrust rearward, while a chromium-finned projectile darted across the rear door, a quaint reminder of 1960s American obsession with all things space age. And those gullwing rear fins pursue a perfect horizontal line along the waist of the car, ending in a rounded flare on the extreme tip of both front fenders. Front and back windshields could have been taken straight out of the cockpit of a Lockheed Lightning. Even the radio antenna was raked at a provocative angle.

GRILLE
The Impala's slatted frontal aspect is its least pleasing facet. Built on a budget, the Venetian blind grille is an eyesore.

FINS
Compared to the '59, the fins on the '60 Impala were tame. Conventional Chevrolet customers did not like the previous model's weird extravagance.

STYLING
Despite the '60 Impala's supposedly quieter styling, no self-respecting American could bear to be without those trendy quad headlights.

HANDLING
With upper and lower A arms and coil springs, the Impala cornered with cinematic tire squeal and plenty of body roll.

SPECIFICATIONS

MODEL Chevrolet Impala (1960)

PRODUCTION Approx. 500,000

BODY STYLE Six-seater, four-door hardtop.

CONSTRUCTION Separate chassis, steel body.

ENGINE Various – 235cid straight-six to 348cid V-8.

POWER OUTPUT 230 hp at 4800 rpm to 335 hp at 5800 rpm.

TRANSMISSION Three-speed manual, two-speed Powerglide, and three-speed Turboglide automatics.

SUSPENSION *Front:* Coil springs and wishbones.
Rear: Coil springs and live axle.

BRAKES Four-wheel drums.

MAXIMUM SPEED 90–135 mph (145–217 km/h)

0–60 MPH (0–96 KM/H) 9–13 sec

0–100 MPH (0–161 KM/H) 20–27 sec

A.F.C. 14–17 mpg

CHEVROLET *Camaro RS Convertible*

RUMORS THAT General Motors had at last come up with something to steal sales from Ford's massively successful Mustang *(see pages 120–23)* swept through the American auto industry in the spring of 1966. Code-named Panther, the Camaro was announced to newspaper reporters on June 29, 1966, reaching showrooms on September 21. The Pony Car building-block philosophy was simple: sell a basic machine and allow the customers to add their own extras.

The trouble was that the Camaro had an option list as arcane as a lawyer's library. From Strato-Ease headrests to Comfort-Tilt steering wheel, the Camaro buyer was faced with an embarrassment of riches. But it worked. Buyers ordered the Rally Sport equipment package for their stock Camaros and suddenly they were kings of the road. Go-faster body striping, hidden headlights, and matte black taillight bezels were all calculated to enhance the illusion of performance pedigree, especially if the buyer could not afford the real thing – the hot Camaro SS.

Z28 CAMARO
Trans Am racing spawned the Z28 Camaro, a thinly veiled street racer designed to take on the Shelby Mustang. Top speed was 124 mph (200 km/h) and 60 mph came up in just 6.7 seconds.

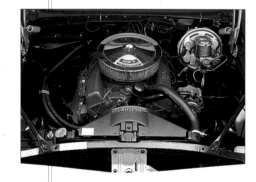

ENGINE
The basic V-8 power plant for Camaros was the trusty small block cast-iron 327cid lump, which, with a bit of tuning, evolved into the 350cid unit of the desirable SS models. Compression ratio was 8.8:1, and it produced 210 hp at 4600 rpm.

327 LABEL
Unlike Europe, where power was measured in cc, American horsepower was all about cubic inches.

INTERIOR
Standard Camaro interiors included color-keyed, all-vinyl trim, Strato-bucket front seats, and color-keyed carpeting. Strato-back bench seat was optional.

NOSE JOB
Lengthening the Camaro's wheelbase created a frontal overhang of 36.7 in (93 cm).

BRAKES
Disc brakes were a popular option and included special vented steel rally wheels.

REAR LIGHTS
All-red taillight lenses with black bezels were an RS feature.

TOP
When the Camaro raised its roof, the purity of line was not disturbed.

BACKUP LIGHTS
On the RS package, back-up lights were moved to the rear valance panel.

GAS CAP
Center-mounted fuel filler had RS emblem inscribed.

CHEVROLET CAMARO RS CONVERTIBLE

The market accepted the Camaro as a solid response to the Mustang. Its styling was cleaner, more European, and less boxy, and it drove better than the Ford. Even so, Camaro sales were considerably less than the Mustang.

INTERIOR
Dash was the usual for the era, with acres of plastic and mock woodgrain veneer. This model has the optional four-speed manual gearbox.

RS PINSTRIPING
Stick-on pinstriping helped flatter the Camaro's curves.

POWER
The 327 V-8 was puny. Real grunt came from the 375 hp 396cid cooking SS version.

CITROËN 2CV

RARELY HAS A CAR been so ridiculed as the Citroën 2CV. At its launch at the 1948 Paris Salon, journalists lashed into this defenseless runabout with vicious zeal. Everyone who was near Paris at the time claimed to be the originator of the quip, "Do you get a can opener with it?" They all missed the point, for this minimal car was not meant to be measured against other cars; its true rival was the farmer's horse and cart, which Citroën boss Pierre Boulanger hoped to replace with his *toute petite voiture* – or very small car. As the Deux Chevaux, it became much more than that and putt-putted into the history books, selling more than five million by the time of its eventual demise in 1990. As devotees of the 2CV say, "You either love them or you don't understand them."

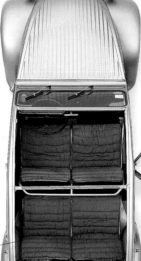

TOUGH TWO-CYLINDER
The original 375cc air-cooled twin, as seen here, eventually grew to all of 602cc, but all versions are genuinely happy to rev flat out all day. They love it.

DOORS
You were lucky to get them; prototypes featured oilcloth door coverings.

CITROËN 2CV
In 1935, Pierre Boulanger conceived a car to woo farmers away from the horse and cart. It would weigh no more than 661 lb (300 kg), carry four people at 37 mph (60 km/h), and run cheaply, going 56 miles on a gallon of gas. The suspension should be supple enough to transport a basket of eggs across a plowed field without breaking a single shell. The car that appears "undesigned" was in fact carefully conceived.

BACK IN FASHION
The two-tone Dolly was a 1985 special edition that, due to strong demand from the fashion-conscious who wanted to be seen in a 2CV, became a standard production model.

SEATS
Minimal, but handy; lightweight, hammock-style seats lift out to accommodate more goods or provide picnic seating.

INSTRUCTIONS ON HOW TO START AND STOP THE 2CV

SOLE INSTRUMENT ON CONSOLE IS AN AMMETER; NO IGNITION KEY

DRIVER FEEDBACK
Who needs banks of aircraft-style instruments anyway? These days they call it driver feedback, but in a classic 2CV you can tell that you are moving because the scenery changes – albeit slowly. In fact there is a speedometer to help reinforce the notion, but in the 2CV's less-is-more idiom the speedometer cable also drives the windshield wipers.

TRUNK
Roll-up canvas trunk lid of the original saved both weight and cost; a metal trunk lid took over in 1957 on French cars.

BODY COLORS
Gray until late 1959, the 2CV later came in Glacier Blue; in 1960, adding green and yellow gave a kaleidoscope of choices.

SURPRISING HANDLING
The tenacious grip of the skinny tires is astonishing, providing an exceptional ride.

HEADLIGHTS
Prewar production prototypes had only one headlight.

SIMPLE CHASSIS
Although designers flirted with notions of a chassis-less car, cost dictated a more conventional sheet steel platform chassis.

ROLL-TOP REASON
The sober design purpose of the roll-top roof was to allow the transportation of tall, bulky objects.

AIR VENT
Fresh air was obtained by opening the vent on the firewall; a mesh strained out the insects and leaves.

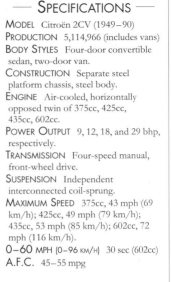

SPECIFICATIONS

MODEL Citroën 2CV (1949–90)
PRODUCTION 5,114,966 (includes vans)
BODY STYLES Four-door convertible sedan, two-door van.
CONSTRUCTION Separate steel platform chassis, steel body.
ENGINE Air-cooled, horizontally opposed twin of 375cc, 425cc, 435cc, 602cc.
POWER OUTPUT 9, 12, 18, and 29 bhp, respectively.
TRANSMISSION Four-speed manual, front-wheel drive.
SUSPENSION Independent interconnected coil-sprung.
MAXIMUM SPEED 375cc, 43 mph (69 km/h); 425cc, 49 mph (79 km/h); 435cc, 53 mph (85 km/h); 602cc, 72 mph (116 km/h).
0–60 MPH (0–96 KM/H) 30 sec (602cc)
A.F.C. 45–55 mpg

DUAL TURN SIGNALS
A good example of the functional design ethos. Why put turn signals on the front and back, when you could give your car "ears" that could be seen front and rear?

BOLT ON
All the body panels simply unbolt, and even the body shell is held in place by only 16 bolts.

SUSPENSION
The sophisticated independent suspension system together with that 2CV trademark, body roll, gave a soft ride.

537-BV-43

CITROËN *Traction Avant*

LOVED BY POLITICIANS, poets, and painters alike, the Traction Avant marked a watershed for both Citroën and the world's motor industry. A design prodigy, it was the first mass-produced car to incorporate a monocoque bodyshell with front-wheel drive and torsion-bar springing, and began Citroën's love affair with the unconventional.

Conceived in just 18 months, the Traction Avant was costly for the French company. By 1934 Citroën had emptied the company coffers, laid off 8,000 workers, and, on the insistence of the French government, was taken over by Michelin, which gave the Traction Avant the backing it deserved. It ran for over 23 years, with more than three quarters of a million sedans, hardtop coupes, and convertibles sold. The world lavished unstinting praise on the Traction Avant, extolling its road-holding, hydraulic brakes, ride comfort, and cornering abilities. Citroën's audacious sedan was the most significant and successful production car of its time, eclipsed only by the passage of 20 years and another *voiture revolutionnaire*, the Citroën DS.

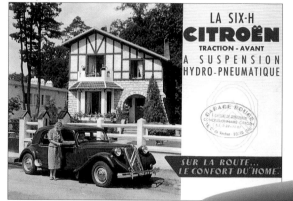

LA SIX-H
CITROËN
TRACTION - AVANT
A SUSPENSION
HYDRO-PNEUMATIQUE

SUR LA ROUTE...
LE CONFORT DU'HOME'.

SUSPENSION ATTRACTION
In 1954, the six-cylinder Traction Avant was known as "Queen of the Road" because of its hydro-pneumatic suspension – a mixture of liquid and gas.

STYLISH DESIGN
The Art Deco door handle is typical of Citroën's obsession with form and function.

SIDE-OPENING HOOD WAS A PREWAR FEATURE

ENGINE REPAIRS MEANT REMOVING THE HOOD COMPLETELY

ENGINE
The Traction's Maurice Sainturat-designed engine was new. "Floating Power" came from a short-stroke four-cylinder unit, with a three-bearing crankshaft and pushrod overhead valves – producing seven French horsepower.

ENGINE, GEARBOX, RADIATOR, AND FRONT SUSPENSION WERE MOUNTED ON A DETACHABLE CRADLE FOR EASY MAINTENANCE

NEW COLORS
In 1953, buyers had the option of gray or blue. Until then all Traction Avants had been black.

FRONT SUSPENSION
All-independent suspension with torsion-bar springing, upper wishbones, radius arms, friction shocks, and worm-and-roller steering (later rack-and-pinion) gave crisp handling.

FRONT WHEEL
Front-wheel drive made for tenacious road holding.

REAR SUSPENSION
*Rear suspension was through a trailing axle with twin
transverse torsion bars, longitudinal radius arms, and hydraulic shocks.*

WINDOW
*Minimal rear
visibility.*

CITROËN TRACTION AVANT

With aerodynamic styling, unit steel body and sweeping
fenders without running boards, the Traction Avant was
a technical and aesthetic tour de force. Yet, despite lavish
praise, it was this great grand routier
that devoured André
Citroën's wealth and
pushed him to his
death bed.

REVISED TRUNK
*In 1952, Citroën dispensed
with the earlier "bobtail"
rear end
and gave the
Traction a
"big trunk."*

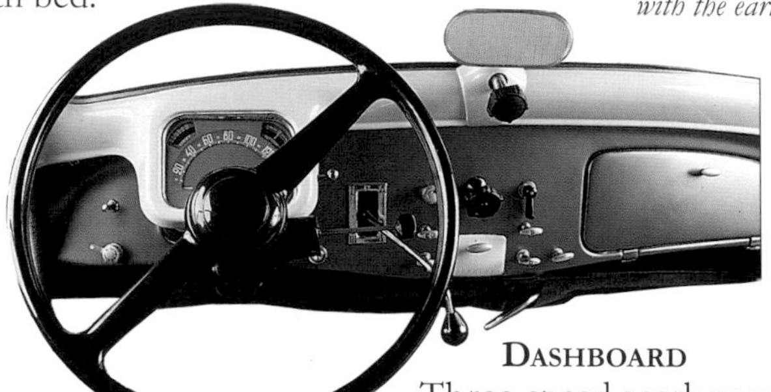

DASHBOARD
Three-speed gearbox was
mounted ahead of the engine,
with synchromesh on second and third. Drive
reached the road by Cardin driveshafts and
constant velocity joints at the axles. The dash-
mounted gearshift (right) lived on in
the DS of 1955 (see pages 72–75).

WHEEL
*Michelin
produced
these Pilote
wheels and
tires for the
Traction.*

SPECIFICATIONS

MODEL Citroën Traction Avant
(1934–55)
PRODUCTION 758,858 (including
six-cylinder)
BODY STYLE Five-seater,
four-door sedan.
CONSTRUCTION Steel front-wheel
drive monocoque.
ENGINE 1911cc in-line four-cylinder.
POWER OUTPUT 46 bhp at 3200 rpm.
TRANSMISSION Three-speed manual.
SUSPENSION Independent front
and rear.
BRAKES Hydraulic drums front
and rear.
MAXIMUM SPEED 70 mph (113 km/h)
0–60 MPH (0–96 KM/H) 25 sec
A.F.C. 23 mpg

CITROËN *DS DECAPOTABLE*

IN 1955, WHEN CITROËN FIRST DROVE prototypes of its mold-breaking DS through Paris, the cars were pursued by crowds shouting "La DS, la DS, voilà la DS!" Few other cars before or since were so technically and stylistically audacious. At its launch, the DS created as much interest as the death of Stalin. Cushioned on a bed of hydraulic fluid, with a semiautomatic gearbox, self-leveling suspension, and detachable body panels, it instantly rendered half the world's cars out of date.

Parisian coachbuilder Henri Chapron produced 1365 convertible DSs using the chassis from the Safari Estate model. Initially Citroën refused to cooperate with Chapron but eventually sold the Decapotable models through its dealer network. At the time the flashy four-seater convertible was considered by many to be one of the most charismatic open-top cars on the market. Today, genuine Chapron cars command three to four times the price of their sedan counterparts.

ENGINE
The DS 21's rather sluggish 2145cc engine developed 109 bhp and was never highly praised, having its origins in the prewar Traction Avant *(see pages 70–71).*

SUSPENSION INACTIVE

AERODYNAMICS
The slippery, streamlined body penetrated the air with extreme aerodynamic efficiency. Body panels were detachable for easy repair and maintenance. Rear fenders could be removed for wheel changing in minutes, using just the car's jack. The novel suspension could be raised to clear rough terrain or navigate flooded roads.

THE DS WAS ACKNOWLEDGED TO HAVE THE FINEST RIDE QUALITY OF ANY CAR IN THE WORLD

SUSPENSION RISING

THE DS WAS NICKNAMED THE "SHARK" BECAUSE OF ITS PRODIGIOUS NOSE

SUSPENSION RAISED

MICHELIN DESIGNED UNIQUE X-TYPE RADIAL PLY TIRES SPECIALLY FOR THE DS

PAST OWNERS OF THE DS INCLUDE GENERAL DE GAULLE, BRIGITTE BARDOT, AND THE POET C. DAY-LEWIS

DESIGN CLASSIC

Smooth Bertone-designed lines have made the Citroën DS a cult design icon and the cerebral choice for doctors, architects, artists, and musicians.

GEAR LEVER

The four-speed semiautomatic gearbox had no clutch and changes were made by hydraulic servo motors; the driver lifted off the accelerator and moved the lever gently along the gate.

DASHBOARD

Bertone's asymetrical dashboard makes the interior look as futuristic as the rest of the car. The single-spoke steering wheel was a Citroën hallmark.

CUSTOMER CHOICE

Because the Decapotable was virtually handbuilt, customers could specify almost any stylistic or mechanical extra.

THE INSIDE WAS AS INNOVATIVE AS THE OUTSIDE, WITH CLEVER USE OF CURVED GLASS AND COPIOUS LAYERS OF FOAM RUBBER, EVEN ON THE FLOORS

CITROEN KNEW THAT HEAVY FRONT-WHEEL DRIVE CARS NEEDED POWER-ASSISTED BRAKES AND STEERING, AND PATENTED THEIR HYDRAULIC SYSTEM AS EARLY AS 1940

ADVERTISEMENT

Citroën's advertising made much of the car's futuristic looks; it was once displayed without wheels to enhance its rocket-ship styling. The London Design Museum once held a special DS exhibition.

THE DISAPPEARING NOSE WAS VERY VULNERABLE TO PARKING MANEUVERS; THIN RUBBER OVERRIDER-TYPE BUMPERS OFFERED SOME PROTECTION

CITROËN'S VISION OF THE FUTURE

Never before in the history of the automobile had a mass market machine achieved such an incredible quantum leap in performance, comfort, and styling.

THE DS'S LIST of innovations was remarkable. Fully independent gas suspension gave a magic-carpet ride, front-wheel drive gave unerring high-speed control and maneuverability, Michelin X-Radial tires contributed high levels of grip, and stopping power was provided by inboard disc brakes with dual circuits. Even gear-shifting and clutch action were aided by hydraulic power-assisted motors, and its sharp rack-and-pinion steering was assisted by high pressure hydraulic power. Add a body style that looked like something out of a Buck Rogers comic and you begin to marvel that all this occurred in 1955, when the novelty of electric razors had just worn off.

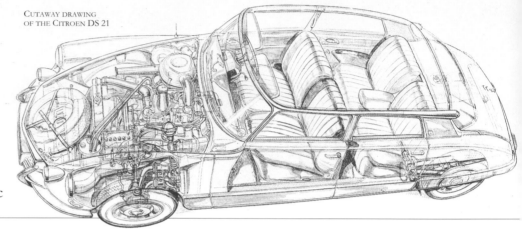

CUTAWAY DRAWING OF THE CITROEN DS 21

CITROËN *DS Decapotable*

HIGH PRAISE
The French philosopher Roland Barthes was captivated by the DS's design and compared its technical pre-eminence to the Gothic flourish of medieval cathedrals.

TURN SIGNALS
The Decapotable's trademark was angled chrome-plated turn signals perched on the rear fenders.

CITROEN'S DOUBLE CHEVRONS ARE MODELED ON HELICAL GEARS

ON ALL DSs THE REAR TRACK WAS NARROWER THAN THE FRONT

DS 21

2724 Y 33

Success came soon for the DS. On the first day of the 1955 Paris Motor Show, 749 orders were taken within 45 minutes, 12,000 within the first day and, by the end of the week, Citroën's prodigy had amassed 80,000 confirmed orders. But the French company had launched the DS too early, prompted by scoop pictures in the French magazine *L'Auto Journal* in 1953. Reliability was patchy – the suspension literally let itself down, Citroën dealers had no technical manuals to work from, and owners, whose expectations were understandably high, limped home crestfallen. In 1962, the image of the DS got a shot in the arm when terrorists attacked President General De Gaulle. Despite being sprayed with bullets and having two flat tires, the presidential DS was able to swerve and speed away to safety.

By the time the DS was deleted from the brochures in 1975, no less than 1½ million had been sold worldwide. For a brief period, the DS fell from grace. In the 1970s, it was eclipsed by the CX, and was seen as overly complicated and difficult to mend. But by the early 1980s, that shape began to recapture the imagination of car enthusiasts, who rightly hailed it as a style icon and a work of art. Championed as the Car of the Century, the DS was unique, a mechanical invention so brilliant that

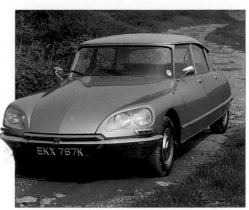

CITROEN DS 21 PALLAS

it stood alone as an inspired vision of the future that owed nothing to conventional wisdom and everything to creative genius.

FRONT SHOT

Low, rakish, and space-age in appearance, the DS was so perfectly styled that it hardly altered shape in 20 years. A major change came in 1967 when the headlights and optional pod spot lights were faired in behind glass covers.

UNLIKE MANY CHAPRON CONVERTIBLES, THIS CAR IS NOT FITTED WITH A CHROME HOOD HANDLE

EARLY EXPOSED HEADLIGHTS MAY HAVE LOOKED GOOD BUT WERE VIRTUALLY USELESS ON LOW BEAM

2724 Y 33

CITROËN *SM*

THE CITROËN SM makes about as much sense as the Concorde, but since when have great cars had anything to do with common sense? It is certainly a flight of fancy, an extravagant, technical *tour de force* that, as a 16-ft (4.9-m) long streamliner, offered little more than 2+2 seating.

The SM bristled with innovations – many of them established Citroën hallmarks – like swiveling headlights and self-leveling hydropneumatic suspension. It was a complex car – too complex, in fact. And of course there was that Maserati V-6 motor. Yet once again Citroën had created an enduringly futuristic car where other "tomorrow cars of today" were soon exposed as voguish fads.

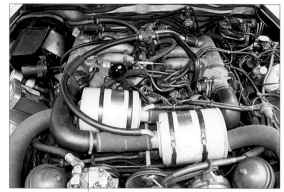

THIS IS THE 2.7-LITER V-6; LATER A 3-LITER AUTO WAS OFFERED, MAINLY FOR THE US MARKET

ENGINE
SM stands for Serié Maserati, and here it is – the exquisite Maserati all-aluminum V-6 engine, weighing just 309 lb (140 kg) and only 12 in (31 cm) long, but producing at least 170 bhp. Capacity was initially kept below 2.8 liters to escape France's punitive vehicle taxation system.

PURELY FUNCTIONAL
This bulge in the tailgate above the rear number plate is for purely functional, aerodynamic reasons. It also suited the deeper license plates used in the US.

REAR CRAMP
Citroën's publicity material tried to hide the fact, but rear-seat legroom and headroom are barely sufficient for two large children.

SUPPORTING ROLE
Like that of most front-wheel-drive cars, the SM's rear suspension does little more than hold the body off the ground.

COMPOUND CURVES
The tinted rear window, with compound curves and heating elements, must have cost a fortune to produce.

ROLLING ALONG
Despite its size and weight the SM can be thrown around like a sports car. It rolls, as here, like a trawler in a heavy sea and, like all front-wheel-drivers, it understeers strongly, but resolutely refuses to let go.

US INFLUENCE
Only the SM's over-elaborate chromed rear "fins" betray the General Motors styling influence.

SKIRTS
Fender skirts were a throwback to an earlier age, but necessary to allow the removal of the rear wheel.

WHEELS
Lightweight wheels reinforced with carbonfiber were optionally available.

IT TOOK PRACTICE
TO DECIDE IN A
HURRY WHAT EACH
OF THE TINY
WARNING LIGHTS
ACTUALLY MEANT

DASHBOARD
The SM's controls owe more to style than
ergonomics. The oval speedometer and
tachometer are visible through the single-spoke
steering wheel, and the perennially confusing
cluster of warning lights *(above)* is to the right.

HARD TO PLACE
*Slim windshield pillars should
have meant excellent visibility
but, in practice, the left-hand-
drive SM was sometimes difficult
to place on the road.*

HEADLIGHTS
The SM had
an array of six
headlights, with
the inner light
on each side
swiveling with
the steering.

WIND CHEATER
*The tapering body is
apparent in this
overhead view.*

BACK TO FRONT
*The SM's engine is mounted
behind the transmission, and
thus well behind the front axle.*

CITROËN SM
The SM's striking low-drag body was
designed by ex-General Motors stylist
Henri de Segur Lauve. The sleek nose
and deep undertray, together with
the noticeably tapered rear
end, endow it with a drag
coefficient of 0.27, still
credible today.

BRAKES
*Inboard front disc
brakes incorporate the
handbrake mechanism.*

DAIMLER *SP250 Dart*

AN ECCENTRIC HYBRID, the SP250 was the car that sank Daimler. By the late 1950s, the traditionalist Coventry-based company was in dire financial straits. Hoping to woo the car-crazy Americans, Daimler launched the Dart, with its odd pastiche of British and American styling themes, at the 1959 New York Auto Show.

Daimler had been making buses out of fiberglass and the Dart emerged with a quirky, rust-free plastic body. The girder chassis was a blatant copy of the Triumph TR2 *(see pages 208–09)* and, to keep the basic price down, necessities like heater, windshield wipers, and bumpers were made extra-cost options. Hardly a great car, the SP250 was a commercial failure. Projected sales of 7,500 units in the first three years dissolved into just 2,644, with only 1,200 going Stateside. Jaguar took over Daimler in 1960 and, by 1964, Sir William Lyons had axed the sportiest car Daimler had ever made.

TRADITIONAL INTERIOR
The cockpit was pure British tradition, with central gauges mounted on an aluminum plate, leather seats and dash, an occasional rear seat, fly-off handbrake, wind-up windows, and thick pile carpets.

TRUNK WAS HUGE DESPITE ACCOMMODATING FUEL TANK AND SPARE WHEEL

VESTIGIAL REAR SEAT COULD JUST ACCOMMODATE ONE CHILD OR A VERY TOLERANT ADULT

ENGINE
The turbine-smooth, Edward Turner-designed V-8 was the Dart's *tour de force*. If you were brave enough, it could reach 125 mph (201 km/h).

SPEED STRAIN
At speed the Dart was hard work; the chassis flexed, doors opened on bends, and the steering was very heavy.

FLUTED FENDERS LOOK GOOD AND GIVE THE BODY EXTRA RIGIDITY

EARLY CARS HAD TO HAVE A STEEL HOOP AROUND THE BULKHEAD TO STOP SKUTTLE SHAKE

FIBERGLASS BODY IS 1 IN (25 MM) THICK IN PLACES

BAD DARTS
The Dart's sales brochure was total misrepresentation. The superlatives ("featherlight handling," "impeccable cornering") betrayed the truth. By 1961, the chassis had to be stiffened to improve the poor roadholding.

STEERING WHEEL
Heavy worm-and-peg steering made maneuvering in tight spaces a real chore. In the 1970s many Darts were converted to the rack-and-pinion type.

RACING DAIMLER
Quick enough in a straight line, corners were the Dart's Achilles heel and it never achieved any significant competitive success. This period shot shows a Dart pirouetting around Brands Hatch in 1962, complete with optional hardtop, bumpers, and badge bar.

GAUGES FOR OIL PRESSURE, FUEL, AMPERAGE, AND ENGINE TEMPERATURE

PADDED LEATHER GLOVEBOX HAD A QUALITY CHROME LOCK

AUTOMATIC OPTION
Borg-Warner was an option but slowed the car down considerably. British police forces who used the Dart still thought it fast enough.

REAR FENDER
Dart development had three phases: 1959–61 A-spec cars came with no creature comforts; April 1961 and later B-specs had standard bumpers, windshield wipers, and chassis modifications; while the last and most refined C-specs, produced from April 1963 to September 1964, boasted a heater and cigar lighter as standard.

DUNLOP RS5 TIRES WERE STANDARD; WIRE WHEELS WERE EXTRA-COST OPTIONS

PROVOCATIVE TWIN EXHAUSTS EMITTED A DEEP BURBLE, RISING TO A THUNDEROUS ACK-ACK AT SPEED

— THE DAIMLER MISFIT —

The Dart belongs here not because it is dynamically brilliant, but because it perfectly chronicles the influence of American styling on British cars of the period.

1950 DAIMLER MAJESTIC

SO PENETRATING was the genius of Harley Earl, General Motors' chief stylist and the man who gave shape to 50 million American cars, that almost every other contemporary carmaker jumped on the bandwagon. The fashion for fins even percolated down to a tiny company like Daimler and there is a sad irony in their fundamental incompatibility. Daimler had been churning out stuffy establishment sedans with all the aerodynamics of church pews. Cars like the Majestic and Conquest Century bore no family resemblance to the rakish Dart and, in trying to seduce the Americans, Daimler alienated the conservative British market as a result.

When it was launched, Dodge, who had registered the trademark Dart, forbid them to use it. And, if that was

CHRYSLER IMPERIAL CROWN SEDAN, WITH REAR FINS RESEMBLING THOSE OF THE LATER DAIMLER DART

not enough, enthusiasts sniggered at the Dart's unhappy styling, which, compared to the smooth MGA, Triumph TR3, and Sunbeam Alpine, looked downright clumsy. With a hefty initial price tag of $3,900, the Dart was not competitive either.

But the Dart's prime attraction was that light, compact, and powerful engine, Britain's only V-8 other than Rolls-Royce's Silver Cloud II unit. The British car magazine *Motor* called the

DAIMLER
SP250 Dart

HOOD FURLED AWAY NEATLY BEHIND REAR SEAT AND WAS COVERED WITH A FABRIC HOOD BAG

CHROME-ON-BRASS REAR LIGHT FINISHERS WERE MONOGRAMMED WITH A DAINTY "D"

QUALITY INSULATION
In the 1950s, few sports cars had windup windows. The Dart had beautifully finished chrome-surrounded glass which, when raised, kept cockpit buffeting to a minimum.

4068 WK

Daimler's engine, "quite exceptional in its torque output and turbine-like smoothness over an incredibly wide range of speeds. Other aspects of the car are quite overshadowed by the performance, and its chassis and coachwork are made to seem undistinguished by the engine which propels them." With aluminum heads and hemispherical combustion chambers, it was a gem of a unit which survived until 1969, providing sterling service as power for the Jaguar Mk II-bodied Daimler 250 sedan.

Underdeveloped and rushed into production, Dart sales were slow. In 1959, Jaguar produced and sold 22,000 cars, while Daimler managed only a few hundred Darts. Never enjoying any reflected glory from racing or celebrity

DAIMLER CONQUEST CENTURY ROADSTER

1961 DAIMLER SP250 DART POLICE CAR

ownership, the only unusual Dart buyers were the British Metropolitan Police, who ran a fleet of around 30 black automatics with brass bells on the front.

The Dart was a 1950s concept born too late to compete with the New Wave of monocoque sports cars headed by the stunning E-Type. It stands as a memorial to both the haphazard 1960s British motor industry and its self-destructive love affair with all things American.

FRONT VIEW

The guppy-style front could never be called handsome but, when 1960s drivers caught it in their rearview mirrors, they knew to move over. The drastic plastic Dart was seriously quick.

FIBERGLASS HOOD HAD A NASTY HABIT OF SPRINGING OPEN AT SPEED

DART HAS MANY DELICATE PERIOD DETAILS, LIKE TINY CHEVRON-SHAPED PARKING LIGHTS PERCHED NEATLY ON BOTH FRONT FENDERS

DATSUN *Fairlady 1600*

Fairlady THE SIMILARITY between the Datsun Fairlady and the MGB *(see page 175)* is quite astonishing. The Datsun actually appeared first, at the 1961 Tokyo Motor Show, followed a year later by the MGB. Hardly a great car in its early 1500cc form, the Fairlady improved dramatically over the years, a foretaste of the Japanese car industry's culture of constant improvement. The later two-liter, twin-carb, five-speed variants of 1967 could reach 125 mph (200 km/h) and even raised eyebrows at American sports car club races.

Aimed at the American market, where it was known as the Datsun 1500, the Fairlady sold only 40,000 in nine years. But it showed Datsun how to make the legendary 240Z *(see pages 84–87),* which went on to become one of the world's best selling sports cars.

EUROPEAN LINES
Higher and narrower than the MGB, the Fairlady had an unmistakable and deliberate European look. However, of the 7,000 1500cc models sold, half went to the United States.

DATSUN FAIRLADY 1600
Low and rakish with classically perfect proportions, the Fairlady has a certain period charm and ranks as one of the best-looking Datsuns produced before 1965. Side views show the car at its best, while the messy rear and cluttered nose do not work quite so well. But compared to some of the awkward Asian offerings of the time, the Fairlady was beautiful.

STYLING
Rear view has echoes of both the MGB and MG TC.

THIRD SEAT
Early Fairladies had a third seat set across the car behind the front bucket seats.

OTHER MODELS

Over nine years Datsun refined the Fairlady until, by the late 1960s, it had evolved into quite a reliable machine.

DATSUN 1500
Early cars had a less-than-willing 1500cc engine which lacked both mid-range heave and top-end power.

DATSUN 2000 ROADSTER
2000s pushed out 145 bhp and boasted a five-speed overdrive gearbox.

MUF 625F

DATSUN DASH

The cockpit was typical of the period, with acres of black plastic. Interestingly, no attempt was made to make the interior harmonize with the Fairlady's traditional exterior lines. Note how the square clock clashes with the circular instruments, plus a steering wheel that would not look out of place in a pickup truck.

SNUG INTERIOR IS DOMINATED BY FULL-LENGTH CENTER CONSOLE.

POINTS OF SALE

Although the Fairlady was aimed at a worldwide market – America in particular – it was never actually listed in Britain.

SPECIFICATIONS

MODEL Datsun Fairlady 1600 (1965–70)
PRODUCTION Approx 40,000
BODY STYLE Two-seater sports convertible.
CONSTRUCTION Steel body mounted on box-section chassis.
ENGINE 1595CC four-cylinder.
POWER OUTPUT 90 bhp at 6000 rpm.
TRANSMISSION Four-speed all-synchro.
SUSPENSION *Front:* independent; *Rear:* leaf springs.
BRAKES Front wheel discs, rear drums.
MAXIMUM SPEED 105 mph (169 km/h)
0–60 MPH (0–96 KM/H) 13.3 sec
0–100 MPH (0–161 KM/H) 25 sec
A.F.C. 25 mpg

ENGINE

The 1595cc 90 bhp power-plant was the mainstay of the Fairlady range until 1970. The simple four-cylinder engine had a cast-iron cylinder block and aluminum head, breathing through twin Hitachi carburetors made under license from SU in England. Later 1600s were uprated to 96 bhp with a five-bearing crankshaft.

BODY PANELS

In common with the MGB, the Fairlady also had bolt-on removable front fenders for easy repair.

FRONT SUSPENSION

Front suspension was independent, courtesy of telescopic shock absorbers, wishbones, and coil springs.

MUF 625F

DATSUN

DATSUN 240Z

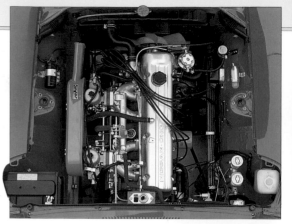

THROUGHOUT THE 1960s, Japanese car makers were teetering on the brink of a sports car breakthrough. Toyota's 2000 GT *(see page 207)* was a beauty, but with only 337 made, it was an exclusive curio. Honda was competing too, with the dainty S600 and S800. As for Datsun, the MGB-lookalike Fairladies were relatively popular in Japan and the United States, but virtually unknown elsewhere. The revolution came with the Datsun 240Z, which at a stroke established Japan on the world sports car stage.

The breakthrough had been in the cards for a while. The E-Type Jaguar *(see pages 140–43)* was not in its first flush of youth. At the lower level, the Austin-Healey 3000 *(see pages 38–39)* was on its last legs; neither was the MGB exactly factory fresh. There was a gaping hole, particularly in the US, and the Datsun 240Z filled it handsomely. It was even launched in the States in October 1969, a month before its official Japanese release, and on a rising tide of Japanese exports to the US it scored a massive hit. It had the looks, performance, handling, and equipment levels – a great value sporting package that outsold all rivals.

ENGINE
The six-cylinder twin-carburetor 2.4-liter engine, developed from the four-cylinder unit of the Bluebird sedan range, provided smooth, reliable power. Japanese buyers had the option of a tax-break 2-liter version, and there were 420 cars built for the Japanese market with a more powerful 24-valve twin-cam 2-liter unit.

Z IDENTITY
The model was launched in Japan as the Fairlady Z, replacing the earlier Fairlady models; export versions were universally known as 240Z and were labeled accordingly.

RACK-AND-PINION STEERING WAS LIGHT AND PRECISE AND ADDED TO DRIVING ENJOYMENT

TRUNK-MOUNTED SPOILER WAS NOT STANDARD 240Z EQUIPMENT IN ALL MARKETS

REAR SIDE WINDOW WAS TINY, BUT WITH NO REAR PASSENGERS NOTHING BIGGER WAS NEEDED

INTERIOR
Cockpit layout was tailored to American tastes of the time, with hooded instruments and beefy controls. The vinyl-covered bucket seats offered generous rear luggage space, but the low seating position marred otherwise excellent visibility.

HANDLING
With independent suspension all around, the 240Z handled well, with a true sporting character to match its beefy good looks. One of the few criticisms was the rough ride.

TASTELESS PLASTIC WHEEL TRIM IS ORIGINAL EQUIPMENT

STYLING CUES

As with the recessed lights at the front, there is an echo of the E-Type Jaguar coupe at the rear, with a little Porsche 911, Mustang fastback, and Aston Martin DBS of 1969 thrown in.

240Z OFFERED EXCELLENT FUEL ECONOMY; YOU COULD GET 30 MPG FROM A 13-GALLON TANK

DATSUN LABEL

Cars were sold in some markets as Nissans, but were labeled as Datsuns in the US and the UK.

DESIGN

The lines of the 240Z were based on earlier styling exercises by Albrecht Goertz, master stylist of the BMW 507 (see pages 48–49).

BALANCE

This view shows that the engine was placed far forwards of the centerline, with the occupants well behind it; yet the Z was noted for its fine balance.

LARGE REAR WINDOW GAVE GOOD REAR VISION

BIG REAR HATCH GAVE MUCH BETTER LUGGAGE ACCESS THAN THE E-TYPE COUPE

STEEPLY RAKED WINDSHIELD AIDED AERODYNAMIC EFFICIENCY

THIN, RUST-PRONE BODY PANELS WERE ONE OF THE FEW THINGS THAT LET THE 240Z DOWN

HOOD WAS UNCLUTTERED BY UNNECESSARY LOUVERS; IT LATER BECAME FANCIER

DATSUN

SPECIFICATIONS

MODEL Datsun 240Z (1969–73)
PRODUCTION 156,076
BODY STYLE Three-door, two-seater sports hatchback.
CONSTRUCTION Steel monocoque.
ENGINE Inline single overhead camshaft six, 2393cc.
POWER OUTPUT 151 bhp at 5600 rpm.
TRANSMISSION All-synchromesh four- or five-speed manual or automatic.
SUSPENSION *Front:* Independent by MacPherson struts, low links, coil springs, telescopic shocks.
Rear: Independent by MacPherson struts, lower wishbones, coil springs, telescopic shocks.
BRAKES Discs front/drums rear.
MAXIMUM SPEED 125 mph (210 km/h)
0–60 MPH (0–96 KM/H) 8.0 sec
A.F.C. 20–25 mpg

JAPANESE SPORTING SUCCESS

When the Datsun 240Z's sleek and aggressive lines broke on the world stage late in 1969, it was a sporting breakthrough that once and for all transformed the image of Japanese automobiles.

AGAINST A RISING tide of postwar recovery and growing Japanese exports, the Datsun 240Z was somehow inevitable. The British sports car invasion of America was, if not quite in retreat, at least losing momentum, and Japanese cars were notching up ever increasing sales in the land of Uncle Sam. In fact, the impetus for the 240Z came from North American Nissan executives who spotted the gap and demanded a true sporting contender to fill it. The first Datsun Fairlady, the SP211 of 1959 (a 1960 model is illustrated), was a pretty car, but really little more than a sporting pretender; its successor, the remodeled,

1952 DATSUN SPORTS ROADSTER

bigger-engined Fairlady SP213 of 1962, was closer to the mark. But, in fact, as early as 1952, Datsun had given expression to its sporting ambitions with a quirky little Sports Roadster. About the only sporting aspect was its fold-flat screen. The 240Z, when it appeared, had an instant pedigree, for it was designed by none other than Albrecht Goertz, master stylist of the beautiful BMW 507 and the shortlived

DATSUN
240Z

DESIGNER ALBRECHT GOERTZ INSISTED THE 240Z SHOULD SEAT TWO 6 FT 3 IN (1.9 M) ADULTS

FIRST-OF-BREED
As with so many long-lived sports cars, the first-of-breed 240Z is seen as the best sporting package – lighter and nimbler than its successors.

RHX 156L

SOPHISTICATED SUSPENSION WAS INDEPENDENT WITH MACPHERSON STRUTS ON ALL FOUR WHEELS

Toyota 2000GT. As if to underline its true sports car status, its evolution is an uncanny mirror of the E-Type Jaguar's, for sporting Datsun devotees generally opt for the purity of the original. The process of fattening up began with the 260Z of 1973–78. With a bigger 2565cc engine to cope with American emission laws, it was not quite as quick as the 240Z and weighed more. In 1974, a stretched 260Z 2+2 was offered. In 1978, the Z-series added more weight and girth with the immensely popular 280ZX.

As for the figures, they speak volumes. Add them all together and you have over a million. In fact, the 240Z alone sold twice as many as the E-Type total of 70,000 in less than half the time. To underline its sports car status, the 240Z

1960 DATSUN FAIRLADY SP2111

TIMO SALONEN'S 240RS, 1983 EAST AFRICA SAFARI RALLY

also accumulated a creditable cabinet of trophies. Its ruggedness earned it a 1–2 in the 1971 East African Safari Rally, and a repeat win in 1973. And in 1983, the 240 name was briefly revived with the Group B competition 240RS, again on the East African Safari.

ULTIMATE 240Z

If you wanted to cut a real swath in a 240Z, the ultimate Samurai performance option had what it takes. Modifications gave six-second 0–60 mph figures.

THE LATER 280ZX OFFERED A POPULAR TARGA OPTION

THE NAME DATSUN – LITERALLY SON OF DAT – FIRST APPEARED ON A SMALL DAT IN 1932

RECESSED FRONT HEADLIGHT TREATMENT IS VERY REMINISCENT OF THE E-TYPE JAGUAR

RHX 156L

DeLorean *DMC 12*

"THE LONG-AWAITED transportation revolution has begun," bellowed the glossy brochures for John Zachary DeLorean's mold-breaking DMC 12. With a unique body of brushed stainless steel, gullwing doors, and an all-electric interior, the DMC was intended as a glimpse of the future. Today it is known as one of the car industry's greatest failures, on a par with Ford's Edsel *(see pages 114–15)*. Despite $130 million in government aid to establish a specially designed factory in West Belfast, DeLorean closed in 1982 with debts of $50 million. As for the hapless souls who bought the cars, they were faced with a litany of quality control problems, from doors that would not open, to windows that fell out. Even exposure in the film *Back to the Future* did not help the DeLorean's fortunes. Success depended on American sales and the company's forecasts were wildly optimistic. After the initial novelty died down, word spread that DeLoreans were dogs and sales completely evaporated.

STARRING ROLE
The 1985 film *Back to the Future* used a DeLorean as a time machine to travel back to 1955; in reality the car was very orthodox.

GULLWINGS
The DeLorean's most celebrated party trick was gullwing doors that leaked and did not open or close properly.

ENGINE
The overhead cam, Volvo-sourced 2.8-liter V-6 engine used *Bosch K-Jetronic* fuel injection, developing 145 bhp. Standard spec was five-speed manual with optional three-speed automatic.

COMPLEX ELECTRONICS WERE DUE TO LAST-MINUTE COST-CUTTING MEASURES

INTERIOR
The leather-clad interior looked imposing, with electric windows, tilting telescopic steering column, double weather seals, air conditioning, and a seven-position climate control function.

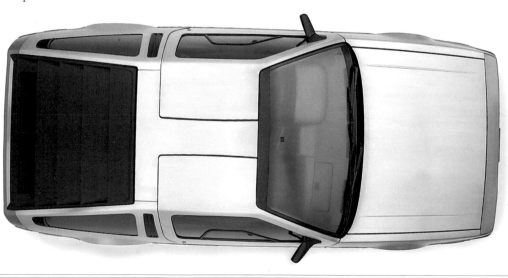

LIGHT FRONT
With rear-engined layout, the weight distribution was split 35 percent front to 65 percent rear.

WHEELS
Custom-made spoked alloys were larger at the back than the front.

DeLorean DMC 12

The DeLorean was targeted at "the bachelor who's made it!" and part of the design brief was that there had to be room behind the front seats for a full set of golf clubs. Designed by Giugiaro and overseen by Colin Chapman of Lotus fame, the gullwing doors and stainless-steel body were cynical marketing ploys which, as everybody involved in the prototype agreed, were more trouble than they were worth.

DISASTER DOORS
Overloaded doors were crammed with locks, glass, electric motors, mirrors, stereo speakers, and ventilation pipery. Held by a puny single gas strut, it was an act of the purest optimism to expect them to work properly.

AIR CONDITIONING
With tiny windows and climate control that regularly failed, temperatures got very hot indeed.

1970S STYLING
By the time of its launch in 1979, the DeLorean was old before its time. '70s styling motifs abound, like the slatted rear window and cubed rear lights.

STAINLESS-STEEL BODY
Brushed-stainless-steel was disliked by Colin Chapman but insisted upon by DeLorean himself. Soon owners found that it was impossible to clean.

SPECIFICATIONS

MODEL DeLorean DMC 12 (1979–82)
PRODUCTION 6,500
BODY STYLE Two-seater rear-engined sports coupe.
CONSTRUCTION Y-shaped chassis with stainless-steel body.
ENGINE 2850cc ohc V-6.
POWER OUTPUT 145 bhp at 5500 rpm.
TRANSMISSION Five-speed manual (optional three-speed auto).
SUSPENSION Independent with unequal length parallel arms and rear trailing arms.
BRAKES Four-wheel discs.
MAXIMUM SPEED 125 mph (201 km/h)
0–60 MPH (0–96 KM/H) 9.6 sec
0–100 MPH (0–161 KM/H) 23.2 sec
A.F.C. 22 mpg

DE TOMASO *Pantera GT5*

AN UNCOMPLICATED SUPERCAR, the Pantera was a charming amalgam of Detroit grunt and Italian glam. Launched in 1971 and sold in North America by Ford's Lincoln-Mercury dealers, it was powered by a mid-mounted Ford 5.7-liter V-8 that could muster 159 mph (256 km/h) and belt to 60 mph in under six seconds. The formidable 350 bhp GT5 was built after Ford pulled out in 1974 and De Tomaso merged with Maserati.

With a propensity for the front lifting at speed, hopeless rear visibility, no headroom, awkward seats, and impossibly placed pedals, the Pantera is massively flawed; yet it is remarkably easy to drive. Handling is poised and accurate, plus there is the wall of power that catapults the car to 30 mph (48 km/h) in less time than it takes to pronounce its name.

ENGINE
The Pantera is really just a big power plant with a body attached. The monster V-8 lives in the middle, mated to a beautifully built aluminum-cased ZF transaxle, which was also used in the Ford GT40 *(see pages 124–27)* and cost more to make than the engine.

INTERIOR
The Pantera requires typical driving position – long arms and short legs. Switches and dials are strewn all over the place, but the glorious soundtracks are just inches from your ears.

PANTERA TRIVIA
Elvis Presley shot his Pantera when it wouldn't start.

LIMITED HEADROOM
Don't buy a Pantera if you are over 5 ft 10 in (178 cm) tall – there is no headroom.

GT5 PANTERA DE

DE TOMASO PANTERA GT5

Fat arches, aggressive GT5 graphics down the flanks, wheels 11 inches wide, and ground clearance you could not slide an envelope under make the Pantera look evil. Americans were not able to buy the real GT5 due to the car's lack of engine-emission controls and had to settle for just the GT5 badges.

┌─────── SPECIFICATIONS ───────┐

MODEL De Tomaso Pantera GT5 (1974–93)
PRODUCTION N/A
BODY STYLE Mid-engined two-seater coupe.
CONSTRUCTION Pressed steel chassis body unit.
ENGINE 5763cc V-8.
POWER OUTPUT 350 bhp at 6000 rpm.
TRANSMISSION Five-speed manual ZF Transaxle.
SUSPENSION All-around independent.
BRAKES All-around ventilated discs.
MAXIMUM SPEED 159 mph (256 km/h)
0–60 MPH (0–96 KM/H) 5.5 sec
0–100 MPH (0–161 KM/H) 13.5 sec
A.F.C. 15 mpg

WIDE NOSE
Top view shows just how wide the nose really is.

THE PANTERA AT SPEED

The huge fender helps rear down-force, but actually slows the Pantera down. At the General Motors Millbrook proving ground in England, a GT5 with the fender in place made 148 mph (238 km/h); without the fender it reached 151.7 mph (244 km/h).

COCKPIT
With the engine so close to the interior, the cabin temperature could get very hot.

WHEEL ARCH
Wheel arches strain outwards to cover 13-in (33 cm) rear tires.

COOLING
Early Panteras would overheat, with the temperature creeping past 230 degrees F.

RAISED TRUNK
Lift-up rear panel gives total engine accessibility for maintenance.

CONSTRUCTION
The underside is old-fashioned welded pressed steel monocoque.

TIRES
Giant Pirelli P7 345/45 rear tires belong on the track and give astonishing road traction.

AERODYNAMICS
With little weight up front, at over 120 mph (193 km/h) the nose would lift and the steering would lighten up alarmingly.

DODGE *Charger* R/T

COLLECTORS RANK THE 1968 Dodge Charger as one of the fastest and best-styled muscle cars of its era. This, the second generation of Charger, marked the pinnacle of the horsepower race between American car manufacturers in the late 1960s. Gasoline was then only 10 cents a gallon, Americans had more disposable income than ever before, and engine capacity was everything to the aspiring car buyer.

With its hugely powerful 7.2-liter capacity engine, the Charger 440 was, in reality, a thinly veiled road racer. The Rapid Transit (R/T) version was a high-performance factory option, which included heavy-duty suspension and brakes, dual exhausts, and wider tires. While idling, the engine produced such massive torque that it rocked the car body from side to side. Buyers took the second generation Charger to their hearts in a big way, with sales outstripping the earlier lackluster model by a factor of six.

STAR OF THE SCREEN
A car with star quality, the Charger featured in the classic nine-minute chase sequence in the film, *Bullitt*. It also had major roles in the 1970s cult movie, *Vanishing Point*, and the American television series, *The Dukes of Hazzard*.

DASHBOARD
The standard R/T cockpit is functional to the point of being stark. There are definitely no distractions here – just a matte black dash with six gauges, a 150 mph (241 km/h) speedometer and, of course, *de rigueur* bucket seats. Factory options included cruise control and wood-grained steering wheel.

COLOR
Options originally included Plum Crazy, Go Mango, and Top Banana.

TURN SIGNAL INDICATOR
Neat styling features include turn signals built into the hood scoop.

ENGINE IS FAST, BUT THIRSTY – JUST 8.1 MPG

LIGHTS
Hazard-warning lights and remote mirrors are both advanced features for 1967.

ENGINE
The wall-to-wall engine found in the R/T Charger is Dodge's immensely powerful 440 Magnum – a 7.2-liter V-8. This versatile powerplant produced maximum torque at a lazy 3200 rpm – making it obscenely quick, yet as docile as a kitten in town traffic.

TIRES
Transferring all the power to the road requires ultrawide 235 x 14 tires.

DODGE CHARGER R/T

The Charger was the creation of Dodge's chief of design, Bill Brownlie. Its clean, voluptuous lines gave this car one of the handsomest shapes of the day. It left you in no doubt as to what this car was all about: guts and purpose. The mean-looking nose, blacked-out grille, and low hood make this the type of car that, if seen in the rear view mirror, would make you move over, fast.

SPECIFICATIONS

MODEL Dodge Charger (1967–70)
PRODUCTION 96,100
BODY STYLE Two-door, four-seater
CONSTRUCTION Steel monocoque body.
ENGINE V-8 7.2-liter.
POWER OUTPUT 375 hp at 3200 rpm.
TRANSMISSION Three-speed Torqueflite auto, or Hurst four-speed manual.
SUSPENSION *Front:* Heavy duty independent; *Rear:* Leaf-spring.
BRAKES Heavy duty, 11 in (280 mm) drums, with optional front discs.
MAXIMUM SPEED 150 mph (241 km/h)
0–60 MPH (0–96 KM/H) 6 sec
0–100 MPH (0–161 KM/H) 13.3 sec
A.F.C. 8.1 mpg

SECURITY
The chrome, quick-fill, racing-style gas cap is attached to the car by wire to stop souvenir-hunters.

REAR VIEW
"Buttress-backed" styling was America's version of a European 2+2 sports coupe.

HEADLIGHTS
These were hidden under electric flaps to give the Charger a sinister grin.

STEERING WHEEL
Its huge size allows the driver to apply plenty of his own torque to turn the car.

ENGINE
The potent engine has enough power to spin the rear wheels in every gear.

ANTIROLL BARS
Enormous antiroll bars 1 in (25 mm) in diameter guarantee that the Charger handles well, despite its size.

NEVADA
OCT 481

FACEL VEGA *II*

WHEN SOMEONE LIKE PABLO PICASSO chooses a car, it is going to look good. In its day, the Facel II was a poem in steel and easily as beautiful as anything turned out by the Italian styling houses. Small wonder then that Facels were synonymous with the 1960s jet setters. Driven by Ringo Starr, Ava Gardner, Danny Kaye, Tony Curtis, François Truffaut, and Joan Fontaine, Facels were some of the most charismatic cars of the day. Even death gave them glamor; the novelist Albert Camus died while being driven in his publisher's FVS in January 1960.

In 1961, the HK 500 was redesigned and given cleaner lines, an extra 6 in (15 cm) in length, and dubbed the Facel II. At 3640 pounds, the II was lighter than the 500, could storm to 140 mph (225 km/h), and squeal from 0–100 mph (161 km/h) in 17 seconds. Costing more than the contemporary Aston Martin DB4 *(see pages 28–29)* and Maserati 3500, the Facel II was as immortal as a Duesenberg, Hispano Suiza, or Delahaye. We will never see its like again.

Early Facels, such as the HK 500, had appalling drum brakes until 1960, when pressure from the press made Facel bolt on Dunlop disc brakes.

FACEL HK 500
The HK 500 was the most popular Facel, with 5.8-liter and 6.2-liter Chrysler V-8s married to three-speed Torqueflite or four-speed Pont-a-Mousson automatic gearboxes.

FABRIC, ROLL-BACK, FULL-LENGTH SUNROOF WAS AN AFTERMARKET ACCESSORY

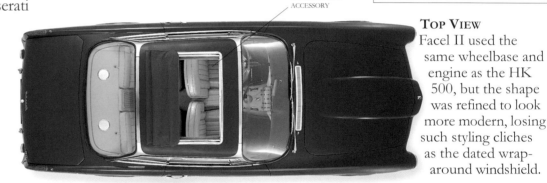

TOP VIEW
Facel II used the same wheelbase and engine as the HK 500, but the shape was refined to look more modern, losing such styling cliches as the dated wrap-around windshield.

SMOOTH LIGHTING
Brake lights are cut out of the rear fenders and help to enhance the Facel's seamless lines.

REAR VIEW
The enlarged rear window gave a much greater glass area than the HK 500 and almost 90 percent visibility, helped by slimmer pillars.

BUMPER IS NOT CHROME BUT RUST-RESISTANT STAINLESS STEEL

HOOD IS HUGE, BUT THEN SO IS THE ENGINE

FACEL WHEELS
Light aluminum, chromed knock-off disc wheels were the most common equipment on Facel IIs. Borrani-Rudge "record" wire wheels were also listed in the brochures, but rarely specified.

PANELS WERE HAND-FINISHED AND MATED TO EACH OTHER TO CREATE A ONE-PIECE LOOK

KNOCK-OFF WHEEL SPINNERS WERE REMOVED WITH A SOFT-HEADED HAMMER

DASH MIGHT HAVE LOOKED LIKE WOOD BUT WAS ACTUALLY PAINTED METAL

MANUAL PONT-A-MOUSSON GEARBOX BEGAN LIFE IN A TRUCK

RAKISH BODY WAS ARTISTICALLY SIMILAR TO THE FACELLIA COUPE

SPECIFICATIONS
MODEL Facel Vega Facel II (1962–64)
PRODUCTION 184
BODY STYLES Two-door, four-seater Grand Tourer.
CONSTRUCTION Steel chassis, steel/light aluminum body.
ENGINE 6286cc cast-iron V-8.
POWER OUTPUT 390 bhp at 5400 rpm (manual) 355 bhp at 4800 rpm (auto).
TRANSMISSION Three-speed Torqueflite automatic or four-speed Pont-a-Mousson manual.
SUSPENSION Independent front coil springs, rear live axle leaf springs.
BRAKES Four-wheel Dunlop discs.
MAXIMUM SPEED 149 mph (240 km/h)
0–60 MPH (0–96 KM/H) 8.3 sec
0–100 MPH (0–161 KM/H) 17.0 sec
A.F.C. 15 mpg

REAR SEATING
The leather rear seat might look inviting, but it is very occasional and folds down to make a luggage platform.

INTERIOR
Steering wheel points straight to the driver's heart. Note the unmistakable aircraft-type panel layout with center gauges and heater controls like hand throttles.

ENGINE
The Facel II was powered by a 6286cc castiron Chrysler V-8, which, when coupled to the rare and balky four-speed manual gearbox, pushed out 390 bhp.

— THE FASCINATING FACEL —

The first products of the Facel stable were known as Vegas, a name deliberately chosen for its American associations.

MADE BETWEEN 1954 and 1955, an early Vega is a rare thing. Only about a dozen survive out of 46 built. In 1956, the Vega was renamed the FVS, this time powered by a 5.5-liter Chrysler V-8 that replaced the 4.6-liter DeSoto unit, but hampered by unpowered drum brakes. Despite the heart-stopping brake pedal, skittish front-end geometry, and suspension reliability glitches, some 357 FVSs were built, with over three quarters of the run going to America.

In terms of finish, image, and quality, Facel Vegas were among the most successful handmade supercars. Body joints were perfectly flush, doors closed like heavy vaults, brightwork was stainless steel, and even the roofline was fabricated from five seamlessly joined sections. Meticulous detailing and engineering panache earned Facel an image of wealthy arrogance, somewhere between a Bentley Continental and a Mercedes-Benz SL. But, more importantly, the HK 500 and Facel II were a unique amalgam of 1950s American and European styling motifs. Facels oozed self-confidence, with huge wraparound windshields, rocketship rear lights, and aircraft interiors, yet they were clothed in a softly curved

FRENCH ADVERTISMENT FOR THE FACEL VEGA EXCELLENCE

tapering body style – France's answer to Detroit's swank tanks.

The third generation FV was the HK 500, launched in 1959, with even more grunt, courtesy of the frenzied

FACEL
Vega II

DIMENSIONS
At 3,640 pounds (30 cwt), 15 ft (4.57 m) long, 6 ft (1.83 m) wide, and only 4 ft 3 in (1.3 m) high, the Facel II aped the girth and bulk of contemporary American iron.

HK 500s HAD A MIRROR ON THE ROOF RAIL; IIs HAD IT MOUNTED ON THE DASH

UNLIKE THE DASHBOARD, THE WOOD-RIM WHEEL WAS THE REAL THING

BADGE
The Facel II represents Facel creator Jean Daninos's last and greatest achievement; few other cars of its era possessed the same cachet.

American horsepower race among GM, Ford, and Chrysler. As soon as one of them came up with another handful of cubic inches, the others did too, and engine sizes became progressively crazier. The first of the HK 500s had a 290 bhp 5.9-liter V-8, which, a year later, was swapped for the hairier 6.3-liter hemihead design, bringing the already commendable maximum speed to a wild 140 mph (225 km/h). Over 500 HKs were produced, the majority with the standard Torqueflite automatic, but some with the awkward Pont-a-Mousson four-speeder. Up to April, 1960, most 500s still had the fade-prone drum brakes of the FVS, later changed to Dunlop discs.

The Excellence, an Olympian 17-ft (5.18-m) long stretched Facel introduced in 1958, was a Quixotic tilt at the R-R Silver Cloud and Mercedes 300 market. Production ceased in 1964 with just 230 cars built and only 13 sold in Britain. Unloved for its great thirst and dropping pillarless doors, the Excellence is now significantly cheaper than any other big Facel. Facel IIs, on the other hand, are considered the most desirable of the breed, with sharper lines and even more power – 390 bhp. Introduced in late 1961, they came with wire wheels, disc brakes, automatic gearshift, and Selectaride shocks. By far the rarest Facel, with only 184 made, IIs are still fiercely admired by Facel fanciers.

The Facellia, a scaled-down HK 500, available as a convertible or coupe, bankrupted Facel. Pont-a-Mousson's first engine-building venture was a

THE FACEL VEGA IN WHICH ALBERT CAMUS DIED, 1960

disaster; the under-developed 1647cc dohc (double overhead camshaft) soon had a reputation as a piston-burner. Even ownership by such celebrities as Joan Collins could not prevent the Facellia's reputation for unreliability, hastening Facel's demise.

PRODIGIOUS HOOD BULGE CLEARED VAST OIL DRUM-LIKE AIR CLEANERS OVER DOUBLE CARBURETORS. DRIVEN FAST, THE FACEL II WOULD DRINK ONE GALLON OF FUEL EVERY TEN MILES

WINDSHIELD IS EVEN MORE STEEPLY RAKED THAN ON THE HK 500

IN THE 1950S, FACEL MADE MOTOR SCOOTERS, JET ENGINES, OFFICE FURNITURE, AND KITCHEN CABINETS

FRONT VIEW

The intimidating front is all grille, because the hot-running castiron V-8 engine needed all the cooling air it could get. HK 500 had four round headlights, but the Facel II's voguish stacked lights were shamelessly stolen from contemporary Mercedes sedans.

FERRARI 250 *GT SWB*

IN AN ERA WHEN FERRARI was turning out some lackluster road cars, the 250 GT SWB became a yardstick, the car against which all other GTs were judged and one of the finest Ferraris ever. Of the 167 made between 1959 and 1962, 74 were competition cars – their simplicity made them one of the most competitive sports racers of the 1950s. Built around a tubular chassis, the 3.0-liter V-12 engine lives at the front, along with a simple four-speed gearbox with Porsche internals. But it is that delectable Pininfarina-sculpted shape that is so special. Tense, urgent, but friendly, those smooth lines have none of the intimidating presence of a Testarossa or Daytona. The SWB stands alone as a perfect blend of form and function. It is one of the world's prettiest cars, and on the track one of the most successful. The SWB won races from Spa to Le Mans, Nassau to the Nürburgring. Which is exactly what Enzo Ferrari wanted. "They are cars," he said, "which the sporting client can use on the road during the week and race on Sundays." Happy days.

HORSE RACING
In the middle 1960s, 250 GTs were cheap enough to be bought by amateurs who raced them at club events.

OVERHEAD VIEW
The car has perfect balance. Form is rounded and fluid and the first 11 SWBs were built in aluminum. Road cars had a steel body and aluminum hood and doors.

COCKPIT IS SNUG AND AIRY BUT FILLS WITH NOISE WHEN YOU TURN THE KEY

GENTLY TAPERING NOSE IS A MASTERPIECE OF THE PANEL BEATER'S ART

RARE LIGHTWEIGHT COMPETITION CARS SUFFERED FROM STRETCHING ALUMINUM

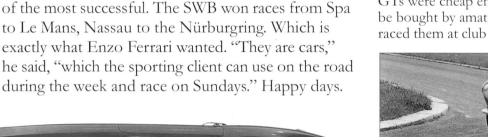

SWB SAT ON ELEGANT CHROME-PLATED BORRANI COMPETITION WIRE WHEELS

ENGINE

The V-12 power unit had a seven-bearing crankshaft turned from a steel bar, one plug per cylinder, and three twin-choke Weber DCL3 or DCL6 carburetors. Progressively more power was extracted from the engine, with output rising from 240 to 295 bhp.

INSTEAD OF AIR CLEANERS, COMPETITION CARS USED FILTERLESS AIR TRUMPETS

SPECIFICATIONS

MODEL Ferrari 250 GT SWB (1959–62)
PRODUCTION 167 (10 rhd)
BODY STYLE Two-seater GT coupe.
CONSTRUCTION Tubular chassis with all-aluminum or aluminum/steel body.
ENGINE 2953cc V-12.
POWER OUTPUT 280 bhp at 7000 rpm.
TRANSMISSION Four-speed manual.
SUSPENSION Independent front coil and wishbones, live rear axle with leaf springs.
BRAKES Four-wheel discs.
MAXIMUM SPEED 147 mph (237 km/h)
0–60 MPH (0–96 KM/H) 6.6 sec
0–100 MPH (0–161 KM/H) 16.2 sec
A.F.C. 12 mpg

SIMPLE INTERIOR

Despite the exotic exterior, the interior is a place of work. Functional dash is basic crackle black with no frills. Sun visors were notably absent.

250 DOMINATION

Stirling Hamil leads Ed Lowther's Corvette in a mid-1960s American club race. For many years the 250 GT dominated hillclimbs and track races at circuits all over the world. The SWB is a small car with wonderfully predictable handling.

COMPETITION VERSIONS HAD LIGHT, BUT EASILY SCRATCHED, PLEXIGLASS WINDOWS. ROAD CARS USED HEAVIER GLASS

EXPANSIVE REAR WINDOW SITS ABOVE ENORMOUS 26-GALLON (120-LITER) GAS TANK

TWIN EXHAUSTS

Two sets of aggressive drainpipe twin exhausts dominate the SWB's rump and declare its competition bloodline.

INTERIOR SEAT

Roll cage and harnesses are concessions to safety. Bucket seats look supportive, but were thinly padded.

AERODYNAMICS

In Pininfarina's wind tunnel with the radiator grille closed, a 250 GT achieved a drag coefficient of only 0.33, a figure that would shame many cars 20 years later.

FERRARI'S LEGEND RACER

Although the 250 GT SWB was based on Ferrari's first real mass produced car, the 250 Europa, it was anything but mainstream. More race than road car, it was soon feted as one of the finest sports cars of the time.

THERE WERE TWO versions of the SWB, the steel-bodied Lusso for the road, or the aluminum-bodied Competizione for the track, and it was on those tortuous tarmac chicanes that the SWB shone. Its most famous win in the UK was with Stirling Moss in the 1960–61 Tourist Trophy. Moss thought it was a "really comfortable grand touring car with good brakes, a super engine and crisp gearbox ... a very well mannered, well balanced car, especially good for Le Mans or any other circuit where one could give it its head."

Yet, despite its loose pretensions towards being a road machine, one walk around the SWB tells you that this is no aimless boulevardier. A racer stripped of all superfluous fat, there were front air scoops to cool the disc brakes, fender air extraction vents for underhood cooling, and reinforced points for racing-type quick-action jacks. Even the gas cap, an aluminum quick-fill variety, was *de rigueur* on all the best Le Mans racers. This was a road rocket in a Savile Row suit, an elegant projectile equally at home crunching up the gravel drive of an English country house or howling around a circuit locked in combat with the Aston Martin DB4GT.

ENZO FERRARI ON THE FRONT OF ITALIAN MAGAZINE, MIRACOLO A MARANELLO, IN 1955

FERRARI
250 GT SWB

RUDIMENTARY REAR WINDOW VENT WAS FOR COCKPIT COOLING

HUGE ALUMINUM GAS CAP WAS FOR FAST FUEL STOPS

DESIGN CREDITS
Soft, compact, and rounded, Pininfarina executed the design, while Scaglietti took care of the sheet metal. The result was one of the most charismatic cars ever produced.

REAR STOPLIGHT AND INDICATORS WERE USED ON MANY OTHER FERRARIS

GUT-WRENCHING THUDS BETRAY THE SWB'S HARD-SPRUNG LIVE AXLE

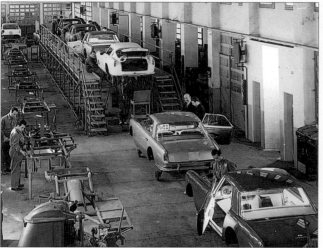

1960s' FERRARI PRODUCTION LINE

km/h), and third saw the needle touching 155 mph (249 km/h), with one more gear to go, enough to give today's V-12s a very bad score. In the 1961 Tourist Trophy at Goodwood, England, Moss won the four-hour race at an average speed of 87.73 mph (141.15 km/h). In the same year he recorded the seventh fastest lap at Le Mans at the time.

great Grand Touring tradition – cars you could drive to the track, annihilate all competitors, and drive home again. It was a true gentleman's sports car.

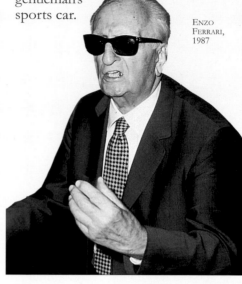

ENZO FERRARI, 1987

With a 4:1 final drive, it would accelerate from standstill to 100 mph (161 km/h) in a head-jerking 14 seconds. First gear was good for 61 mph (98 km/h), second 85 mph (137

One of the first Ferraris with a well-constructed chassis, the 250 GT not only had a lightness and fluidity found in only a handful of the world's most precocious sports cars, but also a stunning beauty. The SWB was one of the final flowerings of that

IMPOSING FRONT

The 250 GT is a polished gem, hugging the road in corners. Front combines beauty and threat with steely grin and squat wheel arch-filling attitude. Nothing is exaggerated for effect.

DRAMATIC SMALL HOOD VENT SUCKED AIR INTO THREE DOUBLE-CHOKE WEBER CARBURETORS

ROAD CARS HAD PRANCING HORSE BADGE IN GRILLE AND VESTIGIAL FRONT BUMPERS

SWEEPING BODY PANELS ARE ALMOST PRICELESS. EACH WAS HAND MADE, WITH SCANT REGARD FOR REPAIR OR REPLACEMENT

FERRARI *308 GTB*

ONE OF THE BEST-SELLING Ferraris ever, the 308 GTB started life with a fiberglass body designed by Pininfarina and built by Scaglietti. Power was courtesy of the 3.0-liter V-8 engine and five-speed gearbox inherited from the 308 GT4. With America the GTB's target market, Federal emission regulations made the GTB clean up its act, evolving into a refined and civilized machine with such high-tech goodies as four valves per cylinder and Bosch K-Jetronic fuel injection. Practical and tractable in traffic, it became the 1980s entry level Ferrari, supplanting the Porsche 911 *(see pages 194–95)* as the standard issue yuppiemobile. In the television detective series *Magnum P.I.*, Tom Sellick gave the 308 prime time exposure and turned it into an aspirational icon. Prices went crazy, but values have softened and a good low mileage 308 is one of the least traumatic and most cost-effective entries into the prancing horse club.

― SPECIFICATIONS ―

MODEL Ferrari 308 GTB (1975–85)
PRODUCTION 712 (308 GTB fiberglass); 2,185 (308 GTB steel); 3,219 (GTS).
BODY STYLE Two-door, two-seater sports coupe.
CONSTRUCTION Fiberglass/steel.
ENGINE Midmounted transverse dohc 2926cc V-8.
POWER OUTPUT 255 bhp at 7600 rpm.
TRANSMISSION Five-speed manual.
SUSPENSION Independent double wishbones/coil springs all around.
BRAKES Ventilated discs all around.
MAXIMUM SPEED 154 mph (248 km/h)
0–60 MPH (0–96 KM/H) 7.3 sec
0–100 MPH (0–161 KM/H) 19.8 sec
A.F.C. 16 mpg

GTS ROOF
The GTB always had a metal roof; the chic GTS had a removable Targa top panel.

FERRARI 308 GTB
The handsome styling is a blend of Dino 246 *(see pages 108–09)* and 365 GT4. The Dino provided concave rear windows and conical air intakes, while the 365 brought double bodyshell appearance with a waistline groove.

ENGINE
The 2926cc V-8 has double overhead cams per bank and four carburetors.

VENTILATION
With the engine at the back, the wide slatted grille scooped up air for brake and interior ventilation.

AERODYNAMICS
Retractable flush-fitting popup headlights keep wind force down on the nose and front wheels.

FERRARI *275 GTB/4*

RACE ENGINE
Type 226 engine was related to the 330 P2 prototypes of the 1965 racing season.

THE GTB/4 WAS A HYBRID made for two short years, 1966 to 1968. With just 350 built, a mere 27 in right-hand drive, it was not exactly one of Ferrari's money-makers. So named for its four camshafts, the GTB still ranks as the finest road car Ferrari produced before Fiat took control of the company.

With fully independent suspension, a musical five-speed gearbox, and a wonderfully fetching Pininfarina-designed and Scaglietti-built body, it was the last of the true Berlinettas. The forerunner of the Daytona *(see page 104)*, the GTB was built more for hard charging than posing. This was Ferrari's first-ever production four-cam V-12 engine and its first road-going prancing horse with an independent rear end. Nimble and compact, with exemplary neutral handling and stunning design, this is probably one of the most desirable Ferraris ever made.

HIDDEN CAP
So as not to clutter the seamless lines, the gas cap was hidden from view inside the trunk.

CARBURETORS
A gentle hood bulge is required to clear the huge air cleaner atop six Webers.

INTERIOR
The interior is cramped, impractical, and trimmed in distinctly unluxurious vinyl.

STYLING
Small trunk, small cockpit, and long nose are classic Pininfarina styling cues – an arresting amalgam of beauty and brawn.

SPECIFICATIONS

MODEL Ferrari 275 GTB/4 (1966–68)
PRODUCTION 350
BODY STYLE Two-seater front-engined coupe.
CONSTRUCTION Steel chassis, aluminum body.
ENGINE 3.3-liter twin overhead-cam dry sump V-12.
POWER OUTPUT 300 hp at 8000 rpm
TRANSMISSION Five-speed all synchromesh.
SUSPENSION All around independent.
BRAKES Four-wheel power-assisted discs.
MAXIMUM SPEED 160 mph (257 km/h)
0–60 MPH (0–96 KM/H) 5.5 sec
0–100 MPH (0–161 KM/H) 13 sec
A.F.C. 12 mpg

FERRARI 275 GTB/4

Prettier than a Jaguar E-Type *(see pages 140–43)*, Aston Martin DB4 *(see pages 28–29)*, or Lamborghini Miura *(see pages 146–47)*, the GTB/4 has a chassis made up of a ladder frame built around two oval tube members.

FERRARI *Daytona*

KNOWN TO EVERY SCHOOLCHILD as the world's fastest car, the classically sculptured and outrageously quick Daytona was a supercar with a split personality. Under 120 mph (193 km/h), it felt like a truck with heavy inert controls and crashing suspension. But once the needle was heading for 140 mph (225 km/h), things started to sparkle. With a romantic flat-out maximum of 170 mph (280 km/h), it was the last of the great front-engined V-12 war horses.

Launched at the 1968 Paris Salon as the 365 GTB/4, the press immediately named it "Daytona" in honor of Ferrari's success at the 1967 24-hour race. Faster than the contemporary Lamborghini Miura *(see page 146)*, De Tomaso Pantera *(see pages 90–91)*, and Jaguar E-Type *(see pages 140–43)*, the chisel-nosed Ferrari won laurels on the race track as well as in the hearts and pockets of wealthy enthusiasts all over the world.

SPECIFICATIONS

MODEL Ferrari 365 GTB/4 Daytona (1968–73)
PRODUCTION 1,426 (165 RHD)
BODY STYLE Two-seater fastback.
CONSTRUCTION Steel/aluminum/ fiberglass body, separate multitube chassis frame.
ENGINE V-12 4390cc.
POWER OUTPUT 352 bhp at 7500 rpm.
TRANSMISSION Five-speed all synchromesh.
SUSPENSION Independent front and rear.
BRAKES Four-wheel discs.
MAXIMUM SPEED 174 mph (280 km/h)
0–60 MPH (0–96 KM/H) 5.4 sec
0–100 MPH (0–161 KM/H) 12.8 sec
A.F.C. 14 mpg

INTERIOR
With hammock-type racing seats, a cornucopia of black-on-white instruments, and a provocatively angled, extra long gear shift, the cabin promises some serious excitement.

CLASH OF THE TITANS
On the track the Daytona did battle with the best and destroyed all competitors. With racing modifications, it not only handled but could muster 190 mph (306 km/h) on the straightaway.

FERRARI 365 GTB/4 DAYTONA
A poem in steel, few other cars could be considered in the same aesthetic league as the Daytona. Beneath the exterior is a skeleton of chrome-molybdenum tubes, giving rigidity and strength. Body panels were hand-hammered on wooden bucks, with no two being exactly the same.

HEADLIGHTS
American safety regulations dictated that the double retractable headlights could be raised in 3 seconds.

SUSPENSION
Double wishbone front suspension was strong enough for hell-raising speeds.

TOURING TRUNK
As a GT car, the Daytona has an accommodating trunk.

WIPERS
The windshield wipers disappear neatly behind the raised edge of the hood.

TOUGH TIRES
200 x 15 G70 Michelin XVRs were the only tires then available to cope with the top speed.

FERRARI *400 GT*

THE FIRST FERRARI ever offered with an automatic transmission, the 400 was aimed at the American market, and was meant to take the prancing horse into the boardrooms of Europe and the US. But the 400's automatic box was a most un-Ferrari-like device, a lazy three-speed GM Turbo-Hydramatic as used in Cadillac, Rolls-Royce, and Jaguar. It may have been the best automatic in the world, but it was a radical departure for Maranello, and met with only modest success.

The 400 was possibly the most discreet and refined Ferrari ever made. It looked awful in Racing Red – the color of 70 percent of Ferraris – so most were finished in dark metallics. The 400 became the 400i GT in 1973 and the 412 in 1985. It became an alternative for the 1980s executive bored with Daimler Double-Sixes and BMW 750s.

SPECIFICATIONS

MODEL Ferrari 400 GT (1976–79)
PRODUCTION 501
BODY STYLE Two-door, four-seater sports sedan.
CONSTRUCTION Steel/aluminum body, separate tubular chassis frame.
ENGINE 4390cc twin ohc V-12.
POWER OUTPUT 340 hp at 6800 rpm.
TRANSMISSION Five-speed manual or three-speed automatic.
SUSPENSION Independent double wishbones with coil springs, rear and front with hydro-pneumatic self-leveling.
BRAKES Four-wheel ventilated discs.
MAXIMUM SPEED 150 mph (241 km/h)
0–60 MPH (0–96 KM/H) 7.1 sec
0–100 MPH (0–161 KM/H) 18.7 sec
A.F.C. 12 mpg

DASHBOARD
The 400's cockpit was a study in luxury, with leather dash and real wood and the option of a second rear air conditioning unit to keep tired tycoons cool. Rear passengers could also benefit from a four-speaker sound system.

pininfarina

PININFARINA BADGE
The Turin-based Pininfarina company is perhaps the most famous name in automotive styling in the world.

HEADLIGHTS
Four headlights were retracted into the bodywork by electric motors.

INTERIOR
The 400 was a genuine 2+2, with ample accommodation for four.

WINDSHIELD
Massive glass area and thin pillars gave the 400 the best visibility of any Ferrari.

MIRROR
Driver's door mirror was remotely controlled from a switch in the interior.

AN-48-TA

TRUNK
Trunk line was raised to limit drag.

FERRARI 400 GT

Apart from the delicate chin spoiler and bolt-on aluminum wheels, the shape was pure 365 GT4 2+2. The rectangular design of the body was lightened by a plunging hood line and a waist length indentation running along the 400's flanks.

FERRARI *365 GT4 Berlinetta Boxer*

THE BERLINETTA BOXER was meant to be the jewel in Ferrari's crown – one of the fastest GT cars ever. Replacing the legendary V-12 Ferrari Daytona *(see page 104)*, the 365 BB was powered by a flat-twelve "Boxer" engine, so named for the image of the horizontally located pistons punching at their opposite numbers. First unveiled at the 1971 Turin Motor Show, the 4.4-liter 380 bhp Boxer was so complex that deliveries to buyers did not start until 1973. The problem was that Ferrari had suggested that the Boxer could top 185 mph (298 km/h), when it could only manage around 170 mph (274 km/h), slower than the Daytona. In 1976 Ferrari replaced the 365 with the 5-liter Boxer 512, yet of the two cars the 365 is faster and rarer, with only 387 built.

TESTING THE STALLION
A handful of prototypes were subjected to extensive testing. This one is recognizable by the roof-mounted antenna. Factory cars had antennas in the windshield.

INTERIOR
An amalgam of racer and grand tourer, the Boxer's cabin was functional yet luxurious, with electric windows and air conditioning.

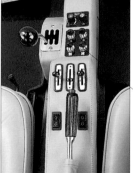

SWITCHES FOR THE POWER WINDOWS AND AIR CONDITIONING

CENTER CONSOLE
The rear-mounted gearbox meant only a small transmission tunnel was needed.

LOWER BODYWORK
This was fiberglass, along with the wheelarch liners and bumpers.

WHEELS
Wheels were the same as on the Daytona – cast light aluminum, with Rudge knock-off hubs.

LOW-SLUNG POSITION
The Boxer engine layout was favored because it allowed the whole car to sit that much lower, giving better aerodynamics and a lower center of gravity.

SPECIFICATIONS

MODEL Ferrari 365 GT4 Berlinetta Boxer (1973–1976)
PRODUCTION 387 (58 rhd models)
BODY STYLE Two-seater sports.
CONSTRUCTION Tubular spaceframe chassis.
ENGINE Flat-12, 4.4 liter.
POWER OUTPUT 380 bhp at 7700 rpm.
TRANSMISSION Five-speed all synchromesh rear-mounted gearbox.
SUSPENSION Independent front and rear.
BRAKES Ventilated front and rear disc brakes.
MAXIMUM SPEED 172 mph (277 km/h)
0–60 MPH (0–96 KM/H) 6.5 sec
0–100 MPH (0–161 KM/H) 15 sec
A.F.C. 14 mpg

FERRARI 365 GT4 BERLINETTA BOXER

In the classic car boom of the mid-Eighties, Boxers changed hands for mad money. The 512 trebled in value before the crash, with the 365 doubling its price. Now both machines have fallen back to realistic levels.

CHASSIS
The Boxer's chassis was derived from the Dino (see pages 108–09), with a frame of steel tubes and doors, bellypan, and nose in aluminum.

COOLING VENT
Slatted hood cooling vent helped keep interior cabin temperatures down.

FERRARI ENGINE

A magnificent piece of foundry art, the flat-twelve has a crankshaft machined from a solid piece of chrome molybdenum steel. Cylinder heads were light aluminum, holding two camshafts each. Instead of timing chains, the 365 used toothed composite belts, an innovation in 1973.

HEART OF THE BEAST

The Boxer 4.4-liter engine could produce an Olympian 380 bhp at 7600 rpm. Note the twin oil filters, one for each bank of six cylinders.

ENGINE POSITION
The entire engine/drivetrain ensemble was positioned longitudinally behind the cockpit.

TIRES
The Boxer was shod with ultrawide Michelin XWX 215/70 tires.

FERRARI *Dino 246 GT*

PRETTY ENOUGH TO STOP a speeding train, the Dino came not from Enzo Ferrari's head, but from his heart. The Dino was a tribute to the great man's love for his son, Alfredino, who died of a kidney disease. Aimed at the Porsche 911 buyer *(see pages 194–95)*, the 246 Dino engine came with only half the number of cylinders usually found in a Ferrari. Instead of a V12 configuration, it boasted a 2.4-liter V-6 engine, yet it was nonetheless capable of a very Ferrari-like 150 mph (241 km/h).

With sparkling performance, small girth, and midengined layout, it handled like a go-kart, and could be hustled around with enormous aplomb. Beautifully sculpted by Pininfarina, the 246 won worldwide acclaim as the high point of 1970s automotive styling. In its day, it was among the most fashionable cars money could buy. The rarest Dino is the GTS, with Targa detachable roof panel. The Dino's finest hour was when it was driven by Tony Curtis in the '70s ITC television series *The Persuaders*. One of the most accessible Ferraris, Dino prices went berserk in the '80s, but are now half that value.

ENGINE
The transversely mounted 2418cc V-6 has four overhead cams and a four-bearing crankshaft; it breathes through three twin-choke Weber 40 DCF carburetors. The engine's distinctive throaty roar is a Ferrari legend.

INTERIOR
The dashboard is suede and strewn with switches, while the cramped-looking interior is actually an ergonomic triumph. Slotting the five-speed gearbox though its chrome gate flows like honey.

AERODYNAMICS
Sweeping roofline is unmistakable from any angle. The Dino's sleek aerodynamic shape helps to give the car its impressively high top speed.

POSITIONING
The engine is positioned in the middle, while the spare wheel and battery are located in the front.

COCKPIT
Interior is cramped, but no one cared with a car that looked this good.

MODEL Ferrari Dino 246 GT (1969–74)
PRODUCTION 2,487
BODY STYLE Two-door midengine sports coupe.
CONSTRUCTION Steel body, tubular frame.
ENGINE Transverse V6/2.4 litre.
POWER OUTPUT 195 bhp at 5000 rpm.
TRANSMISSION Five-speed, all synchromesh.
SUSPENSION Independent front and rear.
BRAKES Ventilated discs all around.
MAXIMUM SPEED 148 mph (238 km/h)
0–60 MPH (0–96 KM/H) 7.1 sec
0–100 MPH (0–161 KM/H) 17.6 sec
A.F.C. 22 mpg

FERRARI 246 GT

Early Dinos were constructed from aluminum, later ones from steel, with the bodies built by Italian designer Scaglietti. Unfortunately, little attention was paid to rust protection. Vulnerable interior body joints and cavities were covered with only a very thin coat of paint and most surviving Dinos will have had at least one body rebuild by now.

COLOR
Metallic brown is a rare color – 75 percent of Dinos were red.

STYLING
The sensuous curves are supplied by Ferrari. The Ferrari badge and prancing horse were added by a later owner.

WINDSHIELD
Windshields do not come much more steeply raked than this one.

EXHAUSTS
Four exhausts mean the V-6 sounds almost as musical as a V-12.

FERRARI *Testarossa*

THE TESTAROSSA was never one of Modena's best efforts. With its enormous girth and overstuffed appearance, it perfectly sums up the 1980s credo of excess. As soon as it appeared on the world's television screens in *Miami Vice*, the Testarossa, or Redhead, became a symbol of everything that was wrong with a decade of rampant materialism and greed.

The Testarossa fell from grace rather suddenly. Dilettante speculators bought it new at $400,000-odd and ballyhooed its values up to a million. By 1988, when this particular car was built, secondhand values were going down the slippery slope, and many an investor stood back in horror as his hedge against inflation shed three-quarters of its value overnight.

1958 FERRARI TESTA ROSSA
Ferrari bestowed on its new creation one of the grandest names from Maranello's glorious racing past – the 250 Testa Rossa, of which only 19 were built for retail customers. The distinctive bodywork by Scaglietti, with its sloping nose separated from the cutaway front wheel arches, was known as "pontoon-fendered."

INTERIOR
The cockpit was restrained and spartan, with a hand-stitched leather dash and little distracting ornamentation. For once a Ferrari's cockpit was accommodating, with electrically adjustable leather seats and air conditioning as standard.

ENGINE
The flat-12 mid-mounted engine was 4942cc, producing 390 bhp at 6500 rpm. With four valves per cylinder, coil ignition, and fuel injection, it was one of the very last flat-12 GTs.

STYLING
Striking radiator cooling ducts obviated the need to pass water from the front radiator to the midmounted engine, freeing the front luggage compartment.

WHEELS
Wheel rims were 8 in (20 cm) in the front and 10 in (25 cm) in the rear.

REAR VENTS

Borrowed from Grand Prix racing experience, these cheese-slicer cooling ducts are for the twin radiators, located forward of the rear wheels to keep heat away from the cockpit.

REAR END TREATMENT
Pininfarina's grille treatment was picked up on the rear end, giving stylistic continuity.

DOOR MIRRORS
Prominent door mirrors on both sides gave the Testarossa an extra 8 in (20 cm) in width.

— SPECIFICATIONS —

MODEL Ferrari Testarossa (1988)
PRODUCTION 1,074
BODY STYLE Midengined, two-seater sports coupe.
CONSTRUCTION Steel frame with aluminum and fiberglass panels.
ENGINE Flat-12 4942cc with dry sump lubrication.
POWER OUTPUT 390 bhp at 6500 rpm.
TRANSMISSION Five-speed manual.
SUSPENSION Independent front and rear.
BRAKES *Front:* disc; *Rear:* drums.
MAXIMUM SPEED 181 mph (291 km/h)
0–60 MPH (0–96 KM/H) 5.3 sec
0–100 MPH (0–161 KM/H) 12.2 sec
A.F.C. 12 mpg

ORIGINAL GRILLES
The Testarossa's distinctive side grilles are now among the most widely imitated styling features

REAR-VIEW MIRROR
The curious, periscopelike rear-view mirror was developed by Pininfarina and manufactured by Gilardina.

FERRARI TESTAROSSA

Design was determined with the help of Pininfarina's full-sized wind tunnel, but enthusiasts were initially cool about the Testarossa's size and shape. Wider than the Ferrari 512 BB, the Corvette *(see pages 62–63),* and the Countach *(see pages 148–49),* it measured a portly 6 ft (1.83 m) across. While this meant a bigger cockpit, the ultrawide door sills collected mud in wet weather and the headlights were inadequate for a 180 mph (290 km/h) road rocket.

AERODYNAMICS
Front spoiler keeps the nose firmly attached to the asphalt, and channels cooling air to the front brakes.

FIAT *500D*

WHEN THE FIAT 500 NUOVA appeared in 1957, long-time Fiat designer Dante Giacosa defended his frugal flyweight by saying, "However small it might be, an automobile will always be more comfortable than a motor scooter." Today though, the diminutive scoot-about needs no defense, for time has justified Giacosa's faith – over four million 500s and derivatives were produced up to the demise of the Giardiniera estate in 1977. In some senses the Fiat was a mini before the British Mini *(see pages 40–41)*, for the baby Fiat not only appeared two years ahead of its British counterpart, but was also 3 in (7.6 cm) shorter. With its very small 479cc two-cylinder motor, the original 500 Nuova was rather frantic. 1960 saw it grow to maturity with the launch of the 500D, shown here, which was pushed along by its enlarged 499.5cc engine. Now, the baby Fiat could almost touch 60 mph (96 km/h) without being pushed over the edge of a cliff.

FIAT'S FIRST BABY
The lineage of the postwar baby Fiat descends from this little mite, the original 500, launched in 1936. To be precise, Fiat called it the 500A, the suffix referring to the airplane engine offices where it was drawn up. But the public instantly dubbed it *Topolino*, or little mouse.

MINIMAL MOTORING
The Fiat 500's interior is minimal but functional. There is no fuel gauge, just a light that illuminates when three-quarters of a gallon remains – enough for another 40 miles (64 km).

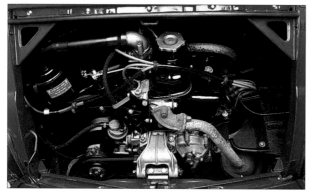

ENGINE
Rear-engined layout, already employed in the Fiat 600 of 1955, saved space by removing the need for a transmission tunnel. The use of an air-cooled engine and only two cylinders in the 500 was a completely new direction for Fiat, and gave an added space-saving bonus by doing away with a radiator. The 500 started with a 479cc engine; the 500D adopted the larger 499cc engine of the 500 Sport, which it replaced. All engines, though, were feisty devils of indefinite flat-out driving.

EARLY "SUICIDE" DOORS

You can tell this Fiat is pre-1965 because of the rear-hinged, so-called "suicide doors." After that the hinges moved to the front in line with more modern practice. The Giardiniera estate kept suicide doors until its demise in 1977.

BACK-TO-FRONT

Some rear-engined cars aped front-engined cousins with fake grilles and air intakes. Not the unpretentious Fiat.

SUNROOF

Some 500s had small fold-back sunroofs. On convertibles the fabric roof with plastic rear screen rolled right back.

FIAT 500D

This pert little package is big on charm. From any angle the baby Fiat seems to present a happy, smiling disposition. When it comes to parking it is a winner, although accommodation is a little tight. Two average-sized adults can fit up front; realistic back-seat permutations are two children, one adult sitting sideways, or a large shopping basket.

DRIVING THE 500

The baby Fiat was a fine little driver's car that earned press plaudits for its assured and nimble handling. Although top speed was limited and the gearbox was a little primitive, the car's poise meant you rarely needed to slow down on clear roads.

"HOOD"

This houses the fuel tank, battery, and spare wheel, with a little space left for a modest amount of luggage.

— SPECIFICATIONS —

MODEL Fiat 500D (1957–77)
PRODUCTION 4 million plus (all models)
BODY STYLES Sedan, convertible. Giardiniera estate.
CONSTRUCTION Unibody/chassis.
ENGINE Two-cylinder air-cooled 479cc or 499.5cc.
POWER OUTPUT 17.5 bhp at 4400 rpm (499.5cc)
TRANSMISSION Four-speed non-synchromesh.
SUSPENSION *Front:* Independent, transverse leaf, wishbones. *Rear:* Independent semitrailing arms, coil springs.
BRAKES Hydraulic drums.
MAXIMUM SPEED 59 mph (95 km/h)
0–40 MPH (0–64 KM/H) 32 sec
A.F.C. 53 mpg

FORD *Edsel*

THE POOR OLD EDSEL, consigned to the dustbin of history as the ultimate clunker. Everyone blames that unfortunate "horse-collar" frontal treatment, but that is only part of the story. Kinder critics say that its aim was true, but the target moved. Conceived when sales of low-end medium-priced cars were booming, the Edsel should have been a winner. Unfortunately, by the time it was officially launched on September 4, 1957, the US auto industry was in a slump, with sales particularly affected in the Edsel's market segment.

The Edsel was also a victim of its own hype. Throughout its conception, the marketing men had gone into overdrive. They forecast 200,000 sales in the first year and predicted they would have to build extra factories to cope with the demand for a car they claimed had cost $250 million to develop. The truth is that in its first year the Edsel set an all-time record for deliveries of a brand new medium-priced model. Yet it fell so short of the grandiose claims that it was almost instantly dubbed a failure. Today the Edsel is an emblem, a comforting reassurance for the little man that mighty corporations can get it wrong. And, of course, its comparative failure marks it as a prized collector's piece.

INTERIOR
Well over 80 percent of Edsel buyers chose automatic transmissions. Some 1958 models featured these transmissions, operated by pushbuttons in the steering wheel hub. This is a 1959 automatic Corsair with padded dash. Less than half of all Edsels had power steering.

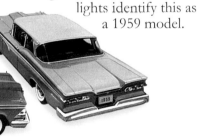

TELLTALE TAILLIGHTS
1958 Edsels had a higher rear light-cluster that one cruel critic likened to an ingrown toenail. The remodeled lights identify this as a 1959 model.

EDSEL MODELS
The Edsel launch lineup featured 18 models in four series, starting with the Ranger and moving up to the Pacer, Corsair, and top-of-the-line Citation. Station wagons were Ranger, Villager, and Bermuda.

EDSEL EXTREMES
The 1958 frontal treatment was more muted than the 1959, shown here with more chrome than a roadside diner.

HYPE HOPES
Edsel's launch was preceded by a massive marketing buildup. The official launch was in September 1957, but sales for the 1958 model year of 63,110 slumped to 44,891 for 1959, then 2,846 for 1960.

LAST EDSEL
1960 model year Edsel was completely restyled with no "horse collar."

FORD EDSEL

The Edsel is no beauty, for sure, but neither is it as ugly as its reputation. The most controversial aspect is the vertical center grille; one comic described the Edsel as an "Oldsmobile sucking a lemon," and it certainly has an unhappy frontal aspect. Its sides, though, are clean, almost elegant. Ford advertising gushed "EDSEL ... already an expression of good taste," but that is surely pushing it a bit.

SPECIFICATIONS

MODEL Ford Edsel (1958–59)
PRODUCTION 108,001 (110,847 including 1960 model year)
BODY STYLES Two- and four-door sedan, two- and four-door hardtop coupe, station wagon, convertible.
CONSTRUCTION Steel body, separate chassis frame.
ENGINES 223cid straight six. V-8s from 292 to 410cid.
POWER OUTPUT 145 hp at 4500 rpm (223cid); 345 hp at 4600 rpm (410).
TRANSMISSION Three-speed manual; two- and three-speed automatic.
SUSPENSION *Front:* Independent, coil springs. *Rear:* Live axle, leaf springs.
BRAKES Drums all around.
MAXIMUM SPEED 90–108 mph (145-174 km/h) depending on engine.
0–60 MPH (0–96 KM/H) 10–17 sec
A.F.C. 10–15 mpg

COLLECTOR PLATES
The collector plate underlines the classic cachet of a car once considered a clunker.

"GUN SIGHTS"
The 1958 Edsel had a "gun-sight" emblem, which was doubled up into two fender-mounted sights in 1959.

OPEN AIR OPTIONS
Convertibles are the rarest of the Edsel family. In 1959, the only ragtop was the Corsair convertible, with a mere 1,343 built.

EDSEL EVOLUTION
For 1959, the headlights were lowered and the hood was much more shelflike. All the chrome took the emphasis away from the "horse collar."

OPTIONS
Dual spotlights were just one in a wide choice of electric and power options ranging from electric windows to power seats.

EDSEL EMBLEM
The car was named after Henry Ford's son, Edsel, who had died in 1943.

BUMPERS
Bumpers on 1959 models are far more substantial; another telltale of the year is the lowered taillight.

FORD *Thunderbird*

LAUNCHED IN 1955 as a stylish, personal sports compact, the Thunderbird broke new ground in American car styling. Against the backdrop of overstyled and overchromed land yachts, Ford came up with an altogether more subtle creation which suggested youth, money, and success. An instant hit, the T-Bird was pitched against the first generation Chevrolet Corvette *(see pages 62–63)*. While the Chevy had an asthmatic straight-six engine, simple fiberglass body, and few creature comforts, the Thunderbird boasted a Mercury V-8, steel body, and wind-up windows. In the showrooms of 1955 the T-Bird annihilated the 'Vette, outselling it 24-to-1 and whetting America's appetite for sports cars. The two-seater Thunderbird of 1955–57 has become a design icon, a romantic piece of 1950s American ephemera that features in the lyrics of half a dozen cult songs and as many movies.

T-BIRD ENGINE
The Thunderbird's cast-iron V-8 breathed through a Holley carburetor and developed 200 hp with three-speed manual transmission and 202 hp with Ford-O-Matic automatic transmission.

HOOD
Fiberglass hardtop was standard, with a rayon convertible hood an extra-cost option at $290.

CARBURETOR SPACE
Hood bulge was for the beefy four-barrel carburetor.

FORD THUNDERBIRD
The Thunderbird was an extremely successful blend of luxury and prestige. The sporting overtones and snug two-seater shape were exactly right for the lifestyles of a new generation of baby boomers.

FORD STYLING
Thunderbird's rear lights, rear fender, and hooded headlights were all styling themes present in other Ford sedans.

RETRO SHAPE
To many, the long hood and short trunk recalled the Lincoln Continental of the early 1940s.

WINDSHIELD
By 1956 curved windshields were fitted to virtually everything.

LOW FRONT
Ground clearance was only 5½ in (14 cm).

SPORTY LABELING
Although Ford's marketeers tried to sell the T-Bird as a sports car, it had a softer image, with comfort and convenience emphasized over raw speed and power.

JET EXHAUST
On the '55 and some '56 models exhausts were routed through the bumper overriders.

BACK END
Rear fender treatment was more restrained than other contemporary American cars and has a definite European feel.

INTERIOR
Dashboard sports a tachometer and high-mount speedometer. 1956 models had softer springs and slower steering than the '55 models. Buyers preferred it that way.

SPECIFICATIONS

MODEL Ford Thunderbird (1955–56)
PRODUCTION 31,786
BODY STYLE Two-door two-seater.
CONSTRUCTION Steel ladder chassis.
ENGINE V-8/4785CC (292cid).
POWER OUTPUT 200 hp at 4400 rpm.
TRANSMISSION Three-speed manual with optional overdrive or automatic.
SUSPENSION *Front:* coil springs; *Rear:* leaf springs.
BRAKES Drums front and rear.
MAXIMUM SPEED 114 mph (183 km/h)
0–60 MPH (0–96 KM/H) 9.5 sec
0–100 MPH (0–161 KM/H) 21 sec
A.F.C. 18 mpg

SUSPENSION
Rear suspension was courtesy of old-fashioned leaf springs under a live rear axle.

FORD *Fairlane 500 Skyliner*

FORD REALLY RAISED the roof with this one, and eyebrows too, for a Ford Fairlane Skyliner pulling up at the curb was an engaging spectacle. All you had to do was flick a switch and watch the amazed faces of onlookers as your Skyliner performed its remarkable and unique retracting hardtop act. The "world's only hide-away retractable hardtop," as Ford billed it, was based on an earlier development project. That plan proved hopelessly grandiose and to redeem the $2 million development costs Ford created the remarkable Skyliner. Ford was pleased with its party trick and gushed in ads that the Skyliner was "just about the most revolutionary change in transportation since the Ford replaced the horse on the American road." Well, not quite. It was a technical tour de force certainly, but also an expensive gimmick whose novelty wore off in three short years. By the end of 1959 the retracting hardtop had disappeared.

LIFTING THE LID
This press ad from 1957 shows how the drama unfolds. To run the show it took 610 ft (186 m) of electrical wire, 10 power relays, 10 limit switches, four lock motors, three drive motors, and eight circuit breakers. Despite its complexity, the mechanism was surprisingly reliable.

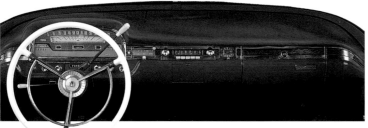

INTERIOR
As the top-of-the-line Fairlane, the glamorous Skyliner was luxuriously appointed, with color coordinated seats and dash, and power-assisted steering and brakes. This 1959 car has Cruise-O-Matic automatic transmission.

ENGINE OPTIONS
All Skyliners were V-8-powered. Base models were 272cid for 1957, then 292cid. The most potent option was a 352cid unit pushing out 300 hp.

SEATING
Hood does not infringe on passenger space; the Skyliner, with benches front and rear, is a spacious six-seater.

FORD FAIRLANE 500 SKYLINER

Each of the three Skyliner model years has its own distinct identity. The original of 1957 had full-length side trim, kinked at the rear of the door to create hips; the full-width grille was a simple slatted affair. In 1958 the trim was revised; the hood received a fake air intake and twin headlights appeared (grille resembled the '58 Thunderbird, *see pages 116–17*). Further revisions followed in 1959 to create this, the final expression of the Skyliner theme.

JET STYLING
1950s rocket ship themes are expressed here by big red rear lights mimicking jet afterburners.

FIN TALE
To you and me they are fins, but Ford called them "high-canted fenders."

LUGGAGE LOCKERS
Retracting hardtop reduced luggage space to a small tub in the center of the trunk.

EXTRA LENGTH
At nearly 17.5 ft (5.3 m) the Skyliner is slightly longer than standard Fairlanes to accommodate the retracting hardtop; extra length is in the rear deck.

SPECIFICATIONS

MODEL Ford Fairlane Skyliner (1957–59)
PRODUCTION 48,394
BODY STYLE Retractable hardtop.
CONSTRUCTION Steel box-section chassis, steel body.
ENGINE Various overhead-valve V-8s. 272cid (1957); 292cid (1958–59). Options of 312, 332 and 352cid V-8s.
POWER OUTPUT 190 hp at 4500 rpm (272cid); 205 hp at 4500 rpm (292cid); 300 hp at 4600 rpm (352cid).
TRANSMISSION Three-speed manual with optional overdrive or Ford-O-Matic automatic.
SUSPENSION *Front:* independent, coil-springs; *Rear:* leaf springs with live axle.
BRAKES Drums all around.
MAXIMUM SPEED 96–100+ mph (154–161+ km/h)
0–60 MPH (0–96 KM/H) 10–18 sec
A.F.C. 14 mpg

FAIRLANE ORIGINS
The car took its name from Henry Ford's mansion, Fair Lane. Up to 1958, the car was called Ford Fairlane 500 Skyliner; in 1959 it became the Ford Fairlane 500 Galaxie Skyliner.

FORD *Mustang*

THIS ONE HIT THE GROUND RUNNING – galloping in fact, for the Mustang rewrote the sales record books soon after it burst onto the market in April 1964. It really broke the mold, for it was from the Mustang that the term "pony car" was derived to describe a new breed of sporty "compacts." The concept of an inexpensive sports car for the masses is credited to dynamic young Ford vice president Lee Iacocca. In reality, the Mustang was more than classless, almost universal in appeal. Its extensive option list meant there was a flavor to suit every taste. There was a Mustang for mothers, sons, daughters, husbands, and even young-at-heart grandparents. Celebrities who could afford a ranch full of thoroughbred race horses and a garage full of Italian exotics were also proud to tool around in Mustangs. Why, this car's a democrat.

MASSIVE AIR CLEANER, HERE IN BODY COLOR, DOMINATES ENGINE BAY

302, 390, 427, AND 428CID OPTIONS WERE SOON ADDED TO THE STANDARD FORD 289 V-8

ENGINE CHOICES
Mustangs were offered with the option of V-8 (289cid pictured) or six-cylinder engines; eights outsold sixes two-to-one in 1964–68. Customers could thus buy the car just for its good looks and make do with 100 bhp – or they could order a highwayburner producing four times that much, and enjoy real sports car performance.

1965 MUSTANG WITH FORD CRUISE-O-MATIC THREE-SPEED AUTOMATIC

THE SPORTS WHEEL IS STANDARD 1965 EQUIPMENT; MUSTANG EMBLEM SERVES AS HORN

INTERIOR
The first Mustangs shared their instrument layout with more mundane Ford Falcons, but in a padded dash. The plastic interior is a little tacky, but at the price, no one was going to complain.

V-SIGN
V-8s advertised engine size and their V configuration. Less powerful sixes kept quiet about their lack of horsepower.

BOTH FRONT AND REAR USE OF CHROME IS RESTRAINED AND TASTEFUL

BANDED, TINTED WINDSHIELD WAS YET ANOTHER OPTION

FRONT DISCS WERE A NEW OPTION FOR 1965

PILLARLESS COUPE
Both front and rear side windows rolled completely out of sight to enhance the hardtop's looks and keep things cool.

RACE WINNER
Mustangs enjoyed success on both sides of the Atlantic. The big engine in a relatively small package meant they were more at home on many European tracks than previous American contenders.

FLANK EXPRESSION
Scalloped, simulated air scoop serves no function but is an enjoyable styling flourish.

POPULAR VINYL-COVERED ROOF OPTION ON THE HARDTOP SIMULATES THE CONVERTIBLE; IT LOOKS LEANER THAN HARDTOPS WITH BODY-COLORED ROOFS

SPECIFICATIONS

MODEL Ford Mustang (1964–68)
PRODUCTION 2,077,826
BODY STYLES Two-door, four-seat hardtop, fastback, convertible.
CONSTRUCTION Unibody chassis/body.
ENGINE Six-cylinder 170cid to 428cid.
POWER OUTPUT 195–250 hp at 4000–4800 rpm or 271 hp at 6000 rpm (289cid).
TRANSMISSION Three- or four-speed manual or three-speed automatic.
SUSPENSION Independent front with coil springs and wishbones; semielliptic leaf springs at rear.
BRAKES Drums; discs optional at front.
MAXIMUM SPEED 110–127 mph (177–204 km/h) (289cid)
0–60 MPH (0–96 KM/H) 6.1 sec (289)
0–100 MPH (0–161 KM/H) 19.7 sec
A.F.C. 13 mpg

STYLING
The Mustang's almost understated styling was a breath of fresh air compared with the extravagant size-is-everything excesses of the 1950s and early 1960s.

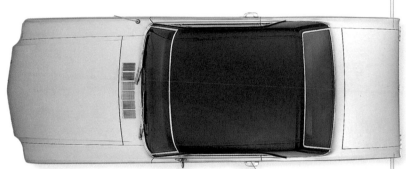

THREE TOPS
In April 1964, first Mustangs were hardtops or convertibles; a fastback coupe arrived in October. Three quarters of 1964–68 cars were hardtops; fastbacks and convertibles split the balance.

LONG DOORS HELPED ENTRY AND EXIT FOR REAR PASSENGERS

THE MUSTANG WAS SO SUCCESSFUL THAT A MICHIGAN BAKER ADVERTISED, "OUR HOTCAKES ARE SELLING LIKE MUSTANGS"

MYRIAD OPTIONS INCLUDED SMALLER WHEELS, WIDER TIRES, WIRE WHEEL COVERS, AND KNOCK-OFF STYLE HUBCAPS

MUSTANG'S MASS APPEAL

The Mustang galloped into the history books almost the moment it was unveiled to the public in April 1964. In one stroke it revived the freedom of spirit of the early sporting Thunderbirds and brought sports car motoring to the masses.

1967 FORD MUSTANG CATALOG

THE UNDISPUTED FATHER of the Mustang is Lee Iacocca, the engineer-turned-salesman whose meteoric career catapulted him to the position of vice president of the Ford Division by 1960. His concept, born of intuitive belief and market research, was for a "personal" Ford. In his early days as sales manager, people had pleaded with him to bring back the two-seater Thunderbird. The idea lodged and grew. The Mustang I prototype of 1962 was a V-4 mid-engined two-seater – pretty, but too exotic. No, Iacocca's Mustang would have to be a practical four-seater.

The Mustang II show car debuted at the US Grand Prix in October 1963, and its rapturous reception gave the production Mustang the green light. Launched with a huge promotional blitz at the New York World's Fair of 1964, it caught the opposition sleeping and hit home with American car buyers. As part of the well orchestrated bally hoo, the first cars in showrooms were auctioned off to the highest bidders. One East Coast customer outbid 14 rivals and slept in the car overnight to ensure that it was not sold from under him while his check cleared.

But there was more to the Mustang than mere hype. Sharing many components with the Ford Falcon to keep costs down, it was an honest

FORD
Mustang

IN 1965, MUSTANG BUYERS SPENT AN AVERAGE $1,000 ON OPTIONS ON TOP OF THE BASE PRICE OF $2,368

CIRCULAR MUSTANG MOTIF NEATLY CONCEALS GAS CAP

DRIVING
All Mustangs are different to drive, with 0–60 mph times ranging from six to a loping 15 seconds.

THIS IS IDENTIFIABLY A FIRST SERIES MUSTANG; CONCAVE REAR END AND DIFFERENT LIGHT CAME IN 1967

CALIFORNIA
588 FNM

bargain. What's more, your Mustang could be as cheap or expensive as you liked. "The Mustang is designed to be designed by you," gushed an early sales brochure. From an entry price of $2,368, you could check the option boxes to turn your "personal" car into a hot-rod costing double that. Some 100,000 were sold in the first four months – Iacocca thought it would take a year.

Limited-edition pace car Mustangs produced in 1979

1966 Shelby Mustang

In fact, it sold 417,471 in its first year, and the total topped a million in 1966. It was a winner on the track and its sporting image was boosted on the road with the Shelby GT350 Mustangs

1970 Ford Mustang Mach 1

from 1965. By 1969, the Mustang was getting bigger and heavier, but the hot Boss and Mach 1 Mustangs preserved the performance image.

And maybe that was the beginning of the end, as the original pony became tethered by emissions regulations. Like the T-bird before it, the Mustang succumbed to middle age.

MUSTANG MYTHOLOGY
Cryptically, the horse on the Mustang grille runs opposite to the way race horses run on US tracks.

PUSHBUTTON RADIO AND ANTENNA WERE ALL PART OF THE OPTION LIST

STIFFER SUSPENSION AND HANDLING KITS COULD BE ORDERED AS AN OPTION

PERFECT FOR CALIFORNIA; SONNY AND CHER HAD A MATCHED PAIR OF "HIS AND HERS" MUSTANGS

FORD *GT40*

FELIC

TO APPLY THE term "supercar" to the fabled Ford GT40 is to demean it; in the modern idiom Jaguar XJ220s, McLaren F1s and Bugatti EB110s are all the acme of supercar superlatives, but when did any one of them win Le Mans outright? The Ford GT40, though, was not only the ultimate road car but also the ultimate endurance racer of its era, a twin distinction no else can match. In fact, the GT40 was so good that arguments are still going on over its nationality, as both Britain and America are proud to claim the honors. Let us call it a joint design project between the American manufacturer and independent British talent, with a bit of Italian and German input as well.

What really matters is that it achieved what it was designed for, claiming the classic Le Mans 24-hour race four times in a row. And there is more to the GT40 than its Le Mans legend. You could, if you could afford it, drive around quite legally on public roads in this 200 mph (320 km/h) projectile. The cockpit might be cramped, but the impracticality of the package is part of the car's extravagance.

Ultimate supercar? No, it is better than that. Ultimate car? Maybe.

WIND CHEATER
The graceful and muscular shape was created in Ford's Dearborn design studios. Essential requirements included a mid-engined layout and aerodynamic efficiency.

INTERIOR
As befits a custom-made racer, the cockpit is designed for business rather than pleasure. Height and width of the door sills make entry and exit a chore, but once in place everything falls to hand. Racers had a side gear-change, road versions a central location.

SHORT NOSE
There is just enough room in this road car for the radiator, spare tire, and a bit of plumbing.

LIP ON TAIL HELPED HIGH-SPEED STABILITY

KNOCK-OFF HUBS FOR QUICK CHANGES; SIMPLE SIX-SPOKED WHEEL FROM 1967

STILL WINNING

GT40s can still be seen in retrospective events such as the 1994 Tour de France rally, which our featured car won. The circuit is the Montlhéry track outside Paris, scene of many minor GT40 successes. The British-owned car proudly displays the British Racing Drivers' Club badge.

LARGE DOORS ALMOST REACH CENTER OF ROOF TO EASE ACCESS

WHEEL WIDTHS VARIED DEPENDING ON RACING REQUIREMENTS

ENGINE LOCATED ALMOST EXACTLY IN MIDDLE OF CAR

PANORAMIC WINDSHIELD GAVE GOOD FORWARD VISION

DESIGN SECRETS

Design of the GT40 was based on an earlier British Lola. Features such as mid-engined layout with gearbox/transaxle at the rear were now standard race-car practice. In Ford's favor were the powerful V-8 engine, plenty of bucks, and Henry Ford II's determination to win Le Mans.

CHANGED APPEARANCE

The front section is the easiest way to identify various developments of the GT40. First prototypes had sharp snouts; squared-off nose, as shown here, first appeared in 1965; the road-going MkIII was smoother, and the end-of-line MkIV rounder and flatter.

MANY RACE CARS DISPENSED WITH FENDER MIRRORS

EARLY VERSIONS AND ROAD CARS HAD DELICATE BORRANI WIRE WHEELS

THIS IS A RACER, BUT ROAD CARS HAD TINY CHROME BUMPERS

B. BELL

COYS INTERNATIONAL HISTORIC FESTIVAL Silverstone

—THE ROAD TO LE MANS—

Le Mans laurels looked a long way off when Ferrari rebuffed Ford's overtures, but with unwavering determination Henry Ford II pursued his goal and created a Le Mans legacy that will live forever.

HENRY FORD'S grandson, Henry Ford II, figured the quickest and easiest way of achieving his ultimate Le Mans goal would be to buy the company that was already doing all the winning in the current endurance classics – Ferrari. The Commendatore, Enzo Ferrari, would not sell to the Americans, so they were forced to look elsewhere. Unsuccessful overtures were also made to Colin Chapman's Lotus in England.

The project finally started to gain momentum when Ford took over a race-car project begun by the small British firm of Lola, which by coincidence used a Ford V-8 racing engine. Other British racing people were hired to join the team based near London and to produce a Ferrari-beater. American input was in the form of the V-8 racing engine, and the distinctive body design. Everything else was created in England, and the

GT40 AT LE MANS, DRIVEN BY MAGLIOLI AND CASSONI

first cars were completed there. But it was American determination which insisted that the cars run at Le Mans in 1964, before they were really ready. They were the fastest cars in the race, but did not have the reliability. On the other hand, the American policy which dictated that the early engines be replaced by a monstrous 7-liter unit for

FORD GT40 Mk1V AT LE MANS IN 1967

FORD *GT40*

FUZZY SLIT ABOVE ENGINE COVER GIVES JUST ENOUGH REAR VISION TO WATCH A FERRARI FADE AWAY

EXHAUST NOTE RISES FROM GRUFF BELLOW TO EAR-SPLITTING YOWL

VITAL STATISTICS

GT, of course, stands for Grand Touring; 40 for the car's height in inches. Overall length was 13 ft 9 in (4.2 m), width 5 ft 10 in (1 .78 m), and unladen weight 1,835 lb (832 kg).

FELIC

1965, brought the first breakthrough – victory in the world championship round at Daytona in Florida.

Still the Le Mans jewel was elusive; the cars again broke down after setting the early pace. But Henry Ford was single-minded, doggedly pursuing his ambition, and it was a matter of third time luck for the Anglo-American enterprise, which finally enjoyed the fruits of its effort

GULF FORD GT40 LE MANS WINNER, 1968

1966 FORD GT40 AT SPA, BELGIUM

with a stunning Le Mans 1-2 finish in 1966. Now that Ford had cracked the formula, it could not be beaten – it won in 1967, 1968, and 1969 as well, when the 24-hour enduro fell to Ford.

The last two victories were achieved after the Ford company, honor satisfied, had withdrawn from the fray and left the operation in the hands of the independent Gulf team. Headed by John Wyer, who had been the first manager of the GT40 racing team, Gulf achieved the incredible distinction of winning at Le Mans two years in a row – with the same car.

GT40's LE MANS VICTORIES
1966: CHRIS AMON (NZ)/BRUCE MCLAREN (NZ); *1967*: A.J. FOYT (US)/ DAN GURNEY (US); *1968*: PEDRO RODRIGUEZ (MEX)/LUCIEN BIANCHI (B); *1969*: JACKY ICKX (B)/JACKIE OLIVER (GB).

THE LUCKY FEW WHO HAVE DRIVEN THE GT40 REPORT PLEASINGLY LIGHT STEERING

DUCTS HELPED HOT AIR ESCAPE FROM RADIATOR

ONE OF THE SEVEN MKIII ROAD CARS WAS ACTUALLY FITTED WITH A TV

FEL IC

GORDON KEEBLE GT

COMPOSITE SKELETON OF SQUARE TUBES

IN 1960, THIS WAS THE MOST electrifying car the British magazine *Autocar & Motor* had ever tested. Designed by Giugiaro in Italy and built in an aircraft hanger in Southampton, it boasted good looks, a fiberglass body, and a 5.4-liter, 300 bhp V-8 Chevrolet Corvette engine *(see pages 62–63).* But, despite plenty of publicity, good looks, epic performance, and a clientele as glamorous as Jackie Kennedy and Diana Dors, the Gordon Keeble was a commercial disaster, with only 104 built.

"The car built to aircraft standards," read the advertising copy. And time has proved the Keeble's integrity; a space-frame chassis, fiberglass body, and that unburstable V-8 has meant that over 90 Gordons have survived, with 60 still in regular use. The Gordon Keeble was born in an era where beauty mattered more than balance sheets. It failed for two reasons. Firstly, the workers could not make enough of them, and secondly, the management forgot to put a profit margin in the price. How the car industry has changed...

SPACE FRAME
The space-frame chassis was finished in February 1960, flown to France, then driven to Turin, where Giugiaro added a handsome GT body.

HIGH-QUALITY BODY
In its day, the Keeble's hand-finished, glass-reinforced plastic body was among the best made.

WINDOWS
Electric windows used the same motors as the Rolls-Royce Silver Shadow.

CARTER FOUR-BARREL CARBURETOR LIVES UNDER RESPLENDENT CHROMED AIR CLEANER

ENGINE
The small block Sting Ray engine, supplied by General Motors, is an aristocrat among American V-8s, delivering a huge 300 bhp of high compression power. Brutal performance means 70 mph (113 km/h) in first gear and a mighty wall of torque which, even when flooring the throttle in top gear, meant you could annihilate most other cars.

LIGHTS
Twin slanted headlights were distinctly sporting in the 1960s.

BUMPERS
The Keeble's delicate three-piece chrome bumpers were specially hand-made.

FEW 555

FUEL TANKS
Twin fuel tanks say much about an era when fuel cost 30 cents a gallon and 15 mpg was considered reasonable.

FEW 555D

— SPECIFICATIONS —

MODEL Gordon Keeble GT (1964–67)
PRODUCTION 104
BODY STYLE Four-seater fiberglass GT.
CONSTRUCTION Multitubular chassis frame, GT body.
ENGINE 5.3-liter V-8.
POWER OUTPUT 300 bhp at 5000 rpm.
TRANSMISSION Four-speed all synchromesh.
SUSPENSION Independent front, de Dion rear end.
BRAKES Four-wheel disc.
MAXIMUM SPEED 141 mph (227 km/h)
0–60 MPH (0– KM/H) 7.5 sec.
0–100 MPH (0–161 KM/H) 13.3 sec.
A.F.C. 14 mpg.

POWER
Despite restrained elegance and concealed twin exhausts, the Keeble could top 140 mph (225 km/h).

GORDON KEEBLE GT

Only 21 when he designed the car, Giugiaro gave the hood a dummy intake scoop and fashionably raked twin headlights. The roof was lengthened and the slant of the C pillar decreased to give wider glass areas and maximum visibility.

FOUR-SPEED CHEVROLET GEARBOX WAS UNBREAKABLE

LAVISHLY EQUIPPED, THE KEEBLE CAME WITH A PUSH-BUTTON RADIO, SEAT BELTS, AND A FIRE EXTINGUISHER

AERO VENTILATION
Built at Eastleigh airport, Southampton, England, many aircraft parts found their way into the Keeble, like this period swivelling ventilation nozzle.

INTERIOR
The inside is like the flight deck of an old luxury jet – quilted aircraft PVC, black-on-white gauges, toggle switches, and that *de rigueur* accessory of all 1960s GT cars, a wood-rimmed steering wheel.

THIS IRONIC BADGE WAS CHOSEN AFTER A TORTOISE WALKED INTO VIEW DURING THE PHOTO SHOOT FOR THE SALES BROCHURE

STYLE
For a '60s design, the Gordon Keeble is crisp, clean, and timeless.

HOLDEN *FX*

AT THE END OF WORLD WAR II, Australia was up against a problem – an acute shortage of cars and a newly discharged army with money to burn. Loaded with government handouts, General Motors-Holden came up with a four-door, six-cylinder six-seater that would eventually become an Australian legend on wheels.

Launched in 1948, the 48-215, more generally known as the FX, was Australia's Morris Minor *(see pages 178–81)*. Tubby, conventional, and as big as a Buick, it had a sweet, torquey engine, steel monocoque body, hydraulic brakes, and a three-speed column shift. Light and functional, the FX so impressed Lord Nuffield (of Morris fame) with its uncomplicated efficiency that he had one shipped to England for his engineers to pull apart. The Australians did not care about the FX's humble underpinnings and bought 120,000 with grateful enthusiasm.

SPEEDOMETER CALIBRATED TO 100 MPH (161 KM/H) WAS A TAD OPTIMISTIC

WHITE STEERING WHEEL WAS AN AMERICAN INHERITANCE

DASHBOARD
The dash echoes the Australian culture for utilitarianism, with central speedometer, two occasional gauges, precise three-speed column changer, and only five switches. The umbrella handbrake and chrome horn ring were holdovers from Detroit design influences.

DOOR HANDLE
The extravagant prewar door handle looked strangely out of place on such an austere shape and was one of the FX's few styling excesses.

FRONT SUSPENSION
Front springing was by tough coil and wishbone with lever arm shocks.

ENGINE
Power came from a sturdy 2170cc cast-iron straight six, which developed a modest 60 bhp, with an integral block and crankcase, pushrod overhead valves, and a single-barrel downdraft Stromberg carburetor.

WARNING
Strident horn mounted behind the front grille was to warn roaming wildlife in the Australian outback.

NSW
TK·377

HANDLING
The Holden was too powerful for its suspension and many ended up on their roofs.

LIGHTING
Simple and unadorned, the FX had no turn signals or parking lights, just a six-volt electrical system with a single rear light.

SPACE
Endlessly practical, the FX had a cavernous luggage compartment.

SPECIFICATIONS

MODEL Holden 48-215 FX (1948–53)
PRODUCTION 120,402
BODY STYLE Six-seater, four-door family sedan.
CONSTRUCTION All-steel Aerobilt monocoque body.
ENGINE Six-cylinder cast-iron 2170cc.
POWER OUTPUT 60 bhp at 4500 rpm.
TRANSMISSION Three-speed manual.
SUSPENSION *Front:* coil and wishbone; *Rear:* leaf spring live axle.
BRAKES Four-wheel hydraulic drums.
MAXIMUM SPEED 73 mph (117 km/h)
0–60 MPH (0–96 KM/H) 27.7 sec
A.F.C. 30 mpg

BROCHURES
General Motors-Holden started life as an Adelaide saddlery and leather goods manufacturer, later diversifying into Holden Motor Body Builders – the sole supplier to General Motors Australia.

ECONOMY
Postwar fuel shortages meant that the Holden was economical.

BODY FLEX
Taxi drivers complained of body flexing – doors could spring open on corners.

MASCOT
Recumbent lion hood mascot gave the FX an illusion of pedigree. In reality, Holden had no bloodline at all.

HOLDEN 48-215 FX

The "Humpy Holden" was a warmed-over prewar design for a small Chevrolet sedan that General Motors US had created in 1938. A Detroit-Adelaide collaboration, the FX emerged as a plain shape that would not date, with high ground clearance for bad roads and dustproof body. It became the standard transportation of the Australian middle classes.

REAR STYLING
Rear fender line was cut into the rear doors but was much milder than Detroit's styling men would have liked. Rear fender skirts made the car look lower and sleeker.

REAR FENDER STONE-GUARDS WERE MADE NOT FROM CHROME BUT RUBBER

CHROME
Lavish Baroque grille looks like a stylistic afterthought.

HUDSON *Super Six*

IN 1948, HUDSON'S FUTURE could not have looked brighter. The feisty independent was one of the first with an all-new postwar design. Under the guidance of Frank Spring, the new Hudson Super Six not only looked stunning, it bristled with innovation. The key was its revolutionary "step-down" design, based on a unibody construction with the floor pan suspended from the bottom of the chassis frame. The Hudson was lower than its rivals, handled with ground-hugging confidence, and with its gutsy six-cylinder engine, outpaced virtually all competitors. In 1951, it evolved into the famous Hudson Hornet, dominating US stock car racing from 1951 to 1954. But the unibody design could not adapt to the rampant demand for yearly revision; the 1953 car looked much like the 1948. In 1954 Hudson merged with Nash, disappearing for good in 1957.

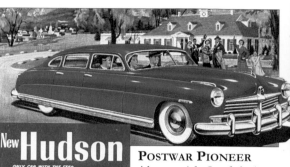

POSTWAR PIONEER
Along with Studebaker, the 1948 Hudson departed from the design of prewar cars. It created a sensation, but its complex structure made it difficult to update.

BIG SIX
The gutsy new 262cid six arrived the same year as the new-style Hudsons in 1948. It made the Hudson one of the swiftest cars on America's roads and, bored out to 308cid for the 1951 Hornet, it became a racing legend.

WOOD-GRAIN DASH
This is not wood at all, but painted metal. Main instruments are a speedometer, and 30-hour windup clock, both later moved in front of the driver. "Idiot lights," rather than gauges, for oil pressure and amperage were a traditional Hudson feature.

THIS IS A RARE RIGHT-HAND DRIVE CAR, ORIGINALLY EXPORTED TO SOUTH AFRICA, NOW IN THE UK

LOW RIDER
Chassis frame runs outside the rear wheels, serving as "invisible side bumpers" and contributing to low height.

HEIGHT
The Super Six stood only 60.4 in (1.53 m) high when contemporary Buicks and Chryslers were more than 15 in (38 cm) taller. Yet Hudson's interior space was exceptional.

LOGO
Hudson triangle dated back to 1909 when department store owner Joseph L Hudson gave his name and financial backing to the venture. White triangle is illuminated.

INTERIOR
All passengers were cradled between axles for comfort. Reviewers raved that rear passengers were treated to a front-seat ride.

SPECIFICATIONS
MODEL Hudson Super Six (1948–51)
PRODUCTION 180,499
BODY STYLES Four-door sedan, Brougham two-door sedan, Club coupe, hardtop coupe, two-door Brougham convertible.
CONSTRUCTION Unit chassis/body.
ENGINE 262cid L-head straight-six.
POWER OUTPUT 121 hp at 4000 rpm.
TRANSMISSION Three-speed manual, optional overdrive; semiautomatic.
SUSPENSION *Front:* independent, wishbones, coil springs, telescopic shocks, antiroll bar. *Rear:* live-axle, semielliptic leaf springs, telescopic shocks, antiroll bar.
BRAKES Hydraulic drums all around.
MAXIMUM SPEED 90 mph (145 km/h)
0–60 MPH (0–96 KM/H) 14–18 sec (depending on transmission)
A.F.C. 15–20 mpg

HUDSON SUPER SIX
It is the smooth beauty of the profile that really marks the Hudson. The design team was led by Frank Spring, a long-time Hudson fixture, whose unusual blend of talents combined styling and engineering. He had also designed airplanes. The new Hudson shape that evolved from a series of wartime doodles was one of the most aerodynamic of its time. The famed "step-down" chassis kept the center of gravity and overall height low without compromising levels of comfort.

MONOBILT
All Hudsons from 1932 had unit chassis and body, Monobilt in company speak. Many figured the Super Six's step-down design made it the safest automobile of its time.

REAR ASPECT
The rear of the Hudson is least pleasing, a slightly settled soufflé; but it is the view most other motorists and stock car racers saw.

SPLIT SCREEN
Each segment of the split screen was curved for partial wraparound effect and good visibility.

JAGUAR *XK120*

A CAR-STARVED BRITAIN, still trundling around in perpendicular, prewar hangover cars, glimpsed the future in October 1948 at the Earl's Court Motor Show in London. The star of the show was the Jaguar Super Sports. It was sensational to look at from any angle, with a purity of line that did not need chrome embellishment. It was also sensationally fast; in production as the Jaguar XK120, it would soon be proven that 120 really did stand for 120 mph (193 km/h), making it the fastest standard production car in the world.

Once again Jaguar boss William Lyons had pulled off his favorite trick: offering sensational value for money compared with anything else in its class. In fact this time there was nothing else in its class. The only trouble was that you could not actually buy one. Lyons had planned the XK120 as a short-production-run, prestige show-stopper, but overwhelming interest at the 1948 show changed all that. Hand-built aluminum-bodied cars dribbled out of the Jaguar factory in 1949, and you needed a name like Clark Gable to get your hands on one. In 1950, tooling for steel-bodied cars was ready and the XK120 took off as an export earner, with over 85 percent of all XK120s going to foreign countries. Today the XK120 is as stunning as ever, still thrilling owners and enthusiasts.

HANDSOME
SMITH DIALS

WALNUT TRIM WAS
A FEATURE OF
HARDTOP COUPES
AND DROPHEADS ONLY

CAT MOTIF
ON IMPOSING
STEERING WHEEL

THE ENGINE
The famed XK six-cylinder engine was designed by Bill Heynes and Wally Hassan, and went on to power the E-type *(see pages 140–43)* and other Jaguars up until 1986. Even this was "styled"; William Lyons insisted it had twin camshafts to make it resemble Grand Prix cars of the 1930s.

CLASSIC SIMPLICITY
Surrounded by leather and thick-pile carpet, you feel good just sitting in an XK120. With its lush interior, purposeful instruments, and the bark of the exhaust from behind, you will hardly notice that it is a little cozy – if not downright cramped.

REAR VIEW
Hardtop coupes had limited rear vision.

SELLING THE DREAM
The original sales brochure for the XK120 used airbrushed photographs of the very first car built.

SPECIFICATIONS

MODEL Jaguar XK120 (1949–54)
PRODUCTION 12,055
BODY STYLES Two-seater roadster, hardtop coupe, and drophead coupe.
CONSTRUCTION Separate chassis, aluminum/steel bodywork.
ENGINE 3442cc twin overhead cam six-cylinder, twin SU carburetors.
POWER OUTPUT 160 bhp at 5100 rpm.
TRANSMISSION Four-speed manual, Moss gearbox with syncromesh on upper three ratios.
SUSPENSION *Front:* independent, wishbones and torsion bars; *Rear:* live rear axle, semielliptic.
BRAKES Hydraulically operated 12-in drums.
MAXIMUM SPEED 126 mph (203 km/h)
0–60 MPH (0–96 KM/H) 10 sec
0–100 MPH (0–161 KM/H) 35.3 sec
A.F.C. 22 mpg

JAGUAR XK120 HARDTOP COUPE

Many rate the hardtop coupe as the most gorgeous of all XK120s, with a roofline and teardrop window reminiscent of the beautiful Bugatti Type 57SC Atlantic. The hardtop model did not appear until March 1951 and is much rarer than the roadster. Even though numbers were trimmed further in the late 1980s' scramble to restore roadsters, their flowing curves and perfect proportions are now more widely appreciated.

PARKING LIGHTS
This is clearly a 1953 XK120 because of the body-colored parking lights fared into the fender. Early XKs had chrome parking light pods.

THE CAT'S PAWS
Skinny cross-ply tires gave more thrills than needed on hard cornering.

WHEELS
Standard wheels were the same steel discs as on the Jaguar sedans. Wire wheels were a popular option and helped to counter alarming fade by reducing heat buildup in the brake drums.

XK120 HALLMARKS
Slim split bumpers and thin grille slats distinguish the XK120 from the thicker bumpered XK140, which superseded it.

JAGUAR *XK150*

THE XK150 APPEARED IN THE SPRING of 1957 and was the most refined of the XK trio. One of the last Jaguars to have a separate chassis, it carried four-wheel Dunlop disc brakes, a 210 bhp version of the legendary XK straight six power plant, and an optional Borg Warner automatic gearbox. The 150 marked the beginning of the civilization of the Jaguar sports car. With its wider girth and with more creature comforts, it was to hold the market's interest until the then-secret E-Type project *(see pages 140–43)* was ready to unveil in 1961.

In the late 1950s, the XK150 was a glamorous machine, almost as flashy as an Aston Martin, but $3,000 cheaper. March 1958 saw more power in the form of the "S" performance package, which brought the 3.4 up to 250 bhp. In 1959 the 3.8's output soared to a heady 265 bhp. Available as a roadster, drophead, or hardtop coupe, the 150 sold 9,400 examples in its four-year run, the rarest model being the XK150S hardtop coupe, with a mere 193 cars built. Despite being eclipsed by the sinewy E-Type, the 150 was charismatic enough to be the personal transportation of '50s racing ace Mike Hawthorn and starlet Anita Ekberg. Currently undervalued, a well-restored 150 costs half the price of the equivalent E-Type and is much more individual.

INTERIOR
The interior was much more refined than previous XKs, with a wrap-around windshield and adjustable steering column. On the last 1960 cars, the turn signal switch was on the steering column instead of the dashboard.

LIGHT INDICATOR
A tiny red peak on the parking light reminded the driver that lights were on.

The XK150 Roadster

SLEEK PROMOTION
Introduced in 1958, the two-seater XK150 Roadster was the last model in the series and also the sportiest. Ever since the 120, all XKs had been a hit in America and the 150 was no exception.

ENGINE
This classic, twin overhead cam design first saw the light of day in 1949, and was phased out in 1986. Some say it is one of the finest production engines of all time. Sturdy, powerful, and handsome, the 3.8 powered the legendary D-Type Jaguars which could top 197 mph (317 km/h).

TIRES
Standard tires were Dunlop crossply RS5s.

REAR VIEW
From the rear, the hardtop has definite sedan lines, with a curved rear window, big wraparound bumper, wide track, and cavernous trunk.

JAGUAR XK150

The gorgeous curved body sits on a conventional chassis. Joints and curves were smoothed off at the factory using lead. The 1950s car industry paid little thought to rustproofing, so all Jaguars of the period are shamefully rust-prone.

WHEELS
Wire wheels were the most common, although steel wheels with hubcaps were available.

BODYWORK
The body is mounted on a massive box-section chassis, which hardly differs from the original XK120 design. All the XK150's body panels were new, with a higher cowl and fender line, wider hood, and broader radiator grille than earlier models.

VENTILATION
Vent in front fender was to provide air to passenger compartment.

HANDLING
XK150s handled well, despite primitive leaf springs and live rear axle.

RACING SUCCESS
Jaguar XKs won laurels all over the world.

SO MUCH FOR SO LITTLE
At $3,600, the 150 was resounding value. This is a very early car wearing a 1958 Coventry-issued registration number, probably a factory demonstrator.

SPECIFICATIONS

MODEL Jaguar XK150 FHC (1957–61)
PRODUCTION 9,400
BODY STYLES Two-seater roadster, drophead, or hardtop coupe.
CONSTRUCTION Separate pressed-steel chassis frame with box section side members.
ENGINE Straight six, twin overhead cam 3442cc or 3781cc.
POWER OUTPUT 190 bhp at 5500 rpm (3.4); 210 bhp at 5500 rpm (3.8); 265 bhp at 5500 rpm (3.8S).
TRANSMISSION Four-speed manual, with optional overdrive, or three-speed Borg Warner Model 8 automatic.
SUSPENSION Independent front, rear leaf springs with live rear axle.
BRAKES Dunlop front and rear discs.
MAXIMUM SPEED 135 mph (217 km/h)
0–60 MPH (0–96 KM/H) 7.6 sec (3.8S)
0–100 MPH (0–161 KM/H) 18 sec
A.F.C. 18 mpg

JAGUAR *C-Type*

THE C-TYPE IS THE CAR that launched the Jaguar racing legend and began a Le Mans love affair for the men from Coventry. In the 1950s, Jaguar boss Bill Lyons was intent on winning Le Mans laurels for Britain, just as Bentley had done a quarter of a century before. After testing mildly modified XK120s in 1950, he came up with a competition version, the XK120C (C-Type) for 1951. A C-Type won that year, failed in 1952, then won again in 1953. By then the C-Type's place in history was assured. It had laid the cornerstone of the Jaguar sporting legend that blossomed through its successor, the D-Type, which bagged three Le Mans 24-hour wins in four years. C-Types were sold to private customers, most of whom used them for racing rather than road use. They were tractable road cars though, often driven to and from races; after their days as competitive racers were over, many were used as high-performance highway tourers.

THE CAT FAMILY
Grille reflects family resemblance to the XK120 production model, which company head Bill Lyons had insisted on.

HOME COMFORTS
Snug-fitting seats supported well during hard cornering.

POWERPLANT
The engine was taken from the XK120 and placed into the competition version. Horsepower of the silky six was boosted each year until some 220 bhp was available.

HOOD IS HINGED FORWARD TO EASE MID-RACE ADJUSTMENTS

ENGINE SNUGGLES NEATLY INTO ITS BAY, READY FOR ACTION

WIRE WHEELS HAVE KNOCK-OFF HUBCAPS FOR QUICK TIRE CHANGES

AERO HERITAGE
Designer Malcolm Sayer's aircraft industry background shows in the smooth aerodynamic styling.

FAST FUELING
Quick-release gas cap was another racing feature, and could save valuable seconds in a race.

ACCESSIBILITY
It was easier to step over the door than open it; passenger did not even get one.

JAGUAR C-TYPE
Jaguar's Bill Lyons dictated that the C-type racer should bear a strong family resemblance to production Jaguars. The Malcolm Sayer body, fitted to a special frame, achieved that aim. The clever blend of beauty and function retained the pouncing-cat Jaguar "look," while creating an aerodynamically efficient tool for the high-speed Le Mans circuit. In racing trim, cars ran with a single windshield; our car has a second full-width windshield.

SPECIFICATIONS

MODEL Jaguar C-Type (1951–53)
PRODUCTION 53
BODY STYLE Two-door, two-seater sports racer.
CONSTRUCTION Tubular chassis, aluminum body.
ENGINE Jaguar XK120 3442cc, six-cylinder, double overhead camshaft with twin SU carburetors.
POWER OUTPUT 200–210 bhp at 5800 rpm.
TRANSMISSION Four-speed XK gearbox with close ratio gears.
SUSPENSION Torsion bars all around; wishbones at front, rigid axle at rear.
BRAKES Lockheed hydraulic drums; later cars used Dunlop discs all round.
MAXIMUM SPEED 144 mph (232 km/h)
0–60 MPH (0–96 km/h) 8.1 sec
0–100 MPH (0–161 km/h) 20.1 sec
A.F.C. 16 mpg

ON THE TRACK

The C-Type was always most at home on the track, though more at Le Mans – where it won the 24-hour classic twice in three attempts – than on shorter circuits such as Silverstone, where this picture was taken in July 1953.

INTERIOR

Cockpit was designed for business, not comfort, but was roomy enough for two adults; passengers were provided with a grab-handle in case the driver thought he was at Le Mans.

LUGGAGE SPACE

A car built for racing does not need to carry baggage; rear deck covers the massive fuel tank.

BRAKE LIGHTS

Brake lights were a racing necessity as well as safety feature for road use, particularly with later disc-braked versions.

PUR 120

SPARE WHEEL

Removable panel in the tail hides the spare wheel.

ATTENTION TO DETAIL

Louvers on the hood help hot air escape; engine cover is secured by quick-release handles and leather safety straps.

SUSPENSION

Telescopic shocks smoothed the ride; C-Type introduced disc brakes to road racing as a secret weapon in 1952, though most examples used drums.

JAGUAR *E-Type*

WHEN JAGUAR BOSS WILLIAMS LYONS, by now Sir William, unveiled the E-Type Jaguar at the Geneva Motor Show in March 1961, its ecstatic reception rekindled memories of the 1948 British launch of the XK120 *(see pages 134–35)*. The E-Type, or XKE as it is known in the US, created a sensation. British motoring magazines had published road tests of preproduction models to coincide with the launch – and yes, the hardtop coupe really could do 150 mph (242 km/h). OK, so the road-test cars were probably tuned a little and early owners found 145 mph (233 km/h) a more realistic maximum, but the legend was born. It was not just a stunning, svelte sports car, though; it was a trademark Jaguar sporting package, once again marrying sensational performance with superb value for money. Astons and Ferraris, for example, were more than twice the price.

HARDTOP
A two-seater hardtop coupe was available from the outset. In 1966, a hardtop two-plus-two with a longer wheelbase was added to the line and it was this longer wheelbase that the V-12 adopted at its launch in 1971.

DETACHABLE HARDTOP WAS AVAILABLE AS A FACTORY OPTION

INTERIM MODEL
Our featured 1965 car is still a Series 1, even though it features the 4.2-liter engine, better brakes, and an all-synchromesh gearbox.

SIMPLICITY OF LINE
Designer Malcolm Sayer insisted he was an aerodynamicist and hated to be called a stylist. He claimed the E-Type was the first production car to be "mathematically" designed.

THIN-BACKED BUCKET SEATS OF THE 3.8S WERE CRITICIZED. IN THE 4.2, AS HERE, THEY WERE GREATLY IMPROVED

TELL TAIL
The thin bumpers with lights above are an easy giveaway for E-Type spotters. In 1968, with the introduction of the Series 2, bulkier light clusters appeared below the bumpers.

WIRE WHEELS WERE STANDARD ROAD WEAR FOR SIX-CYLINDER E-TYPES; STEEL DISCS WERE FITTED TO V-12S

XK ENGINES

The twin-overhead cam, six cylinder was a development of the original 3.4-liter XK unit fitted to the XK120 of 1949. First E-Types had a 3.8-liter unit, then 4.2 after 1964. Configuration changed in 1971 to a new V-12.

TRIPLE SU CARBURETORS ON UK SIXES; LESS OOMPH FROM TWIN STROMBERGS ON SOME US CARS

ENGINE ACCESS LOOKS GOOD, BUT WATCH YOUR HEAD

SPECIFICATIONS

MODEL E-Type Jaguar (1961–74)
PRODUCTION 72,520
BODY STYLES Two-seater roadster and hardtop coupe, 2+2 hardtop coupe.
CONSTRUCTION Steel monocoque.
ENGINE 3781cc straight six; 4235cc straight six; 5343cc V-12.
POWER OUTPUT 265 to 272 bhp.
TRANSMISSION Four-speed manual, optional automatic from 1966.
SUSPENSION *Front*: independent, wishbones, and torsion bar; *Rear*: independent, coil and radius arm.
BRAKES Discs all around.
MAXIMUM SPEED 150 mph (241 km/h), 3.8 & 4.2; 143 mph (230 km/h) 5.3.
0–60 MPH (0–96 КМ/Н) 7–7.2 sec.
0–100 MPH (0–161 КМ/Н) 16.2 sec (3.8)
A.F.C. 16–20 mpg

HANDLING

Jaguar designed an all-new independent setup at the rear. Handling in the wet and on the limit is often criticized, but for its day the E-Type was immensely capable.

RACING

Although intended as a roadgoing sports car, light-weight and racing E-Types performed creditably on the track in the hands of amateurs.

CENTER PANEL HINGES FOR ACCESS TO ELECTRICS

3.8s HAD ALUMINUM-FINISHED CENTER CONSOLE PANEL AND TRANSMISSION TUNNEL

COCKPIT

The interior of this Series 1 4.2 is the epitome of sporting luxury, with leather seats, wood-rim wheel, and an array of instruments and toggle switches – later replaced by less sporting and less injurious rocker switches.

WITH NO SUN VISORS, TINTED GLASS IS DESIRABLE

LOUVERS ARE NOT FOR LOOKS; E-TYPES, PARTICULARLY EARLY ONES, TENDED TO OVERHEAT IN HOTTER CLIMATES

HOOD

On a sunny day, the view over the long hood from the driving seat is one of the great motoring sensations – but not in congested traffic.

STANDARD FOUR-WHEEL DISC BRAKES WERE PART OF THE SPEC FROM FIRST E-TYPES

— THE EXHILARATING JAGUAR —

Most enthusiasts would settle for any E-Type Jaguar, but through the years the curvaceous Cat transformed, and for the later part of its life Americans had to make do with detoxed XKEs as emissions laws emasculated the wild Cat.

FIXED-HEAD E-TYPE AT GENEVA MOTOR SHOW, 1961

E – IT IS ONLY A LETTER, but when you attach it to the trunk lid of a sporting Jaguar it stands for exhilaration, excitement, ecstasy, and entertainment.

1955 JAGUAR D-TYPE

E also comes after D and that is where all these sporting superlatives have their roots, in the D-Type sports racers of the 1950s that dominated Le Mans with wins in 1955, '56 and '57.

In its early development stages, the E-Type was seen as a successor to the D-Type (and the rare XKSS roadgoing D-Type), but as Jaguar abandoned racing, the road-car project developed along different lines. There

was no doubt though, that racing had improved the breed. For a start, the lovely lines of the E-Type displayed a direct lineage from the D-Type. That is no surprise as the C, D, and E-Types were penned by aerodynamicist Malcolm Sayer. Under the skin, the E-Type chassis evolved from the D-

JAGUAR
E-Type

AS LEGISLATORS GANGED UP ON THE E-TYPE, THESE ELEGANT LIGHTS WERE REPLACED BY BULKIER ITEMS

ULTIMATE E
The 4.2 is often seen as the most complete driving package, but most prized are the first 3.8s, especially the earliest "flat-floor" models.

HDU 555C

THIS BULGE LOOKS PURPOSEFUL, BUT IS NOTHING MORE IMPORTANT THAN THE FUEL TANK DRAIN PLUG

Type's monocoque and front-subframe structure. Of course there were the four-wheel disc brakes and that fabulous XK six cylinder overhead cam engine.

The impact the shape made at its launch on March 15, 1961, at the Geneva Motor Show is now the stuff of Jaguar lore. Those first E-Type roadsters and hardtop coupes, produced until June 1962, are now referred to as "flat-floor" models, and are the most prized of all. In fact, their flat floor was something of a flaw, as recessed foot wells were later incorporated to increase comfort for taller drivers. In 1964, the 4.2-liter engine supplanted the 3.8. It was slightly more torquey and now had an

1972 JAGUAR E-TYPE SERIES 3

all-synchromesh box. One of the many E-Type watersheds was in 1967 with the so-called Series 1½ models, which lost those characteristic headlight covers in the interests of better illumination. From there, US Federal safety regulations took control and the Series 2 featured altered bumpers and lights. By now the Cat was

putting on weight and girth. In 1971, as US emission regulations were increasingly strangling the Cat's performance, the Series 3 emerged with a 5.3-liter V-12 based on the layout of the longer 2+2 hardtop. Production ceased in 1974, ending a distinguished life and a remarkable export success story. For every three E-Types built, two were exported – most of those to the US. There is one more telling fact, when deciding on which E-Type to choose. The 150 mph (242 km/h) performance of the very first 3.8-liter E-Types was never matched by later models.

CONVERTIBLE COUNT

Hardtop coupes actually accounted for a little over half of all E-Type production, yet the roadster was the major export winner, with most going to the US.

UNUSUAL AND SPORTY-LOOKING TRIPLE WIPERS GAVE WAY TO A TWO-BLADE SYSTEM WITH THE 1971 V-12

THE STYLISH BUT INEFFICIENT LENS COVERS WERE REMOVED IN 1967

HDU 555C

JENSEN *Interceptor*

THE JENSEN INTERCEPTOR was one of those great cars that comes along every decade or so. Built in a small Birmingham, England, factory, a triumph of tenacity over resources, the Interceptor's lantern-jawed looks and tire-smoking power made the tiny Jensen company a household name. A glamorous cocktail of an Italian-styled body, American V-8 engine, and genteel British craftsmanship, it became the car for successful swingers of the late 1960s and 1970s.

The Interceptor was handsome, fashionable, and formidably fast, but its tragic flaw was a singlefigure appetite for fuel – 10 mpg if you enjoyed yourself. After driving straight into two oil crises, a worldwide recession, and suffering serious losses from the ill-starred Jensen-Healey project, Jensen filed for bankruptcy in 1975 and finally closed its doors in May 1976.

ADWEST POWER STEERING WAS ALSO USED IN THE CONTEMPORARY JAGUAR XJ6

INTERIOR
Road testers complained that the Interceptor's dash was like the flight deck of a small aircraft, but the interior was beautifully hand-made with the finest leather and plush Wilton carpets.

BODYWORK
Bodies were all-steel, with scant attention paid to corrosion proofing.

SUSPENSION
Front suspension was coil spring, wishbone and lever arm shocks borrowed from the Austin Westminster.

TIRES
Original skinny Dunlop RS5 Crossplies had, by 1968, changed to wider Dunlop SP Radials.

ENGINE
The lazy Chrysler V-8 of 6.2 liters gives drag strip acceleration along with endless reliability. With one huge carburetor and only a single camshaft, the Interceptor has a simple soul.

GEARING
Most Interceptors were automatic apart from 24 ultra rare cars fitted with four-speed manual gearboxes.

JENSEN INTERCEPTOR
The Interceptor's futuristic shape hardly changed over its 10-year life span and was widely acknowledged to be one of the most innovative designs of its decade. The rear window lifted up to reveal a large luggage compartment.

STYLING
The classic shape was crafted by Italian styling house Vignale. From bare designs to running prototype took just three months.

LAMBORGHINI *Espada*

FERRUCCIO LAMBORGHINI'S AIM OF out-Ferrari-ing Ferrari took a sidestep with the four-seater Espada. It was a first and a last for the tractor manufacturer turned dream-maker; the first and only true four-seater Lamborghini, and the last of the front-engined cars, along with the Jarama. Perhaps underrated today, it was nevertheless the biggest-selling Lamborghini ever until the Countach *(see pages 148–49)* overtook it.

With the design constraint of seating four adults in a VIP road rocket, the Espada was never going to have conventional 2+2 beauty, but it is still an exhilarating executive express. Propelled by the Miura's muscular four-liter V-12, the fastest boardroom on wheels will eat up the autostrada at 140 mph (225 km/h) all day long. Where other cars are merely labeled GTs, this Bertone beauty needs no acronyms on its rump to excel as the epitome of the term Grand Tourer.

SPECIFICATIONS

MODEL Lamborghini Espada (1968–78). S1 1968–70; S2 1970–72; S3 1972–1978.
PRODUCTION 1,217
BODY STYLE Two-door, four-seater fastback sedan.
CONSTRUCTION Pressed-steel platform frame, integral steel body with aluminum hood.
ENGINE Four-cam V-12 of 3929cc.
POWER OUTPUT 325–365 bhp at 6500 rpm.
TRANSMISSION Five-speed manual or, from 1974, Chrysler TorqueFlite auto.
SUSPENSION All independent by unequal-length wishbones & coil springs.
BRAKES Discs on all four wheels.
MAXIMUM SPEED 150–155 mph (241–249 km/h)
0–60 MPH (0–96 KM/H) 7.8 sec
0–100 MPH (0–161 KM/H) 16 sec
A.F.C. 10–15 mpg

EXECUTIVE LUXURY
Sumptuous fittings included leather upholstery and electric windows. The dash improved on later cars, as seen here.

SMOOTH POWER
The engine was borrowed from existing models – the 400GT and the Miura. Power from the 4-liter V-12 grew from 325 bhp for the first models, through 350 bhp for the S2, to 365 bhp for the last of the S3s.

FAT FEET
Fat tires, supple ride, and a fine chassis add up to exceptional handling.

DEEP BREATHS
Six greedy twin-choke Webers gulp in air through hood air ducts.

POISE
Four headlights, blacked-out grille, and low stance make for a formidable road presence.

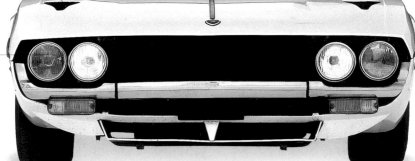

LAMBORGHINI ESPADA
The Espada's styling was created by Marcello Gandini from Bertone's "Marzal" show car. Lamborghini's first true passenger car could carry four people comfortably, as long as two of them were not too tall.

LAMBORGHINI *Miura*

THE LAUNCH OF the Lamborghini Miura at the 1966 Geneva Motor Show was the decade's driving sensation. Staggeringly beautiful, technically pre-eminent, and unbelievably quick, it was created by a triumvirate of engineering wizards all in their twenties. For the greater part of its production life the Miura was considered the most desirable car money could buy, combining drop-dead looks, awesome performance, and unerring stability, as well as an emotive top speed of 175 mph (282 km/h).

From its dramatic swooping lines – even Lamborghini thought it was too futuristic to sell – to its outrageously exotic colors, the Miura perfectly mirrored the middle 1960s. But, as the oil crises of the 1970s took hold, the Miura slipped into obscurity, replaced in 1973 by the unlovely, and some say inferior, Countach *(see pages 148–49).*

INTERIOR
The cockpit is basic but finely detailed, with a huge Jaeger speedometer and tachometer. Six minor gauges on the left of the console tell the mechanical story. Only the gearbox is a disappointment, with a trucklike, sticky action that does not do the Miura's gorgeous engine justice.

ALUMINUM GEAR-LEVER GATE IS A HAND-MADE WORK OF ART

ENGINE
The V-12 4.0-liter engine was mid-mounted transversely to prevent the car's wheelbase from being too long. The gearbox, final drive, and crankcase were all cast in one piece to save space. Beneath all that pipery slumber 12 pistons, 4 chain-driven camshafts, 24 valves, and 4 carburetors.

BERTONE DESIGN
Long, low, and delicate, the Miura is still considered one of the most handsome automotive sculptures ever.

TAIL-END ACTION
Because the Miura sits so low, it displays virtually zero body roll; therefore there is little warning before the tail breaks away.

SOUND INSULATION
In an attempt to silence a violently loud engine, Lamborghini put 4 in (10 cm) of polystyrene insulation between engine and cabin.

FRONT-END LIFT
Treacherous aerodynamics meant that approaching speeds of 170 mph (274 km/h) both front wheels could actually lift off the ground.

LIGHT POWERHOUSE
The Miura has a very impressive power-to-weight ratio – output of 385 bhp, yet it weighs only 2,646 lb (1,200 kg).

LAMBORGHINI MIURA SV

In looks and layout the mid-engined Lambo owes much to the Ford GT40 *(see pages 124–27)*, but was engineered by Gianpaulo Dallara. At the core of the Miura is a steel platform chassis frame with outriggers front and rear to support the major mechanicals. The last-of-the-line SV was the most refined, with more power, a stiffer chassis, and redesigned suspension. Other changes included wider wheels and a different rear fender profile.

GAS CAP
The gas cap hides under one of the hood slats.

HEADLIGHT POSITION
The car was so low that headlights had to "pop-up" to raise them high enough for adequate vision.

SV MARQUE
The Miura SV is the most desirable of the species, with only 150 built.

AIR DUCTS
Ducts in front of the rear wheels channel air for cooling the rear brakes.

LIGHTS
Standard Miura headlights were shared by the Fiat 850.

LAMBORGHINI *Countach 5000s*

THE COUNTACH IS a prodigious antique. First unveiled at the 1971 Geneva Motor Show as the Miura's replacement, it was engineered by Giampaolo Dallara and breathtakingly styled by Marcello Gandini of Bertone fame. For a complicated, hand-built car, the Countach delivered all the reliable high performance that its swooping looks promised. In 1982, a 4.75-liter 375 bhp V-12 was shoehorned in to give the upcoming Ferrari Testarossa *(see pages 110–11)* something to reckon with. There is no mid-engined car like the Countach. The engine sits longitudinally in a multi-tubular spaceframe, with fuel and water carried by twin side-mounted tanks and radiators. Weight distribution is close to 50/50, which means that the Countach's poise at the limit is legendary. On the down side, it takes forever to get used to the extra wide body, visibility is appalling, steering is heavy, gear selection difficult and, for all its tremendous cost, the cockpit is cramped, with luggage space restricted to an overnight bag. Yet such faults can only be considered as charming idiosyncrasies when set against the Countach's staggering performance – a howling 187 mph (301 km/h) top speed and a 0–60 belt of 5 seconds.

NOT ONE BUT FOUR
Everything on the Countach is built on a grand scale. Four exhausts, four camshafts, 12 cylinders, six 45DCOE Webers, a rev line of 8000 rpm, 26-gallon fuel tank, single figure thirst, and the widest track of any car on the road.

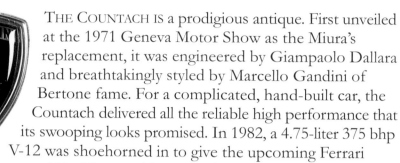

MANEUVERABILITY
Reversing the Countach is like launching the Queen Mary. Preferred technique is to open the door and sit on the sill while looking over your shoulder.

WHEELS
Steamroller-like 12J five-porthole aluminum wheels sit on ultra-low profile Pirelli P7 tires.

CELEBRATIONS

The 25-year anniversary of Lambo production in 1985 was celebrated with the 5000S and the elite Quattrovalvole 5000S.

BODY VULNERABILITY
Scant body protection means that most Countachs acquire a tapestry of scars and scratches that require the cost of a Ford Escort to repair.

INTERIOR
The cabin is crude, with unsubtle interior architecture. Switches and stalks are Fiat- and Lancia-sourced.

HANDLING
The Countach goes exactly where it is pointed with unerring precision thanks to almost perfect weight distribution.

SOUND EFFECTS
Inches away, all occupants are able to hear exactly what this engine has to say.

SPECIFICATIONS

MODEL Lamborghini Countach (1973–90)
PRODUCTION Approx 1,000
BODY STYLE Mid-engined, two-seater sports coupe.
CONSTRUCTION Aluminum body, space-frame chassis.
ENGINE 4754cc four-cam V-12.
POWER OUTPUT 375 bhp at 7000 rpm.
TRANSMISSION Five-speed manual.
SUSPENSION Independent front and rear with double wishbones and coil springs.
BRAKES Four-wheel vented discs.
MAXIMUM SPEED 187 mph (301 km/h)
0–60 MPH (0–96 KM/H) 5.1 sec
0–100 MPH (0–161 KM/H) 13.3 sec
A.F.C. 9 mpg

DOORS
Pivoting doors are works of art that worked perfectly from the earliest prototypes.

LAMBORGHINI COUNTACH 5000S

The shape is a riot of creative genius that ignores all established rules of car design. Air scoops behind the body's side windows break up the wedge-shaped line and form a readymade indent for a compact door catch and an ideal hand-hold for the huge gullwing doors. Under the aluminum panels nestles a birdcage spaceframe chassis of great complexity.

LANCIA *Aurelia* B24 *Spider*

BEAUTY IS MORE THAN just skin deep on this lovely little Lancia, for underneath those lean Pininfarina lines, the Aurelia's innards bristle with innovative engineering. For a start there is the compact aluminum V-6. Designed under Vittorio Jano, the man responsible for the great racing Alfas of the 1920s and '30s, this free-revving, torquey little lump was the first mass-produced V-6. The revolution was not just at the front though, for at the back were the clutch and gearbox, housed in the transaxle to endow the Aurelia with near perfect weight distribution. Suspension, although hardly run-of-the mill, was typically Lancia, with the front sliding pillars that Lancia had first employed in the 1920s.

These innovations were first mated with the Pininfarina body in 1951, with the Aurelia B20 GT coupe. And the point of it all becomes clear when you climb behind the wheel, for although the Aurelia was never the most accelerative machine, its handling was so impeccable that 40 years on it still impresses with its cornering poise. The B20 GT is often credited as the first of the new breed of modern postwar GTs. With the B24 Spider you got fresh air too, and today this charismatic roadster is the most prized of this illustrious family.

FLEXIBLE V-6
Aurelias featured an all-aluminum unit that grew from 1754cc to 1991cc and then 2451cc, which was fitted to the B24 Spider. The flexible 60-degree V-6 could pull the Spider from 20 mph (32 km/h) in top gear, yet ran to 5500 rpm.

ELEGANT, ADJUSTABLE NARDI STEERING WHEEL WAS STANDARD EQUIPMENT ON THE SPIDER

SPARTAN INTERIOR
The panel has just three major dials and a clutch of switches on a painted metal dash. It was devoid of the walnut-leather trimmings that British car makers of the time considered essential for a luxury sports car.

LUGGAGE ROOM
The Aurelia Spider scored well in luggage-carrying capabilities compared with other two-seaters of the time.

TWIN TAILPIPE
As you pile on the revs, the throbbing, gruff sound rises to a rich gurgle that is singularly tuneful from the twin exhausts.

ROADHOLDING
Handling, the Spider's best feature, was helped by racing tires being fitted as part of the original spec.

BALANCE
For perfect balance, the weight of the engine was offset by locating clutch and gearbox in a unit with the differential at the rear.

CROSSED FLAGS
These represent the joint input of Lancia, responsible for design and manufacture of the mechanical parts, and Pininfarina, who not only styled the body but also built the cars.

RIGHT-HAND DRIVE
Until the Aurelia, Lancia had eccentrically persisted with right-hand steering, even for the Italian market. The adoption of left-hand drive makes this right-hander a real rarity.

─ **SPECIFICATIONS** ─

MODEL Lancia Aurelia B24 Spider (1954–1956)

PRODUCTION 330

BODY STYLE Two-seater sports convertible.

CONSTRUCTION Monocoque with pressed steel and box-section chassis frame.

ENGINE Twin-overhead-valve aluminum alloy V-6, 2451cc.

POWER OUTPUT 118 bhp at 5,000 rpm.

TRANSMISSION Four-speed manual.

SUSPENSION Sliding pillar with beam axle and coil springs at front, De Dion rear axle on leaf springs.

BRAKES Hydraulic, finned aluminum drums, inboard at rear.

MAXIMUM SPEED 112 mph (180 km/h)

0–60 MPH (0–96 KM/H) 14.3 sec

A.F.C. 22 mpg

LANCIA AURELIA B24 SPIDER

The Spider bears a passing family resemblance to the Aurelia sedan, and even more so to the GT models. Neither of the closed versions had the wraparound windshield though, or the equally distinctive half-bumpers; the Spider's radiator grille was a slightly different shape, too. The curvaceous Pininfarina profile is characterized by the sweeping front fenders and long luggage compartment. High-silled monocoque construction meant small doors; the Spider had a basic hood with plastic side-screens.

SPIDER SPOTTING
The Spider's hood-top air-scoop was a unique feature among Aurelia models.

LANCIA STRATOS

THE LANCIA STRATOS was built as a rally-winner first and a road car second. Fiat-owned Lancia took the bold step of designing an all-new car solely to win the World Rally Championship and, with a V6 Ferrari Dino engine *(see pages 108–09)* on board, the Stratos had success in 1974, '75 and '76. Rallying rules demanded that at least 500 cars be built, but Lancia needed only 40 for its rally program; the rest laid unsold in showrooms across Europe for years. Never a commercial proposition, the Stratos was an amazing mix of elegance, hard-charging performance, and thrill-a-minute handling.

RALLY SUCCESS

Lancia commissioned Bertone to build a rally weapon, and the Stratos debuted at the 1971 Turin Show. Despite scooping three World Championships, sales of Stratos road cars were so slow that they were still available new up until 1980.

INTERIOR

The Stratos is hopeless as a day-to-day machine, with a claustrophobic cockpit and woeful rear vision. The width of 67 in (1.72 m) and the narrow cabin mean that the steering wheel is virtually in the middle of the car.

ENGINE

Factory rally versions had a four-valve V-6 engine.

REAR COWL

Molded fiberglass rear cowl lifts up by undoing two clips, giving access to midships-mounted power plant.

DEEP WINDOWS

Plastic side windows are so deeply recessed within the bodywork that they can be fully opened without causing any wind turbulence.

SHARP END

Flimsy nose section conceals spare wheel, radiator, and twin thermostatically controlled cooling fans.

WHEELS

Campagnallo aluminum wheels with Pirelli P7F tires — F stands for a softer compound to give a gentler loss of adhesion.

LANCIA STRATOS

Shorter than a Mk II Escort, and with the wheelbase of a Fiat 850, the stubby Stratos wedge looks almost as wide as it is long. Front and back are fiberglass with a steel center section.

COMFORT
Truncated cabin is cramped, cheap, nasty, and hot.

WEIGHT
The Stratos is a two-thirds fiberglass featherweight, tipping the scales at a little over 2,000 lb (908 kg).

WINDSHIELD
Windshield is cut from thin cylindrical glass to avoid distortion.

ENGINE
Lifted straight out of the Dino 246, the 190 bhp transverse, mid-mounted V-6 has four chain-driven camshafts spinning in aluminum heads, which sit just 6 in (15 cm) from your ear. Clutch and throttle are incredibly stiff, which makes smooth driving an art form.

SLATS
A 1970s fad, matte black plastic rear window slats do little for rearward visibility.

REAR SPOILER
Raised rear spoiler does its best to keep the rear wheels stuck to the road like lipstick on a collar.

BERTONE

SUSPENSION
Rear springing was by Lancia Beta-style struts, with lower wishbones, and had anti-dive and anti-squat geometry.

LOTUS *Elite*

IF EVER A CAR WAS A MARQUE landmark, this is it. The Elite was the first Lotus designed for road use rather than out-and-out racing, paving the way for a string of stunning sports and GT cars that, at the least, were always innovative. But the first Elite was much more than that. Its all-fiberglass construction – chassis as well as body – was a bold departure which, coupled with many other innovations, marked the Elite as truly exceptional, especially considering the small-scale operation that created it. What's more, its built-in Lotus race-breeding gave it phenomenal handling and this, together with an unparalleled power-to-weight ratio, brought an almost unbroken run of racing successes. It also happens to be one of the prettiest cars of its era; in short, a superb GT in miniature.

WINDOW DESIGN
The door shape did not allow for conventional windup windows. Wing windows opened, but on early cars the main side windows were fixed. This later car has a catch to allow outward opening.

CUBBY-HOLES APLENTY WERE PROVIDED TO SUPPLEMENT TRUNK SPACE

SE (SPECIAL EQUIPMENT) MODELS HAD A SILVER ROOF AS A "DELETE OPTION"

QUICK-RELEASE FUEL CAP WAS AN OPTION MANY CHOSE

LOW DRAG
Low frontal area, with air intake below the bumper lip, was a major contribution to Elite speed and economy. Drag coefficient was 0.29, a figure most other manufacturers would not match for 20 years.

LENGTH IS ONLY 12 FT (3.66 M), YET THE TRUNK IS VERY USABLE; SPARE WHEEL IS IN THE CABIN

BOTH FRONT AND REAR BUMPERS HID BODY MOLDING SEAMS

FIBERGLASS FACTS
Fiberglass was used to avoid both the tooling costs of traditional construction and to build in lightness. In reality, the Elite was not cheap to produce but, at around 1,300 lb (590 kg), it was certainly light.

INTERIOR

Even tall owners were universal in their praise for driving comfort. The award-winning interior is crisp and neat, with light, modern materials. Main instruments were a speedometer reading to 140 mph (225 km/h) and an 8000 rpm tachometer.

OUTLINE OF INSTRUMENT PANEL MIMICS PROFILE OF THE ELITE BODY

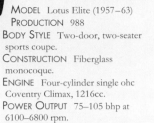

WOOD-RIM WHEEL IS THE ONE TRADITIONAL TOUCH ON THE INTERIOR

SPECIFICATIONS

MODEL Lotus Elite (1957–63)
PRODUCTION 988
BODY STYLE Two-door, two-seater sports coupe.
CONSTRUCTION Fiberglass monocoque.
ENGINE Four-cylinder single ohc Coventry Climax, 1216cc.
POWER OUTPUT 75–105 bhp at 6100–6800 rpm.
TRANSMISSION Four-speed MG or ZF gearbox.
SUSPENSION Independent all around; wishbones and coil springs at front and MacPherson-type "Chapman strut" at rear.
BRAKES Discs all around (inboard at rear).
MAXIMUM SPEED 118 mph (190 km/h)
0–60 MPH (0–96 KM/H) 11.1 sec
A.F.C. 35 mpg

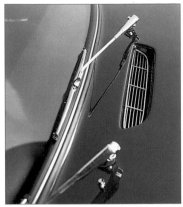

VENTILATION

Built-in cockpit ventilation system was fed by an intake on the cowl; outlet vents were above the rear window.

CIRCUIT SUCCESS

Elites were seen on the track even before they were available for sale. They were uncatchable in their class, claiming Le Mans class wins six years in a row from 1959 to 1964, and often embarrassing bigger GT Ferraris and Jaguars.

COVENTRY CLIMAX ENGINE BADGE SHOWS LADY GODIVA, WHO PARADED NAKED THROUGH THE CITY'S STREETS

ENGINE

The lightweight 1216cc four-cylinder engine was developed by Coventry Climax from its successful racing units. Power rose from an initial 75 bhp to 83 bhp in the second series, but over 100 bhp was possible with options.

THE COVENTRY CLIMAX ENGINE WAS DEVELOPED FROM A WARTIME FIRE-PUMP ENGINE

CONCEALED STEEL HOOP AROUND WINDSHIELD ADDED STIFFNESS AND GAVE SOME ROLLOVER PROTECTION

CONTEMPORARY ROAD TESTS RECORDED A REMARKABLE 25 MPG AT A STEADY 100 MPH (161 KM/H)

48-SPOKE CENTER-LOCK DUNLOP WIRE WHEELS WERE STANDARD

THE FIRST LOTUS FOR THE ROAD

Against the odds the elegant Elite launched the tiny Lotus company into the world of production car manufacturing with a blend of almost amateur enthusiasm, race-bred engineering expertise, dedication, and sure intuition.

THE ELITE WAS THE brainchild of company founder and great racing innovator, Anthony Colin Bruce Chapman. The elegant coupe was a remarkable departure for the small company – and, to most, a complete surprise when it appeared at the London Motor Show in October 1957. Even more surprising was the nature of the package, for it was not professionally styled, but drawn up initially by a friend of Chapman's, Peter Kirwan-Taylor, an accountant and design hobbyist.

It bristled with innovation too, for its fiberglass monocoque – not just body – was an amazing industry first. The engine was the lightweight Coventry Climax unit that Chapman knew well in competition Lotuses. It really was developed from a wartime fire-pump engine. Suspension was derived from the Lotus Formula 2 car of 1956, with that elegant weight-saving Chapman strut at the rear. The result was a light fantastic, so nimble and precise that it

gave road users an insight into racing car dynamics. On the race track it was a giant-killer.

That is the glory of the Elite, but in reality, customers had to wait to find out. The Elite was already a race winner, but the first customer cars – only two of them – did not go out

COLIN CHAPMAN AT TRACKSIDE

LOTUS
Elite

AT ITS LAUNCH, THE ELITE COST MORE THAN A JAGUAR XK150

MANY ELITES FROM 1961 ONWARD WERE SOLD AS NEAR-COMPLETE KITS, WHICH, THE ADVERTISING SAID, COULD BE ASSEMBLED IN 25 MAN-HOURS

STRESSED ROOF
The roof was part of the Elite's stressed structure, which meant that popular calls for a convertible – especially from America – could not be answered.

TINY DOOR HANDLE IS LITTLE MORE THAN A HOOK

LJC 322

COLIN CHAPMAN, LOTUS SUPREMO

until December 1958, more than a year after the launch. And the Elite's exceptional qualities came at an exotic price, initially a little more than a Jaguar XK150, and twice the price of an MGA. In the end, it was a triumph that 988 were built at all, against a backdrop of early production problems and Lotus' characteristically convoluted finances and organization – even the production total is far from certain.

But the ultimate testimony to the Elite is the number of survivors – at least 660, possibly 750. It had made its mark and when the end came, the American magazine *Road & Track* published a full-page obituary that serves as a fine epitaph: "A beautiful design was the Elite ... one that seems certain to be looked back upon as a landmark of some sort in automobile design. Without question it was the best, if not the very best looking Grand Touring car ever built." But it was also a beginning. Built along with the Elite was the cult-status Lotus 7, and the Elite laid the foundations for future Lotuses – the Elan, then Europa, Elite again, Eclat, Esprit, and back to a new Elan.

LOTUS 7

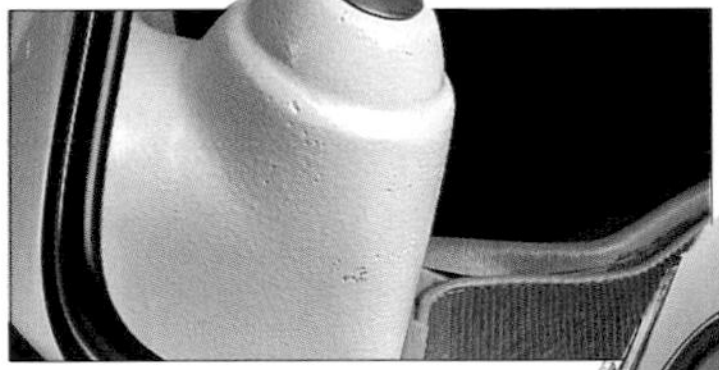

SUSPENSION STRUT
Curious conical bulges cover the coil springs and telescopic shocks.

AIR CHEATER
The Elite's aerodynamic makeup is remarkable considering that there were no full-scale wind tunnel tests, only low-speed airflow experiments. Height of just 46 in (1.17 m) helped, as did the fully enclosed undertray below.

A 2-LITER ENGINE WAS TOYED WITH FOR A WHILE, BUT IT UPSET THE ELITE'S FINE BALANCE

LJC 322

LOTUS *Elan Sprint*

THE LOTUS ELAN RANKS as one of the best handling cars of its era. But not only was it among the most poised cars money could buy, it was also drop-dead gorgeous. Conceived by engineering genius Colin Chapman to replace the race-bred Lotus 7, the Elan sat on a steel backbone chassis, was clothed in a slippery fiberglass body, and was powered by a 1600cc Ford twin-cam engine. Despite a high price tag, critics and public raved and the Elan became one of the most charismatic sports cars of its decade, selling over 12,000 examples.

Over an 11-year production life, with five different model series, it evolved into a very desirable and accelerative machine, culminating in the Elan Sprint, a 120 mph (193 km/h) banshee with a sub-seven second 0–60 time. As one motoring magazine of the time remarked, "The Elan Sprint is one of the finest sports cars in the world." Praise indeed.

ENGINE
The "Big Valve" engine in the Sprint pushed out 126 bhp and blessed it with truly staggering performance. Twin 40 DCOE Weber carburetors were hard to keep in tune. The ribbed cam covers were designed to prevent oil leaks. Power assisted disk brakes provided tremendous stopping power.

CLASSY INTERIOR
The Sprint's interior accommodation was refined and upmarket, with all-black trim, wood veneer dashboard, and even electric windows. Safer recessed rocker switches were a legal requirement in most markets.

WHEEL RESPECT
Colin Chapman's signature on the aluminum steering wheel.

TRUNK SPACE
The Elan was popular as a touring car because, despite housing the battery, its trunk was larger than average.

HEADLIGHTS
The pop-up headllights worked via a vacuum system, but often failed.

SPORTY PIPE
The rakishly angled exhaust left no doubt about the car's performance.

LOTUS ELAN SPRINT
The two-tone paint with dividing strip was a popular factory option for the Sprint. The red and gold combination had racing associations – the same color scheme as the Gold Leaf racing team cars. Everyone agreed that the diminutive Elan had an elfin charm.

WRAP-AROUND BUMPERS
Front bumper was foam-filled fiberglass. The Elan was one of the first cars to be fitted with bumpers that followed the car's contours.

SPECIFICATIONS

MODEL Lotus Elan Sprint (1970–73)
PRODUCTION 1,353
BODY STYLE Two-seater drophead.
CONSTRUCTION Steel box section backbone chassis.
ENGINE Four-cylinder twin overhead cam, 1558cc.
POWER OUTPUT 126 bhp at 6500 rpm.
TRANSMISSION Four-speed manual.
SUSPENSION Independent front and rear.
BRAKES Discs all around.
MAXIMUM SPEED 121 mph (195 km/h)
0–60 MPH (0–96 KM/H) 6.7 sec
0–100 MPH (0–161 KM/H) 15 sec
A.F.C. 24 mpg

STYLING
Perfectly proportioned from any angle, the Elan really looked like it meant business.

WORLD CHAMPION BADGE
Never slow to sing its own praises, Lotus fitted many Elans with this badge as a reminder of the company's string of Grand Prix victories.

WORLD CHAMPION CAR CONSTRUCTORS 1970 1968 1965 1963

SPRINT

MASERATI *Ghibli*

MANY RECKON THE GHIBLI is the greatest of all road-going Maseratis. It was the sensation of the 1966 Turin Show, and 30 years later is widely regarded as Maserati's ultimate front-engined road car, a supercar blend of luxury, performance, and stunning good looks that never again quite came together so sublimely on anything with the three-pointed trident. Pitched squarely against the Ferrari Daytona *(see page 104)* and Lamborghini Miura *(see page 146)*, it outsold both. Its engineering may have been dated, but it had the perfect pedigree, with loads of grunt from its throaty V-8 engine and a flawless Ghia design. It is an uncompromised supercar, yet it is also a consummate continent-eating grand tourer with 24-karat panache. Muscular and perhaps even menacing, but not overbearingly macho, it is well mannered enough for the tastes of the mature super-rich with hectic social timetables. There will only be one dilemma; do you take the windy back roads or blast along the autoroutes? Why not a bit of both.

GHIBLI NAME
Like the earlier Mistral, the Ghibli takes its name from a regional wind.

QUAD-CAM
The potent race-bred quad-cam V-8 is even-tempered and undemanding, delivering loads of low-down torque and accelerating meaningfully from as little as 500 rpm in fifth gear. The "dry sump" arrangement allowed for a low hood-line.

FOUR GREEDY TWIN-CHOKE WEBER CARBS SIT ASTRIDE THE V-8

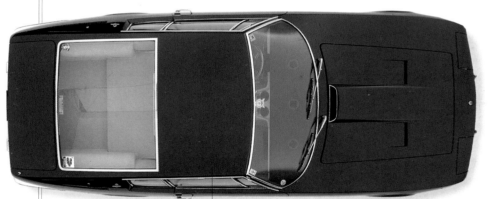

OPEN MASER
Most prized of all Ghiblis are the 125 convertible Spiders.

WIDE VIEW
The front windshield is huge but the big hood can make the Ghibli difficult to maneuver.

STEERING
Power steering was a later, desirable option.

HIDE-AWAY HEADLIGHTS
Pop-up headlights improve looks when not needed, but take their time to pop up.

LIFT OFF
Wide front has a tendency to lift above 120 mph (193 km/h) as the steering can become disconcertingly light.

TRIDENT
Masers are instantly recognizable by the three-pointed trident.

FLIGHT DECK
A cliché certainly, here you really do feel you are on an aircraft flightdeck. The high center console houses air-conditioning, which was standard Ghibli equipment.

MASERATI GHIBLI SS
The Ghibli's dramatic styling is uncompromised, a sublime and extravagant 15 ft (4.57 m) of attitude that can only accommodate two people. From its blade-like front to its short bobbed tail, it looks fast even standing still. It has also aged all the better for its lack of finicky detail; the Ghibli's detail is simple and clean, worn modestly like fine, expensive jewelry.

> ### SPECIFICATIONS
>
> **MODEL** Maserati Ghibli (1967–73)
> **PRODUCTION** 1,274
> **BODY STYLE** Two-door sports coupe or open Spider.
> **CONSTRUCTION** Steel body and separate tubular chassis.
> **ENGINE** Four-cam 90-degree V-8, 4719cc, 4930cc (SS).
> **POWER OUTPUT** 330 bhp at 5000 rpm (4719cc), 335 bhp at 5500 rpm (4931).
> **TRANSMISSION** ZF five-speed manual or three-speed Borg-Warner auto.
> **SUSPENSION** Wishbones and coil-springs at front; rigid axle with radius arms/semi-elliptic leaf springs at rear.
> **BRAKES** Girling discs on all four wheels.
> **MAXIMUM SPEED** 154 mph (248 km/h), 168 mph, SS (270 km/h)
> **0–60 MPH** (0–96 KM/H) 6.6 sec, 6.2 sec (SS)
> **0–100 MPH** (0–161 KM/H) 15.7 sec
> **A.F.C.** 10 mpg

THIRSTY
The Ghibli was a gasoline guzzler, but when was there an economical supercar?

EARLY GIUGIARO
Coachwork by Ghia was one of the finest early designs of its brilliant young Italian employee, Giorgetto Giugiaro.

MASERATI *Kyalami*

MASERATI 300S
Maserati's racing bloodline goes back to 1930, when it won five Grand Prix events in a row. After the war, Juan Fangio trounced the opposition in the legendary 250F, and the 300S sports-racing car went on to secure success at Le Mans.

THE 1970s PRODUCED some automotive lemons. It was a decade when bare-faced label engineering and gluttonous V-8 engines were all the rage, and nobody cared that these big bruisers cost three arms and a leg to run. The Kyalami is one such monument to excess, a copy of the De Tomaso Longchamp with Maserati's all-aluminum V-8 on board instead of Ford's 5.8 liter cast-iron lump.

The Kyalami was meant to take on the Jaguar XJS but failed hopelessly. Plagued with electrical gremlins, this was a noisy, bulky, and unrefined machine that was neither beautiful nor poised. Yet for all that, it still sports that emotive trident on its nose and emits a deep and strident V-8 bark. The Kyalami might not be a great car but most of us, at least while looking at it, find it hard to tell the difference.

REAR LIGHTS
Dainty rear light clusters were borrowed from the contemporary Fiat 130 Coupe.

GVV 255X

MASERATI KYALAMI
Maserati designer Pietro Frua retouched the De Tomaso Longchamp design, turning it into the Kyalami. He gave it a new lower nose with twin lights, full width hood, new rubber-cap bumpers with integral turn signals, and deleted the extractor vents from the C-pillars. By the time he had finished, the only shared body panels were the door panels.

THIRSTY
The Kyalami guzzled liquid gold at the rate of 14 miles per gallon.

ENGINE

The engine is a four-cam, five-bearing 4.9-liter V-8, with four twin-choke Weber carburetors, propelling the Kyalami's bulk to a touch under 150 mph (241km/h). Physically imposing, the vast air cleaner and cam covers come in crackle black as opposed to the usual polished Italian aluminum. Transmission was five-speed manual or three-speed automatic.

INTERIOR

The cabin is a study of 1970s tastelessness, with leather seats and Alcantara dash top. Quality control was poor and many components, like the Ford steering column, came from European parts bins.

STYLING

Basic design was originally penned by Tom Tjaarda for De Tomaso and was unit construction with a pressed-steel body and a chassis that turned out rather too boxy and angular for its own good.

TIRES

The Kyalami generates lots of commotion and bump thump from fat 205/70 Michelins.

STEERING

Power-assisted steering robs the car of much needed accuracy and feel.

NOT A PRETTY FACE

The frontal aspect is mean but clumsy. The three-part front bumper looks cheap, while the Maserati grille and trident seem to have been bolted on as afterthoughts.

SPECIFICATIONS

MODEL Maserati Kyalami 4.9 (1976–82)
PRODUCTION 250 approx
BODY STYLE Two-door, 2+2 sports sedan.
CONSTRUCTION Steel monocoque body.
ENGINE 4930cc all-aluminum V-8.
POWER OUTPUT 265 bhp at 6000 rpm.
TRANSMISSION Five-speed ZF manual or three-speed Borg Warner automatic.
SUSPENSION Independent front with coil springs and wishbones. Independent rear with double coils, lower links, and radius arms.
BRAKES Four-wheel discs.
MAXIMUM SPEED 147 mph (237 km/h)
0–60 MPH (0–96 KM/H) 7.6 sec
0–100 MPH (0–161 KM/H) 19.4 sec
A.F.C. 14 mpg

MAZDA RX7

THE RX7 ARRIVED in American showrooms in 1978 and sales promptly went crazy. Even by importing 4,000 a month, Mazda could not cope with demand and waiting lists stretched towards the horizon. For a while, RX7s changed hands on the black market for as much as $3,000 above retail price. By the time production ceased in 1985, nearly 500,000 had found grateful owners, making the RX7 the best selling rotary-engined car of all time.

Cheaper than the Porsche 924 and Datsun 280Z, the RX7 sold on its clean European looks and Swiss watch smoothness. Inspired by the woefully unreliable NSU Ro80 *(see page 182)*, Mazda's engineers were not worried about the NSU's ghost haunting the RX7. By 1978, they had completely mastered rotary-engine technology and sold almost a million rotary-engined cars and trucks. As always, the Japanese took a good idea and made it even better. These days the RX7 is becoming an emergent classic – the first car to make Felix Wankel's rotary design actually work and one of the more desirable and better made sports cars of the 1970s.

ENGINE
The twin-rotor Wankel engine developed 135 bhp in later models, although oil consumption was always high. Reliable, compact, and easy to tune, there was even an electric winch on the bulkhead to retract the choke if owners forgot to push it back in.

INTERIOR
Cockpit and dashboard are tastefully orthodox, with a handsome three-spoke wheel and five-gauge instrument cluster.

EUROPEAN STYLING
For a Japanese design, the RX7 was atypically European, with none of the garish over-adornment associated with other cars from Japan. Occasional rear seats and hatchback rear window helped in the practicality department.

SUSPENSION
Rear suspension was in the best European sports car tradition – wishbones and a Watt linkage.

HANDLING
Fine handling is due to near equal weight distribution and the low center of gravity.

HEADLIGHT
Popup headlights helped reduce wind resistance and add glamor. But, unlike those on the Lotus Esprit and Triumph TR7, the Mazda's always worked.

MAZDA RX7
Originally planned as a two-seater, Mazda had to include a small rear seat in the RX7 as Japanese law stated that all cars had to have more than two seats to encourage car sharing. The RX7's slippery, wind-cheating shape penetrated the air well, with a drag coefficient of only 0.36 and a top speed of 125 mph (201 km/h). Smooth aerodynamics helped the RX7 feel stable and composed with minimal body roll. The body design was perfect from the start and in its seven-year production run few changes were made to the slim and balanced shape.

REAR DESIGN
Original design used a one-piece rear tailgate like the Porsche 944, but economics dictated an all-glass hatch instead.

ENGINE FLAWS
The Wankel-designed rotary engine has two weak points – low speed pull and fuel economy.

HOOD
The RX7's low hood line could not have been achieved with anything but the compact rotary engine, which weighed only 312 lb (142 kg).

BRAKES
Both front and rear brakes were well cooled with ventilated discs and finned rear drums.

MERCEDES *300SL Gullwing*

WITH ITS GORGEOUS gullwing doors raised, the Mercedes 300SL looked like it could fly. And with them lowered shut it really could, rocketing beyond 140mph (225 km/h) and making its contemporary supercar pretenders look ordinary. Derived from the 1952 Le Mans-winning racer, these mighty Mercs were early precursors of modern supercars like the Jaguar XJ220 and McLaren F1 in taking racetrack technology to the streets. In fact, the 300SL can lay a plausible claim to being the first true postwar supercar. Awkward to enter, hot once you were inside, noisy, and with twitchy high-speed handling strictly for the "advanced motorist," it was sublimely impractical – it is a virtual supercar blueprint. It was a statement, too, that Mercedes had recovered from wartime devastation. Mercedes was back, and at the pinnacle of that three-pointed star was the fabulous 300SL, the company's first postwar sports car.

SLANT SIX
The engine was canted at 50 degrees to give a low hood-line. It was also the first application of fuel injection in a production car.

GULLWING DOORS ARE MADE OF ALUMINUM AND ARE SURPRISINGLY LIGHT TO LIFT WITH HELP FROM HYDRAULIC SUPPORTS

GULLWING DOORS
The car's most famous feature was the roof-hinged gullwing doors. With the high and wide sills, they were a functional necessity, rather than a finnicky design flourish.

REAR VISION IS GOOD, BUT ALL THAT GLASS CAN TURN THE COCKPIT INTO A HOT HOUSE

AERODYNAMICS
Detailed attention to aerodynamics was miles ahead of anything else at the time and helped make the 300SL the undisputed fastest road car of its era.

SEDAN-BASED REAR SUSPENSION COMPROMISED HIGH-SPEED HANDLING AND COULD SURPRISE YOU IN A BIG WAY

IN BRITAIN YOU COULD BUY TWO-PLUS JAGUAR XK140s FOR ONE GULLWING. IN THE US IT COST THE SAME AS NEARLY TWO CORVETTES

SOME SAY STEEL DISC WHEELS WERE PUT ON TO KEEP COSTS DOWN, BUT THEY ALSO LOOK MORE MUSCULAR THAN FRAGILE WIRE WHEELS

PRECISION INTERIOR

In the Fifties, the bechromed dash was pure sci-fi. The large two-spoked white wheel gives a good view of the dials. On some cars, mostly for the US, the wheel tilted to ease access and became known as "the fat man's wheel."

PASSENGER AND DRIVER GET EQUAL SHARE OF THE CLOCK.

AERODYNAMIC STYLING

Mercedes insisted that the "eyebrows" over the wheel arches were aerodynamic aids; it is more likely they were US-aimed styling touches.

SPECIFICATIONS

MODEL Mercedes-Benz 300SL (1954–57)
PRODUCTION 1,400
BODY STYLE Two-door, two-seat coupe.
CONSTRUCTION Multitubular space-frame with steel and aluminum body.
ENGINE Inline six-cylinder overhead camshaft, 2996cc.
POWER OUTPUT 240 bhp at 6100 rpm.
TRANSMISSION Four-speed all synchromesh gearbox.
SUSPENSION Coil springs all around, with double wishbones at front, swinging half-axles at rear.
BRAKES Finned aluminum drums.
MAXIMUM SPEED 135–165 mph (217–265 km/h), depending on gearing.
0–60 MPH (0–96 KM/H) 8.8 sec
0–100 MPH (0–161 KM/H) 21.0 sec
A.F.C. 18 mpg

IF YOU FLIP IN A GULLWING THERE IS NO GETTING OUT UNTIL SOMEONE COMES ALONG

ROAD CARS DEVELOPED 240 BHP, MORE EVEN THAN THE RACING VERSIONS OF JUST TWO YEARS EARLIER

PIPEWORK ON THE SIDE IS FOR FUEL INJECTION

PRODUCTION ENGINE

The engine was derived originally from the 300-Series 3-liter sedans, then developed for the 1952 300SL racer. Two years later it was let loose in the road-going Gullwing, with fuel injection in place of carburetors.

STAR IDENTITY

The massive three-pointed star dominated the frontal aspect and was repeated in enamel on the hood edge.

ENGINE BAY COULD GET VERY HOT, SO GILL-LIKE SIDE VENTS WERE MORE THAN A MERE STYLING MOTIF

HD·WD 34

SILVER WAS THE OFFICIAL GERMAN RACING COLOR

The Flight of the Gullwing

The might of Mercedes had been brought low by the ravages of war, but the launch of the staggering 300SL Gullwing prototype at the 1954 New York Auto Show also announced to the world that Mercedes was back – with a bang.

MERCEDES' RECOVERY had been based on its trademark solid and well-engineered sedans, but with the Gullwing, its proud sporting tradition was once more in full flight. The awesome Silver Arrows were no longer just a misty memory of yesterday's podium glory; here in the 300SL was tomorrow's supercar, today.

The Gullwing is certainly magical and bathed in its own folklore, which centers on the involvement of a New York sports car importer with a coast-to-coast smile – Max Hoffman.

STIRLING MOSS AT START OF 1955 MILLE MIGLIA

In 1952, Mercedes stormed back into autosports with a space-frame chassised car that

STIRLING MOSS AT THE 1955 MILLE MIGLIA

did not allow for conventional doors. Its engine was a development of the 3-liter engine of the 300-Series sedans. This aluminum-bodied car was called the 300SL – SL stood for Super Leicht – and it was right straight out of the box. In its first race, the 1952 Mille Miglia, it finished second, snatched outright victory at the Berne Grand Prix, took a 1–2 at Le Mans, won at the Nürburgring, and finished the year with 1–2 in the Carrera Panamericana Mexican road race. Mercedes had proved its point, and in 1954 concentrated on Grand Prix goals.

MERCEDES
300SL Gullwing

SMOOTH REAR
The Gullwing's smooth styling extended to the uncluttered rear; the trunk lid suggests ample luggage space, but this was not the case.

REAR VIEW GIVES A GOOD IDEA OF THE WIDTH OF THE SILL

COZY COCKPIT BECAME PRETTY HOT; AIR VENTS AT REAR HELPED REMOVE STALE AIR

LIMITED SPACE
With the spare tire mounted atop the fuel tank, there was very little room for luggage.

HD·WD·34

MERCEDES AT THE 1955 MILLE MIGLIA

But the 300SL Gullwing was about to enter a new life. Max Hoffman was so convinced of the 300SL's appeal that he was willing to back up his word with a large order, if Mercedes would build them. The road-going 300SL was clearly based on the racer, with the addition of luxury refinements. Hoffman's hunch was right, for over half of the 1400 Gullwings built from 1954 to 1957 went straight to American customers. As Gullwing

ON THE TRACK AT THE 1955 MILLE MIGLIA

production wound down in 1957, a roadster version was introduced, which lasted until 1963.

Meanwhile, something that looked like a Gullwing was making waves again in autosports. It was the 300SLR of 1955, which with its straight-eight actually owed more to the Mercedes W196 Grand Prix car. It won the Targa Florio, and, in the hands of Stirling Moss, the 1955 Mille Miglia.

The 300SL reestablished Mercedes' position at the pinnacle of sporting excellence. Yet it had a wider appeal, for wherever the jet setters gathered there also seemed to be a 300SL nearby, often drawing more camera flashes than the stars themselves. A youthful King Hussein of Jordan owned one, along with Stirling Moss, British comedian Tony Hancock, and numerous film stars.

But the story did not end there, for in 1969 gullwings appeared again on a Mercedes; but the rotary-engined C111 was a research project that was never seriously contemplated for production.

300SL ROADSTER

As Gullwing production wound down, Mercedes introduced the 300SL Roadster, which from 1957 to 1963 sold 1,858, compared to the Gullwing's 1,400. From 1955 to 1963 the 190SL Roadster served as the "poor man's" 300SL.

ALL GULLWINGS WERE ONLY AVAILABLE IN LEFT-HAND DRIVE

ONE HOOD BULGE WAS FOR AIR INTAKES, THE OTHER FOR AESTHETIC BALANCE

MOST OF THE BODY WAS MADE OF STEEL, BUT HOOD, TRUNK LID, AND DOORS WERE ALUMINUM

HD·WD 34

MERCEDES *280SL*

THE MERCEDES 280SL has mellowed magnificently. In 1963, the new SLs took over the sporting mantle of the aging 190SL. Named W113 in Mercedes parlance, they evolved from the original 230SL, through the 250SL, and on to the 280SL. The most remarkable thing is how modern they look. With their uncluttered, clean good looks, it is hard to believe that the last one was made in 1971. Underneath the timelessly elegant sheet metal, they were based closely on the earlier "fintail sedans," sharing even the decidedly unsporting recirculating ball steering.

Yet it is the looks that mark this Mercedes as something special. The enduring design, with its distinctive so-called "pagoda roof," is credited to Frenchman Paul Bracq. Some macho types may dismiss it as a "woman's car" and it is certainly not the most hairy-chested sporting Mercedes. But this well-manicured car is a beautifully built boulevardier that will induce a sense of supreme self-satisfaction on any journey.

SL MOTIF
In Mercedes parlance, the S stood for Sport or Super, L for Leicht (light) and sometimes Luxus (luxury), although at well over 3,000 lb (1,362 kg) it was not particularly light.

US-MARKET CARS HAD A MILDER CAMSHAFT

BRAKES ARE POWER ASSISTED

ENGINE
The six-cylinder overhead camshaft engine saw a process of steady development starting in July 1963, with the 2281cc, 150 bhp, 230SL. In December 1966 came the 2496cc 250SL, with the same power but slightly more torque. From January 1968 to March 1971 the final 2778cc, 170 hp 280SL shown here was produced.

CITY SLICKER
With standard power steering and a turning circle of less than 33 ft (10 m), the SL handled city streets with aplomb.

SPECIFICATIONS

MODEL Mercedes-Benz 280SL (1968–71)
PRODUCTION 23,885
BODY STYLE Two door, two seat convertible with detachable hardtop.
CONSTRUCTION Pressed-steel monocoque.
ENGINE 2778cc inline six; two valves per cylinder; single overhead camshaft
POWER OUTPUT 170 bhp at 5750 rpm.
TRANSMISSION Four- or five-speed manual, or optional four-speed auto.
SUSPENSION *Front:* Independent, wishbones, coil springs, telescopic shocks. *Rear:* Swing axle coil springs, telescopic shocks.
BRAKES Front discs & rear drums.
MAXIMUM SPEED 121 mph, auto (195 km/h)
0–60 MPH (0–96 KM/H) 9.3 sec
0–100 MPH (0–161 KM/H) 30.6 sec
A.F.C. 19 mpg

SAFE SUSPENSION
Swing axle rear suspension was tamed to provide natural understeer.

OPTIONAL THIRD
The SL was essentially a two-seater, although a third, sideways-facing rear seat was available as a (rare) optional extra.

CLAP HANDS
Windshield wipers are of the characteristic "clap hands" pattern beloved by Mercedes.

MERCEDES 280SL

The most distinctive design feature of the 280SL is the so-called "pagoda-roof" removable hardtop. It is said to have evolved from the need to provide relatively deep windows for a more balanced side view of the car, without at the same time making it look topheavy from the front or rear. The layout also provided a remarkably efficient way of keeping rain away.

LEATHER LOOK
Seats were trimmed in leather-look vinyl or, at extra cost, real leather.

TRADEMARK LIGHTS
"Stacked" headlights are unmistakable Mercedes trademarks. Each outer lens concealed one headlight, turn signal and parking lights.

CHROME BUMPER
The full width front bumper featured a central recess just big enough for a standard license plate; the quality of the chrome, as elsewhere on the car, was first class.

THE D-SHAPED HORN RING ALLOWS AN UNOBSTRUCTED VIEW OF THE INSTRUMENTS

ILLUMINATED HEATER CONTROLS ARE COMMON TODAY, BUT IN THE 1960s WERE A STEP FORWARD

ONLY THE 280 AUTOMATIC AND SOME OF THE LAST 250s HAD THE ILLUMINATED GEARSHIFT SHOWN HERE

INTERIOR
With the huge steering wheel (albeit attached to an energy-absorbing column), the painted dash, and the abundance of chrome, the interior is one area where the 280SL shows its age. It is still elegant, though. Relatively few cars were ordered with manual gearboxes, underlining the public perception of the SL as more a grand tourer than a genuine sports car.

MG *TC*

EVEN WHEN IT WAS NEW, the MG TC was not new. The TC, introduced in September 1945, displayed a direct lineage back to its prewar ancestors. If you were a little short on soul, you might even have called it old fashioned. Yet it was a trailblazer, not in terms of performance, but in opening up new export markets. Popular myth has it that American GIs stationed in England fell in love with these quaint sporting devices, when they left for home they were eager to take a little piece of England with them.

Whatever the reality, it was the first in a long line of MG export successes. The average American family car of the time could drag a TC off the line, but there was simply nothing remotely like this TC toy car coming out of Detroit. It had a cramped cockpit, harsh ride, and minimal creature comforts, but when the road got twisty the TC could show you its tail and leave soft-sprung sofa-cars lumbering in its wake. Yet it was challenging to drive, and all the more rewarding when you got it right. Mastering an MG was a thrill in its own right, for in a TC you did not need to joust with other jalopies; the TC and its cracking exhaust note were enough to give you hours of solo driving enjoyment.

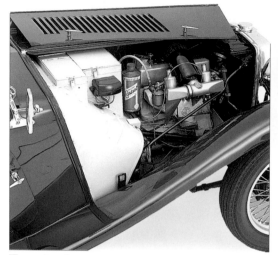

ENGINE ACCESS
Ease of accessibility and maintenance was another of the TC's attractions. The XPAG engine, first used on some TB Midgets in 1939, then became standard on MGs until it was replaced by a 1500cc version in 1955.

POWER BOOST
Though not a factory option, Shorrock superchargers were often fitted.

ALTHOUGH OVER 2,000 WERE SOLD IN AMERICA, ALL TCS WERE RIGHT-HAND DRIVE

RACERS' FAVORITE
The TC was a popular race car, especially in the US, where it launched many careers and one world champion, Phil Hill.

COCKPIT
Roomier than earlier Midgets, the TC cockpit was still more cramped than less sporting contemporaries.

SPORTING DIALS
Big Jaeger dials were in true British sporting tradition; the driver got the tachometer, while the speedometer was in front of the passenger. Closeup *(right)* shows the warning light that came on if you exceeded Britain's 30 mph (48 km/h) town speed limit.

FBT 112

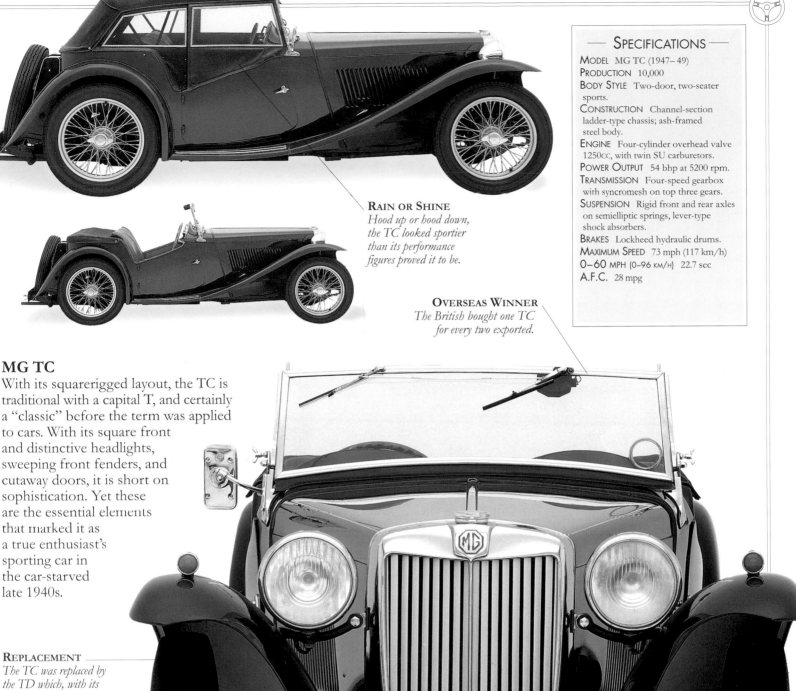

RAIN OR SHINE
*Hood up or hood down,
the TC looked sportier
than its performance
figures proved it to be.*

SPECIFICATIONS

MODEL MG TC (1947–49)
PRODUCTION 10,000
BODY STYLE Two-door, two-seater
   sports.
CONSTRUCTION Channel-section
   ladder-type chassis; ash-framed
   steel body.
ENGINE Four-cylinder overhead valve
   1250CC, with twin SU carburetors.
POWER OUTPUT 54 bhp at 5200 rpm.
TRANSMISSION Four-speed gearbox
   with syncromesh on top three gears.
SUSPENSION Rigid front and rear axles
   on semielliptic springs, lever-type
   shock absorbers.
BRAKES Lockheed hydraulic drums.
MAXIMUM SPEED 73 mph (117 km/h)
0–60 MPH (0–96 KM/H) 22.7 sec
A.F.C. 28 mpg

OVERSEAS WINNER
*The British bought one TC
for every two exported.*

MG TC

With its squarerigged layout, the TC is
traditional with a capital T, and certainly
a "classic" before the term was applied
to cars. With its square front
and distinctive headlights,
sweeping front fenders, and
cutaway doors, it is short on
sophistication. Yet these
are the essential elements
that marked it as
a true enthusiast's
sporting car in
the car-starved
late 1940s.

REPLACEMENT
*The TC was replaced by
the TD which, with its
smaller disc wheels, and
chrome hubcaps and
bumpers, was considered
less pure by some
aficionados. The export
trend begun by the TC took
off with the TD, which sold
three times the number.*

FBT 112

MGA

LAUNCHED IN SEPTEMBER 1955, the MGA was the first of the modern sporting MGs. The chassis, engine, and gearbox were all new, as was the smooth, Le Mans-inspired bodywork. Compared to its predecessor – the TF, which still sported old-fashioned running boards – the MGA was positively futuristic. Buyers thought so too, and being cheaper than its nearest rivals, the Triumph TR3 and Austin-Healey 100, helped MG sell 13,000 cars in the first year of production. The company's small factory at Abingdon, near Oxford, managed to export a staggering 81,000 MGAs to America. The car also earned an enviable reputation in competition, with the Twin Cam being the most powerful of the MGA engines.

SPECIFICATIONS

MODEL MGA (1955–62)
PRODUCTION 101,081
BODY STYLES Two-door sports coupe.
CONSTRUCTION Steel.
ENGINE Four-cylinder/1489cc; 1588cc; 1622cc (Twin Cam).
POWER OUTPUT 72 bhp; 80 bhp; 85 bhp.
TRANSMISSION Four-speed manual.
SUSPENSION *Front:* Independent . *Rear:* Leaf-spring.
BRAKES Rear drums, front discs. All discs on De Luxe and Twin Cam.
MAXIMUM SPEED 100 mph (161 km/h); 113 mph (181 km/h) Twin Cam.
0–60 MPH (0–96 KM/H) 15 sec (13.3 sec Twin Cam)
0–100 MPH (0–161 KM/H) 47 sec (41 sec Twin Cam)
A.F.C. 20–25 mpg

HORN BUTTON IS LOCATED IN THE CENTER OF THE DASHBOARD AND CAN BE WORKED BY EITHER DRIVER OR PASSENGER

LIMITED SPACE
The trunk is deceptively shallow and filled by the spare wheel.

DASHBOARD
The simple dashboard has no glove compartment, but the MG badge and center grille are for a radio and speaker. Passengers have a map light, but little else.

NO HANDLES
The uncluttered design means no door handles – doors are opened by pulling a cable reached from inside the car.

WHEELS
Perforated steel wheels are standard.

HAND-FINISHED
Although the MGA's steel panels were hand-pressed, bodies were finished by hand and no two are quite the same.

VENTILATION
The chromed, shroud-panel vents at the front are for engine bay ventilation.

ENGINE
The tough B-Series, pushrod engine goes well and lasts forever. A heater unit in front of the bulkhead was an optional extra.

MGA
The slippery, wind-cheating shape of the MGA was created for racing at Le Mans – an early prototype achieved 116 mph (223 km/h). Production MGAs were very similar and the smooth hood and sloping fenders aid both top speed and fuel consumption.

STARTING HANDLE
Hole is for a starting handle.

BSK 215

MG*B*

WIDELY ADMIRED FOR its uncomplicated nature, timeless good looks, and brisk performance, the MGB caused a sensation back in 1962. The now famous advertising slogan "Your mother wouldn't like it" was quite wrong. She would have wholeheartedly approved of the MGB's reliability, practicality, and good sense.

In 1965 came the even more practical hardtop MGB GT. These were the halcyon days of the MGB – chrome bumpers, leather seats, and wire wheels. In 1974, in pursuit of modernity and US safety regulations (the US was the MGB's main market), the factory gave the B ungainly rubber bumpers, a higher ride height, and garish striped nylon seats, making the car slow, ugly, and unpredictable at the limit. Yet the B became the best-selling single model sports car ever, finding 512,000 grateful owners throughout the world.

SPECIFICATIONS

MODEL MGB Tourer (1962–80)
PRODUCTION 512,243
BODY STYLE Steel front-engined two seater with aluminum hood.
CONSTRUCTION One-piece monocoque bodyshell.
ENGINE Four-cylinder/1798cc.
POWER OUTPUT 92 bhp at 5400 rpm.
TRANSMISSION Four-speed with overdrive.
SUSPENSION *Front:* Independent coil; *Rear:* Semielliptic leaf springs.
BRAKES Lockheed discs front, drums rear.
MAXIMUM SPEED 106 mph (171 km/h)
0–60 MPH (0–96 KM/H) 12.2 sec
0–100 MPH (0–161 KM/H) 37 sec
A.F.C. 25 mpg

AGELESS DESIGN
The MGB's shape was a miracle of compact packaging. One-piece steel monocoque bodyshell was strong and roomy.

MIRROR SUPPORT
The line down the center of the windshield is a mirror support rod.

DASHBOARD
This is vintage traditionalism at its best. Leather seats, crackle black metal dash, nautical-sized steering wheel, and minor controls are strewn about the dash like boulders with scant thought for ergonomics. The radio speaker is almost Art Deco.

EBW 45B

ADDITIONAL HOOD
To supplement the hood a fiberglass detachable hardtop was an option in 1962.

SOFT TOP
Early cars had a "packaway" hood made from ICI Everflex.

HOOD
Hood is made out of lightweight aluminum.

SUSPENSION
Front suspension was coil spring with wishbones, and dated back to the MG TF of the 1950s.

MGB TOURER
All MGBs had the simple 1798cc B-series four-cylinder engine with origins going back to 1947. This Tourer's period charm is enhanced by the rare Iris Blue paintwork and seldom seen pressed-steel wheels – most examples were fitted with optional spoked wire wheels.

MORGAN *Plus Four*

IT IS REMARKABLE THAT THEY still make them, but there are many men with cloth caps and corduroys who are grateful that they do. Derived from the first four-wheeled Morgans of 1936, this is the car that buoyed Morgan after the war while many of the old mainstays of the British motor industry wilted around it. Tweedier than a Scottish moor on the first day of the grouse shooting season, it is as quintessentially British as a car can be. It was a hit in America and other foreign countries. It has also remained the backbone of the idiosyncratic Malvern-based company that refuses to move with the times. Outdated and outmoded it may be, but there is still a very long waiting list to purchase a Morgan. First introduced in 1951, the Plus Four, with a series of Standard Vanguard and Triumph TR engines, laid the foundations for the modern miracle of the very old-fashioned Morgan Motor Company.

LIKE ALL FOUR-WHEELED MORGANS, THE PLUS FOUR HAD A TWO-PIECE HOOD WITH A PIANO HINGE IN THE MIDDLE

OTHER MODELS

Today, the company builds just two cars: the four-cylinder Ford Zetec-engined Plus Four, with a top speed of 111 mph (179 km/h), and the Plus Eight.

MORGAN PLUS EIGHT
The 3.5-liter Rover V-8-engined Plus Eight is slower today, at 121 mph (195 km/h), than it was 20 years ago, but accelerates to 60 mph (96 km/h) in just 6.1 seconds.

ENGINE
The later Triumph TR3A 2138cc engine, as here, gave increased torque. The 2138cc engine was available in the TR3A from summer 1957. The earlier Triumph 1991cc engine was still available for those wishing to compete in classes below two liters.

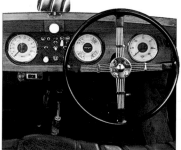

INTERIOR
From 1958 onward, all Plus Fours had wider cockpits with a new dash, identifiable by the cubbyhole on the passenger's side. Speedometer, switches, warning lights, and minor gauges were grouped in a central panel on the dash.

"SUICIDE" DOORS
The earlier two-seat drophead coupe retained rear-hinged "suicide" doors with framed, sliding windows, but the sleeker two- and four-seat sports models had front-hinged doors with removable sidescreens.

ON THE RACK
Morgans have limited luggage capacity, so many owners fitted external racks.

LIGHT WORK
Headlights are big, bold affairs set in pods on the front fenders, but sidelights are about as visible as a pair of lightning bugs.

REAR ILLUMINATION
Rear lights have never been a Morgan strong point. Amber signals are a good 6 in (15 cm) inboard of the stop/tail lights, and are partially obscured by the luggage rack.

SPECIFICATIONS

MODEL Morgan Plus Four (1951–69)
PRODUCTION 3,737
BODY STYLES Two- and four-seater sports convertible.
CONSTRUCTION Steel chassis, ash frame, steel and aluminum outer panels.
ENGINE 2088cc overhead valve inline four (Vanguard); 1991cc or 2138cc overhead valve inline four (TR).
POWER OUTPUT 105 bhp at 4700 rpm (2138cc TR engine).
TRANSMISSION Four-speed manual.
SUSPENSION *Front:* Sliding stub axles, coil springs, and telescopic shocks. *Rear:* Live axle, semielliptic leaf springs, and lever-arm shocks.
BRAKES Drums front and rear; front discs standard from 1960.
MAXIMUM SPEED 100 mph (161 km/h)
0–60 MPH (0–96 KM/H) 12 sec
A.F.C. 20–22 mpg

MORGAN PLUS FOUR

The second generation Plus Four was the first of what are generally considered the "modern looking" Morgans – if that is the right expression for a basic design which, still in production today, dates back to 1936. Distinguishing features are the cowled radiator grille and, from 1959 onward, a wider body (as here) to provide more elbow room for driver and passenger.

HOOD
The dramatically tapering hood meant limited engine access.

WHERE'S THE CATCH?
Traditional latches – two for each hood half – are among the most tactile features of the Plus Four.

MIRROR POSITION
Doors were the only sensible places for exterior rear view mirrors; the tops of the front fenders were miles away.

TRADITIONAL ASH FRAME

The current four-cylinder Morgan is built in exactly the same manner as most of its predecessors. The chassis is made from "Z"-section steel members, and on it sits a 94- or 114-piece wooden framework (two- and four-seat cars, respectively) clothed in a mixture of steel and aluminum panels.

SUSPENSION
The Plus Four retained a simple sliding-pillar front suspension.

FULL-UP POSITION

COUP DE VILLE POSITION

BEST OF BOTH WORLDS

Unlike most convertible cars, the Plus Four has a hood that can be partially folded back. It provides fresh air without being too drafty.

MORRIS MINOR MM *Convertible*

THE MORRIS MINOR is a motoring milestone. As Britain's first million seller it became a "people's car," staple transportation for everyone from midwives to builder's suppliers. Designed by Alec Issigonis, the genius who later went on to pen the Austin Mini *(see pages 40–41)*, the new Series MM Morris Minor of 1948 featured the then-novel unit chassis-body construction. The 918cc side-valve engine of the MM was rather more antique, a hang-over from the pre-war Morris 8.

Its handling and ride comfort more than made up for the lack of power. With independent front suspension and crisp rack-and-pinion steering it embarrassed its rivals and even tempted the young Stirling Moss into high-speed cornering antics that lost him his license for a month. Of all the 1.5 million Minors the most prized are the now rare Series MM convertibles. Rag-tops remained part of the Minor model line-up until 1969, two years from the end of all Minor production. So desirable are these open tourers that in recent years there has been a trade in rogue rag-tops, chopped sedans masquerading as original factory convertibles.

TURN SIGNALS
With no door pillars above waist height, semaphore turn signals were mounted lower down on the tourers; flashers eventually replaced semaphores in 1961.

RAG-TOP RARITY
Convertibles represent only a small proportion of Minor production. Between 1963 and 1969 only 3,500 soft-tops were produced, compared with 119,000 two-door sedans.

CHOICE OF MODELS
At its launch the Minor was available as a two-door sedan and as a convertible (Tourer). Four-door, wagon, van, and pick-up complete the range.

ORIGINAL MM TOURER HAD SIDE CURTAINS, REPLACED BY GLASS REAR WINDOW IN 1952

MORRIS BEAM COUNTERS DICTATED OLD-FASHIONED LIVE AXLE AND LEAF SPRINGS AT REAR

BODY WIDTH

At 61 in (155 cm) the production car was 4 in (10 cm) wider than the prototype.

DASHBOARD

This simple early dashboard was never really updated, but the speedometer was later moved to the central console.

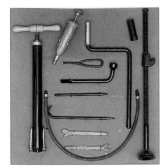

TOOLED UP

A complete original tool kit is a rarity, a prize companion piece for any owner.

THE SPRUNG-SPOKE STEERING WHEEL IS TRADITIONAL, BUT RACK-AND-PINION STEERING GIVES A CRISP, LIGHT FEEL

MINOR MOTORS

The original 918cc side-valve engine was replaced progressively in 1952 and 1953 by the Austin A-series 803cc overhead valve engine, then by the A-series 948cc, and finally the 1098cc.

— SPECIFICATIONS —

MODEL Morris Minor (1948–71)
PRODUCTION 1,620,000
BODY STYLES Two- and four-door sedan, two-door convertible (Tourer), wagon (Traveller), van, and pick-up.
CONSTRUCTION Unit body/chassis; steel.
ENGINE Straight-four, 918cc, 803cc, 948cc, and 1098cc.
POWER OUTPUT 28 bhp (918cc); 48 bhp (1098cc).
TRANSMISSION Four-speed manual.
SUSPENSION Torsion bar independent front suspension; live-axle leaf-spring rear.
BRAKES Drums all around.
MAXIMUM SPEED 62–75 mph (100–121 km/h)
0–60 MPH (0–96 KM/H) 50+ sec for 918cc, 24 sec for 1098cc.
A.F.C. 36–43 mpg

UNDER-HOOD SPACE AND EASY ENGINE ACCESS MAKE THE MINOR A DIY FAVORITE

EVEN ON CROSS-PLY TIRES THE ORIGINAL MINOR WON PRAISE FOR ITS HANDLING AND COMPETED WITH DISTINCTION IN THE MONTE CARLO RALLY

— BRITAIN'S FIRST MILLION SELLER —

The Morris Minor owes much of its success to the singular vision of one shy man, Alex Issigonis, the Greek-born son of an itinerant marine engineer.

UNDER THE PATRONAGE of Morris vice-chairman, Sir Miles Thomas, the young and talented Alex Issigonis, already a respected suspension engineer, was entrusted with the task of developing a small new Morris.

Prototypes of the car that was to become the Morris Minor had already been built in 1943. Back then it was to be called the Mosquito, but the name was abandoned in the ramp up to its launch as several other companies claimed rights to the name. Issigonis had wanted a flat-four water-cooled engine and his rear suspension was also compromised, but the car that made its debut at Britain's first post-war motor show, in London in 1948, was still very much his in concept, design, and execution – he had even designed the door handles. The Jaguar XK120 *(see pages 134–35)* was the show-stopper, the car that everyone wanted, but the Morris Minor was the car ordinary people needed. Unusually for a small utility car, its merits were appreciated quite early on, even though

WORLDWIDE MINOR EXPORTS, FROM 1950S SALES BROCHURE

MORRIS
Minor MM
Convertible

MINOR
WATERSHED
The split windshield was replaced by a curved glass in 1956.

BOTH FRONT AND REAR FENDERS ARE EASILY REPLACED, BOLT-ON ITEMS

LGO 786

THE FILLET IN THE BUMPER IS ANOTHER EXAMPLE OF THE WIDENING OF THE BODY

THE MILLIONTH MINOR ROLLS OFF THE PRODUCTION LINE

Morris boss Lord Nuffield dismissed it as a "poached egg." But there was no stopping the Minor. After its official launch as a two-door sedan and convertible Tourer, a four-door sedan, van, pick-up, and Traveller wagon followed, so that in one guise or another the Minor met the needs of every ordinary motorist.

On December 22, 1960, the millionth Minor was made, spawning a limited edition of 349 Minor Millions, painted a sudden lilac and badged "Minor 1000000" on the rear.

As the Minor's fortune's dimmed through the Sixties until its eventual demise in 1971, another Issigonis design, the Mini *(see pages 40–41)*, was on the rise. The Mini eventually outstripped the Minor's 1,620,000 sales total to become Britain's best-seller ever, but the Minor will always be remembered as Britain's first million seller and its first "people's car."

EXTRACT FROM A 1950s FRENCH SALES BROCHURE – "THE BEST LITTLE CAR IN THE WORLD"

LA PETITE VOITURE LA PLUS AVANTAGEUSE DU MONDE

"LOW LIGHTS"
In 1950, the headlights on all Minors were moved to the top of the fenders. Earlier models such as our featured car are now dubbed "low lights."

STARTER HANDLE
Most Minor engines are willing starters, but all models to the end of production came with a starter handle in the tool kit.

SYMBOLS OF AN OX AND A FORD REPRESENT MORRIS'S HOME TOWN OF OXFORD

ISSIGONIS WAS ORIGINALLY A SUSPENSION ENGINEER AND INDEPENDENT FRONT SUSPENSION IS A CREDIT TO HIS GENIUS

ORIGINAL SLIMLINE BUMPERS LATER ACQUIRED OVER-RIDERS AS THE MODEL WAS UPDATED

LGO 786

NSU *Ro80*

INTERIOR
Power steering was by ZF. Dashboard was a paragon of Teutonic efficiency which would later be mirrored by Mercedes and BMW. With no transmission tunnel or driveshaft, plenty of headroom, and a long wheelbase, rear passengers found the Ro80 thoroughly accommodating.

ALONG WITH THE Citroën DS *(see pages 72–75)*, the NSU Ro80 was ten years ahead of its time. Beneath that striking, wind-cheating shape was an audacious two rotor engine, front-wheel drive, disc brakes, and a semiautomatic clutchless gearbox. In 1967, the Ro80 won the acclaimed "Car of the Year" award and went on to be hailed by many as "Car of the Decade." Technical preeminence aside, it also handled like a racer. But NSU's brave new Wankel power unit was flawed and, due to acute rotor tip wear, would expire after only 15–20,000 miles (24–32,000 km). NSU honored its warranty claims until it went broke. Eventually Audi/VW took over, axing the Ro80 in 1977.

TO AVOID OVER-REVVING THE ENGINE, A WARNING BUZZER WOULD SOUND AT 7000 RPM

ENGINE HAD TWO SPARK PLUGS PER ROTOR AND BREATHED THROUGH SOLEX TWO-STAGE CARBURETORS

ENGINE POSITION
Engine was mounted on four progressive-acting rubber mounts with telescopic shocks on each side of the gearbox casing.

ENGINE
Designed by Felix Wankel, the brilliant twin rotor engine was equivalent to a two-liter reciprocating piston unit. Drive was through a torque converter with a Fichel & Sachs electro-pneumatic motor to a three speed NSU gearbox.

CORNERING
The Ro80's stability, roadholding, ride, steering, and dynamic balance were exceptional, and far superior to most sports and GT cars.

NSU RO80
In 1967, the Ro80 looked like a vision of the future with its low center of gravity, huge glass area, and sleek aerodynamics. The high rear end, widely imitated a decade later, held a huge, deep trunk.

LIGHTS
Hella headlights give fine nighttime light.

BRAKES
ATE Dunlop with twin circuits and inboard discs at the front.

WHEELS
Five-spoke aluminum wheels were optional.

HYU 975K

UPX 37F

SPECIFICATIONS

MODEL NSU Ro80 (1967–77)
PRODUCTION 37,204
BODY STYLE Front engine five-seater sedan.
CONSTRUCTION Integral chassis with pressed steel monocoque body.
ENGINE Two rotor Wankel, 1990cc.
POWER OUTPUT 113.5 bhp at 5500 rpm.
TRANSMISSION Three speed semiautomatic.
SUSPENSION Independent all around.
BRAKES Four wheel discs.
MAXIMUM SPEED 112 mph (180 km/h)
0–60 MPH (0–96 KM/H) 11.9 sec
0–100 MPH (0–161 KM/H) 25 sec
A.F.C. 20 mpg

PANHARD *PL17 Tigre*

PANHARD WAS ONE of the world's oldest names in car manufacturing, dating back to 1872. But by 1955 it had lost its upmarket image and had to be rescued by Citroën, which eventually bought it out completely in 1965. The Dyna, produced after the war in response to a need for a small, practical, and economical machine, had an aluminum alloy frame, bulkhead, and horizontally opposed, air-cooled, two cylinder engine.

In 1954, the Dyna became front-wheel drive, with a bulbous but streamlined new body. The 848cc flat twin engine was a gem and in post-1961 Tigre form pushed out 60 bhp; this gave 90 mph (145 km/h), enough to win a Monte Carlo Rally. Advertised as "the car that makes sense," the PL17 was light, quick, miserly on fuel, and years ahead of its time.

EFFICIENT DESIGN
Simple design meant fewer moving parts, more power, and more miles to the gallon.

DESIGN
Front-wheel drive guaranteed stability and safety, with class-leading space for an 848cc car.

ENGINE
The engine design dates back to 1940. Cylinders were cast integral with their heads in light aluminum, cooling fins and cast iron liners. Heads had hemispherical combustion chambers and valve gearing incorporating torsion bars. Carburetor was Zenith 38 NDIX twin choke.

STEERING
The steering was rack and pinion, with only two turns lock-to-lock and large Bendix hydraulic brakes.

PANHARD PL17 TIGRE
With its aerodynamically shaped body, Panhard claimed the lowest drag coefficient of any production car in 1956. Emphasis was on weight saving and, despite its quirky looks, the PL17 was a triumph of efficiency.

INTERIOR
The unusual interior had bizarre oval-shaped pedals, column shifter, and an unsuccessful collection of American styling themes.

SPECIFICATIONS

MODEL Panhard PL17 Tigre (1961–64)
PRODUCTION 130,000 (all models).
BODY STYLE Four door, four seater sports sedan.
CONSTRUCTION Separate chassis with steel and aluminum body.
ENGINE 848cc twin horizontally opposed air cooled.
POWER OUTPUT 60 bhp at 5800 rpm.
TRANSMISSION Front-wheel drive four-speed manual.
SUSPENSION Independent front with twin transverse leaf, torsion bar rear.
BRAKES Four-wheel drums.
MAXIMUM SPEED 90 mph (145 km/h)
0–60 MPH (0–96 KM/H) 23.1 sec
A.F.C. 38 mpg

PEUGEOT *203*

COMPARED TO THE SCORES of upright postwar sedans that looked like church pews, Peugeot's 203 was a breath of fresh air. As well as being one of the French car maker's most successful products, the 203's monocoque body and revolutionary engine set it apart. In its day, the 1290cc overhead valve powerplant was state-of-the-art, with an aluminum cylinder head and hemispherical combustion chambers, said to be the inspiration for the famous Chrysler "Hemi" unit. With a range that included two- and four-door cabriolets, a family wagon, and a two-door coupe, the French really took to the 203, loving its tough mechanicals, willing progress, and supple ride. By its demise in 1960, the 203 had broken records for Peugeot, with nearly 700,000 sold.

PEUGEOT 203 AT THE MONTE CARLO RALLY
In the '50s there were plenty of firms who could give the 203 more urge. Many were tuned and campaigned by amateurs in rallies like the Monte Carlo.

TURN SIGNAL
The 203's turn signals were operated by a vacuum from the inlet manifold.

INTERIOR
With postwar steel in short supply, aluminum was used to good effect in the under-dash handbrake and column-mounted gear changer. The handsome fastback body gave plenty of cabin room.

ROOMY
Clever use of space meant 203 was spacious.

PEUGEOT'S LION LABEL DATES BACK TO 1906, WHEN ROBERT PEUGEOT STARTED UP HIS OWN COMPANY CALLED LION-PEUGEOT

PAINTWORK
A high gloss finish was achieved with several coats of synthetic lacquer.

ENGINE
The 49 bhp ohv pushrod engine was the 203's most advanced feature. With wet piston liners, low compression ratio, and aluminum head, it was smooth, free-revving and long-lasting. The four-speed gearbox is really a three with overdrive. The basic design was still used in the 1980s for Peugeot's 1971cc 505 model.

OAA 950

PEUGEOT 203 CABRIOLET

The 203 Cabriolet turned out as a 2+2 but was originally planned to have a rumble seat. Colors were cheerful pastels instead of dull grays and blacks.

SPECIFICATIONS

MODEL Peugeot 203 (1948–60)
PRODUCTION 685,828
BODY STYLES Two-door coupe, two- or four-door convertible, family wagon.
CONSTRUCTION All-steel monocoque rigid one-piece body shell.
ENGINE Four-cylinder ohv 1290cc.
POWER OUTPUT 42–49 bhp at 3500 rpm.
TRANSMISSION Four-speed column change with overdrive.
SUSPENSION Transverse leaf independent front, coil spring rear with Panhard rod.
BRAKES Drums all around.
MAXIMUM SPEED 73 mph (117 km/h)
0–60 MPH (0–96 KM/H) 20 sec
A.F.C. 20–35 mpg

WINDSHIELD WIPERS

"Clap hand" windshield wipers may look dated, but the motor was so robust that it was still in use 43 years later on the tailgate wiper of the 504 model.

BUDGET INTERIOR

Interior was built to a budget with rubber mats, metal dash, and cloth seat facings.

SMART DESIGN

The hood swings up on counterbalanced springs and the front grille comes away by undoing a wing nut.

STYLING

These stylish sweeping curves were influenced by the 1946 Chevrolet.

GAS TANK

This was concealed under a flush-fitting flap – unheard of in 1948.

PEUGEOT 203

Widely acclaimed at the 1948 Paris Motor Show, the 203's slippery shape was wind tunnel tested in model form and claimed to have a rather optimistic drag coefficient of just 0.36 – lower than a modern Porsche 911 *(see pages 194–95)*. Quality touches abound, such as the exterior brightwork in stainless steel and integral mounting points for a roof rack.

TRUNK

A vast trunk with a low-loading sill made the 203 the ideal family car.

OAA 950

PLYMOUTH *Barracuda*

BACK IN 1964, IT WAS Ford's Mustang *(see pages 120–23)* that gave its name to a new breed of sporty compact. But Chrysler was quick with its own "pony car," the Plymouth Barracuda, launched for the 1965 model year. Admittedly, Chrysler had hastily revised its Valiant tooling to reach the starting gate in the pony car stakes, but there is no doubt the Barracuda was a worthy contender. Over the years it grew in stature, and in 1970 really came of age with a complete redesign that was altogether more purposeful-looking. The Barracuda never matched the Mustangs and Camaros *(see pages 66–67)* in sales terms, but it attracted a loyal band of followers with its clean, lean looks. It was a brief flowering though, for the Barracuda's fate was sealed when insurance companies took exception to muscle cars and government emission laws started to strangle the performance. The fuel crisis of 1973–74 finished it off once and for all.

INTERIOR
Many ordinary buyers were attracted by Plymouth successes on the NASCAR stock-car circuit and having tried out the cockpit, valued the "race-bred" features. These included a three-spoke wood rim steering wheel, 150 mph (241 km/h) speedometer, and high-backed bucket seats with headrests.

STREAMLINING
Attention to aerodynamics included retractable antenna, streamlined door mirrors, and hidden windshield wipers.

WIDE DOORS
The huge doors give access to low front seating and make rear entry manageable.

GO-FASTER PINS
External hood pins are a racing-style accessory.

HEMI OPTION
One engine option was the famous Chrysler Hemi, so named for its hemispheral combustion chambers.

OVERHEAD VIEW
From the top the Barracuda could be a different car; compared to its slim and lean side aspect the top view is almost completely rectangular.

SLOPING TAIL
The first Barracudas had a glass-filled roof sloping gently back to the tail. The hardtop option, introduced as part of the 1970 redesign, became more popular.

SHARED SHELL
The Barracuda shared the same bodyshell as another Chrysler pony car, the Dodge Challenger.

SPECIFICATIONS

MODEL Plymouth Barracuda (1970–74)
PRODUCTION 102,786
BODY STYLES Two-door fastback coupe, convertible, or hardtop.
CONSTRUCTION Unibody shell.
ENGINE Inline six, 224cid, or 90-degree V-8, 318cid, 339cid, 383cid, 426cid, or 440cid.
POWER OUTPUT 110–145 hp at 4000 rpm (six), 150–390 hp (V-8).
TRANSMISSION Torqueflite automatic or four-speed manual.
SUSPENSION *Front:* independent, unequal length wishbones, with torsion bar and antiroll bar. Live rear axle, semielliptic leaf springs.
BRAKES *Front:* disc; *Rear:* drums.
MAXIMUM SPEED 137 mph (220 km/h)
0–60 MPH (0–96 KM/H) 5.9 sec (7212cc)
A.F.C. 10–23 mpg

PLYMOUTH BARRACUDA

The Plymouth Barracuda range was developed from the Valiant to become Chrysler's prime pony car contender. With its rivals, the 'Cuda shared the then-popular two-door coupe styling on a short-wheelbase chassis. The post-redesign, second-generation cars, built to 1974, are favored by many devotees. This is a top-of-the-line Cuda 440, with the biggest (7.2-liter) engine and special bodywork package. Power and handling options made Barracudas great performers.

NAME ORIGINS
The name came from Plymouth Rock, where the first white settlers landed.

"SHAKER HOOD"
Engine options ranged from "small" six to V-8 of seven liters plus. The air cleaner for the triple carburetors protruded through the hood, and could be seen vibrating; hence the term "shaker hood" for this feature.

PONTIAC *Trans Am*

THE BIG-HEARTED Pontiac Trans Am was born in those heady days when America's "big three" (Ford, General Motors, and Chrysler) built bold-as-brass, brawny machines. GM's Pontiac Division, under the dynamic John Z. DeLorean, adopted a sporting image across its whole range in this era. The first Pontiac "muscle car" was the 1964 GTO *(see pages 190–91)*, followed in 1967 by the Firebird "pony car." Pontiac raced this in the Trans Am championship and before long a higher-performance version was put on sale, with go-faster stripes, trunk spoiler, and sports cockpit.

But the classic Pontiac Trans Am was much more, with a stiffened chassis and better brakes to cope with the 350 hp engine. By the mid-1970s, the fuel crisis and US emission laws turned it from a roaring lion into a tame pussycat.

HOLLYWOOD STAR
The Trans Am was a Hollywood favorite, a four-wheeled film star in its own right. One of its biggest roles was in *Smokey and the Bandit*, in which it upstaged Burt Reynolds. The Firebird, on which the Trans Am was based, was made famous in the television detective series, *The Rockford Files*.

SPORTS CONTROLS
Leather-rimmed steering wheel, floor shift, grooved dashboard, and bucket seats make the Trans Am cockpit about as sporting as that of any American car – even if the seats are vinyl trimmed.

PONTIAC CALLED THIS INSTRUMENT PACKAGE ITS "RALLY CLUSTER"; IT WAS OPTIONAL ON SOME OTHER PONTIACS

BIG V-8s (400 OR 455 CID) PROVIDED TRANS AM POWER

AROUND 350 HP WAS AVAILABLE FROM THE VARIOUS ENGINE OPTIONS, BUT 1973 EMISSION LAWS TAMED THE BEAST

FRONTAL FEATURE
All post-1964 Pontiacs were quickly identifiable from the front by the divided air intake. The 1969–73 "bull-nose" Trans Am was more attractive head on than some of its successors, which almost became cartoon versions of the original. Early Trans Ams all came with white paintwork and blue flashes.

PARKING LIGHTS
Front parking lights were a distinguishing feature of the very first Trans Ams, as the early base Firebird models had none.

DLR 305 MASSACHUSE

PONTIAC TRANS AM

Clean Trans Am styling was welcomed by at least some sectors of the American market as a departure from the finned and chromed monsters which still made up the bulk of Detroit production at the time. Family resemblance to other GM "pony cars" of the time, such as the Chevrolet Camaro *(see pages 66–67)* and Pontiac's own Firebird, is clear, sharing their chic Coke-bottle shape.

DEBUT
The first Trans Ams appeared in 1969, two years after the Firebird.

FIREBIRD
The logo was based on Indian firebird legend; it is often affectionately referred to as a "chicken" or even "dead eagle."

FISHER BODYWORK
Fisher was the coachbuilding division of GM; the logo appeared on top-line models.

SPECIFICATIONS

MODEL Pontiac Firebird Trans Am (1969–73)

PRODUCTION 12,097

BODY STYLE Two-door, four-seat sports coupe.

CONSTRUCTION Steel-bodied monocoque with engine subframe.

ENGINE 90-degree V-8, 400cid; 455cid option from 1971.

POWER OUTPUT 345 hp at 5400 rpm (400cid); 335 hp at 4800 rpm (455cid).

TRANSMISSION Three- or four-speed manual or Hydramatic automatic.

SUSPENSION Independent front by wishbones and coil springs, beam axle on semielliptic leaf springs at rear.

BRAKES *Front:* Power-assisted front discs; *Rear:* drums.

MAXIMUM SPEED 112–132 mph (180–212 km/h) depending on spec.

0–60 MPH (0–96 KM/H) 5.4–6.0 sec.

A.F.C. 10–15 mpg

BULL-NOSE
Post-1973 models were given a more sloping front end.

RACING MIRRORS
Streamlined mirrors were another tell-tale Trans Am feature.

HIDDEN WIPERS
The Trans Am's concealed windshield wipers aided aerodynamic efficiency and enhanced the uncluttered appearance of the whole package.

HARD TOP
Although convertible Firebirds were freely available at the time, only eight rag-top Trans Am versions were built, all in the first year of production.

LUGGAGE SPACE
Small by US standards, but bigger than most European cars.

REAR VIEW
Another advantage over many European sporting cars was adequate rear visibility.

PONTIAC

TRANS AM

TRANS AM

DLR 3055 D
MASSACHUSETTS

PONTIAC *GTO*

THE CAR THAT STARTED the whole muscle car movement was really just a piece of corporate defiance. When General Motors clamped down on performance cars, Pontiac chief engineer John Z. DeLorean skirted the edict by simple "hot-rod" methods, placing the biggest engine available into its medium-sized Tempest Le Mans range. The GTO immediately hit home, especially in the youth market, and it was the first to offer near-race performance and roadholding in a full-sized car. Americans lined up to buy: 207,000 chose the GTO option in the first three years. From the original option package, the GTO was elevated to a separate Tempest model in 1966, and became a model in its own right in 1968. It faded back into the Le Mans line in 1972, but in the course of its joyride, the GTO had created a uniquely American expression of performance driving.

Speak softly and carry a GTO

IMAGES OF ADVERTISING
In this 1966 advertisement, the GTO was described as "A Pontiac in a saber-toothed tiger skin." Whatever it meant, the GTO upheld Pontiac's recent strong following in the youth market.

INTERIOR
The interior looks more like a speedboat than a car. The Tempest was a six seater with front bench; Tempest Le Mans, on which the GTO was based, was a five seater with separate front seats.

WALNUT GRAIN DASH

WIPER MOVE
For the 1968 facelift, disappearing wipers cleaned up the cowl area.

POWER TOP
Apart from the first few, all GTO convertibles came with power-operated top.

GTO NICKNAME
The GTO very quickly earned the nickname of "Goat," as it was agile for its size.

HARD FACTS
Pillarless hardtop coupes often outsold convertibles by nearly 10 to 1.

TIRE CHOICE
For many production years, GTO buyers could choose between red-line or whitewall-stripe tires.

SPACIOUS
Bowling-alley rear deck enclosed spacious trunk.

HEADLIGHTS
Twin lights were horizontal in 1964, then vertical for 1966 and 1967, before reverting to side-by-side format in line with GM design trends.

PONTIAC GTO

While the GTO was by no means a giant in American terms, at a little over 17 ft (5.18 m) long, it was a step up in size from the "pony cars" of the period. With routine annual updates, GTO spotters can identify model years with ease. The car featured here is from 1966; the grille, different from the preceding and following year models, is one giveaway. The slab sides of 1965 have a "Coke bottle" treatment. After various facelifts, an all-new design appeared for 1970. From 1969 to 1971, the ultimate GTO was the "The Judge," with all top GTO options as standard. They are rare too – only 11,000 were built.

POWER BULGE
Hood scoop in various forms easily distinguished the GTO from the Tempest Le Mans.

SPECIFICATIONS

MODEL Pontiac GTO (1964–71)
PRODUCTION 497,122
BODY STYLES Two door, five seat coupe, hardtop, or convertible.
CONSTRUCTION Semi-unit chassis/body.
ENGINE V-8; 326cid, 389cid, 400cid, or 456cid.
POWER OUTPUT 250–280 hp at 4600–4800 rpm; 325 hp at 4800 rpm; 335–350 hp at 5000 rpm; 360 hp at 5000 rpm.
TRANSMISSION Three- or four-speed manual; two-speed automatic.
SUSPENSION *Front:* independent, coil springs. *Rear:* live axle, coil springs, upper and lower trailing arm links.
BRAKES Drums all around, front discs from 1968.
MAXIMUM SPEED 135 mph (217 km/h)
0–60 MPH (0–96 KM/H) 6.6 sec
A.F.C. 8–12 mpg

GRAN TURISMO
The GTO name ("Gran Turismo Omologato") was hijacked by GM from Ferrari.

ENGINE
GTO engines were always the most powerful in the Pontiac range. This 1966 car has that year's standard GTO 389cid V-8 (6.5-liter), pumping out 335 hp.

Porsche 356B

Volkswagen Beetle designer Ferdinand Porsche may have given the world the "people's car," but it was his son Ferry who, with longtime associate Karl Rabe, created the 356. These days a Porsche stands for precision, performance, purity, and perfection, and the 356 is the first chapter in that story. Well not quite. The 356 was so named because it was actually the 356th project from the Porsche design office since it was set up in 1930. It was also the first car to bear the Porsche name. Postwar expediency forced a make-do reliance on Beetle underpinnings, but the 356 is much more than a Bug in butterfly's clothes. Its rear-engined layout and design descends directly from the father car, but in the athletic son the genes are mutated into a true sporting machine. A pert, nimble, tail-happy treat, the pretty 356 is the foundation stone of a proud sporting tradition.

Track Record
Here Porsches are seen retro racing at Palm Springs, California in 1990. The first Porsche 356s distinguished themselves immediately with a 1951 Le Mans class win and a 20th overall finish. Since then, Porsche has always been associated with performance, boasting an enviable track and rally victory tally.

Split-screen Deceit
On convertibles, the rear view mirror is attached to a slim chrome bar that gives a deceptive split-screen appearance from the front.

1949 Porsche 356
This original incarnation of the 356 has slimmer wheels, split screen, lower bumpers, and is a more bulbous shape.

Redesign
On the 356B, headlights and bumpers moved higher up the fender.

Interior
The interior is delightfully functional, unfussy, unfaddish, and, because of that, enduringly fashionable. Below the padded dash are the classic green-on-black instruments. Seats are wide and flat, and the large, almost vertical, steering wheel has a light feel. Passenger gets a grab handle.

Transmission lock was a useful security fitting available on later cars

Slick Changes
The lever is long, but the patented Porsche split-ring synchromesh gives smooth changes with quick and positive engagement.

DYU 40C

EXTRA LUGGAGE
With limited luggage accommodation in the front, the rear rack provides useful extra luggage space.

ACCESS COVER
Not a covered jacking point but an access cover to allow you to retrieve the torsion bar.

BRAKES
Drum brakes gave way to four-wheel discs with the 356C in 1963.

PORSCHE 356B SUPER 90

The first Porsche 356 was a triumph of creative expediency and inspired engineering, taking basic VW Beetle elements to create a new breed of sports car. Aficionados adore the earliest cars, often affectionately dubbed "jelly molds," and, like a jelly settling on a plate, the shape settled and spread out over the years to become flatter and sleeker.

EXHAUSTS
On the 356B, twin exhausts exit on each side through bumper overriders.

ENGINE

The rear-engined layout was determined by reliance on VW Beetle mechanicals and running gear. The flat-four engine, with its so-called "boxer" layout of horizontally opposed cylinders, is not pure Beetle, but a progressive development. Engines grew from 1086cc producing 40 bhp, to 1996cc in the final versions. This is the 1582cc engine of the 1962 356B.

SPECIFICATIONS

MODEL Porsche 356B (1959–63)

PRODUCTION 30,963

BODY STYLES Two-plus-two hardtop coupe, convertible, and Speedster.

CONSTRUCTION Unit steel body with integral pressed steel platform chassis.

ENGINE Aircooled, horizontally opposed flat four 1582cc.

POWER OUTPUT 90 bhp at 5500 rpm (Super 90).

TRANSMISSION Four-speed manual, all synchromesh, rear wheel drive.

SUSPENSION *Front:* Independent, trailing arms with transverse torsion bars and anti-roll bar. *Rear:* Independent, swing half axles, radius arms, and transverse torsion bars. Telescopic shocks.

BRAKES Hydraulic drums all around.

MAXIMUM SPEED 110 mph (177 km/h)

0–60 MPH (0–96 KM/H) 10 sec

A.F.C. 30–35 mpg

PORSCHE *Carrera 911 RS*

AN INSTANT LEGEND, the Carrera RS became the classic 911, and is hailed as one of the ultimate road cars of all time. With lighter body panels and bare bones interior trim, the RS is simply a featherweight racer. The classic flat-six engine was bored out to 2.7 liters and equipped with uprated fuel injection and forged flat-top pistons – modifications that helped to develop a sparkling 210 bhp.

Porsche had no problem selling all the RSs it could make. A total of 1,580 were built and sold in just 12 months. Standard 911s were often criticized for tail-happy handling, but the Carrera RS is a supremely balanced machine. Its race-bred responses offer the last word in sensory gratification. With one of the best engines ever made, an outstanding chassis, and 150 mph (243 km/h) top speed, the RS can rub bumpers with the world's finest. Collectors and Porsche fans consider this the pre-eminent 911, with prices reflecting its cult-like status, The RS is the original air-cooled screamer.

INTERIOR
Touring or road versions of the RS had creature comforts like sunroof, electric windows, and radio cassette. Large central tachometer and "dog-leg" gear shift are RS trademarks. Leather seats and steering wheel are non-standard later additions.

RACING 911
The RS outclassed everything else on the track, winning the Daytona 24-hours in 1973 and beating heavyweights like the Ferrari 365 GTB/4.

ENGINE
The bored-out, air-cooled 2.7-liter opposed six produces huge reserves of power. Externally, it is identifiable only by extra cylinder cooling fins. Internally, things are very different from the stock 911 unit.

WINDSHIELD
Steeply raked glass helps the 911's wind-cheating shape.

GoldStar

LIGHTS
Classic slanted headlights betray 911's VW Beetle origins.

VENTILATION
Cockpit ventilation is through tiny louvers above the rear window.

WHEEL ARCHES
Rear wheel arches are flared to accommodate 7-in (18-cm) rims.

SPECIFICATIONS

MODEL Porsche Carrera 911 RS (1972–73)

PRODUCTION 1,580

BODY STYLES Two door, two seater coupe.

CONSTRUCTION Thin-gauge steel panels.

ENGINE Flat-six, 2687cc.

POWER OUTPUT 210 bhp at 5100 rpm.

TRANSMISSION Close-ratio, five-speed manual.

SUSPENSION Front and rear torsion bar.

BRAKES Ventilated discs front and rear, with aluminum calipers.

MAXIMUM SPEED 150 mph (243 km/h)

0–60 MPH (0–96 KM/H) 5.6 sec

0–100 MPH (0–161 KM/H) 12.8 sec

A.F.C. 23 mpg

PORSCHE CARRERA 911 RS 2.7

The plastic bumpers, thin steel bodywork, and lightweight "Glaverbell" glass help the RS to weigh in at just over 1,984 lb (900 kg). Standard Porsches tip the scales at 2,194 lb (995 kg). In addition, the weight distribution and rear engine layout demand some very gentle treatment of the throttle. Handle the 911 roughly and it will understeer, eventually breaking away with savage violence. 911s need great respect in the rain.

TARGA STAMP
The 911 Targa had a lift-out roof panel and built-in roll bar. But enthusiasts preferred the Beetle-backed lines of the closed 911.

INTERIOR
Racing RSs do not even have headlining, sun visors, or sound-proofing.

REAR SPOILER
The RS has a fiberglass Burzel rear spoiler, fitted to reduce rear-end lift at speed. This boosted the RS's maximum speed by 2 mph (3 km/h).

RENAULT *Alpine A110*

THE RENAULT ALPINE A110 may be diminutive in its proportions but it has a massive and deserved reputation, particularly in its native France. Although wearing the Renault label, this pocket rocket is a testimony to the single-minded dedication of one man – Jean Redélé, a passionate sports car enthusiast and son of a Dieppe Renault agent. As he took over his father's garage he began to modify Renault products for competition, then develop his own machines based on Renault engines and mechanicals. The A110, with its fiberglass body and backbone chassis, was the culmination of his effort, and from its launch in 1963 went on to rack up a massive list of victories in the world's toughest rallies. On the public roads, it had all the appeal of a thinly disguised racer, as nimble as a mountain goat, with sparkling performance and just about the most fun you could have this side of a Lancia Stratos *(see pages 152–53).*

SAFETY CUT OUT
External cut out switches are a competition requirement, allowing outsiders to switch off the engine to prevent fire in an accident.

INTERIOR
Instrument layout is typical of sports cars of the period, and the stubby gear lever is handily placed for ease of operation. Getting in and out was not easy though, because of the low roof and high sills. Examples built for road rather than race use lacked the racing seats but were better trimmed and were still fun cars to drive.

ALPINE ACTION
The Alpine was most at home in rally conditions and won everything on the world stage, including a staggering 1–2–3 at the 1971 Monte Carlo Rally. The picture shows this featured car on the way to winning the Millers Oils RAC Rally Britannia in England in November 1994.

COMPACT SIZE
It is a compact little package just 44.5 in (1.16 m) high, 60 in (1.5 m) wide, and 151.5 in (3.85 m) in length.

Richard Tyzack
Mick Briggs

MILLERS OILS
RAC International Historic Rally of Great Britain

104

LEFT HOOKERS
Sadly for British enthusiasts, the Alpine A110 was only available in left-hand drive.

RENAULT ENGINES
Myriad engine options mirrored Renault's offerings but, in Alpine tune – by Gordini or Mignotet – it really flew. First models used Dauphine engines, progressing through R8 and R16 to R12 power. This 1967 car sports the 1442cc unit. Engines were slung behind the rear axle, with drive taken to the gearbox in front of the axle.

RENAULT ALPINE A110

Squat, nimble and slightly splay-footed on its wide tires, the Alpine looks purposeful from any angle. Climb into that tight cockpit and you soon feel part of the car; start it up and there is a delicious barrage of noise. On the move, the sting in the Alpine's tail is exhilarating as it buzzes behind you like an angry insect. The steering is light too, and the grip tenacious, but when it does let go that tail wags the dog in a big way. Its singular appearance remained intact through its production life, with only detail changes to the trim, which these days is hard to find.

NAME
Cars were known at first as Alpine Renaults, then became Renault Alpines as Renault influence grew.

TRUNK AJAR
Competition versions had engine covers fixed slightly open to aid cooling.

SPECIFICATIONS

MODEL Renault Alpine A110 Berlinette (1963–77)
PRODUCTION 8,203
BODY STYLE Two-seater sports coupe.
CONSTRUCTION Fiberglass body integral with tubular steel backbone chassis.
ENGINE Four cylinder, 13 options ranging from 956cc to 1796cc.
POWER OUTPUT 51–170 bhp (depending on engine size).
TRANSMISSION Four- and five-speed manual, rear-wheel drive.
SUSPENSION *Front:* Coil springs all around, with upper/lower control arms. *Rear:* Trailing radius arms and swing-axles.
BRAKES Four-wheel discs.
MAXIMUM SPEED 132 mph (212 km/h) 1595cc.
0–60 MPH (0–96 KM/H) 8.7 sec (1255cc)
A.F.C. 27 mpg

ROLLS-ROYCE *Silver Cloud*

IN 1965, $8,000 BOUGHT a large house, 11 Austin Minis, eight Triumph Heralds, or a Rolls-Royce Silver Cloud. The Rolls that everybody remembers was the ultimate conveyance of landed gentry and captains of industry. But, by the early '60s, Britain's social fabric was shifting. Princess Margaret announced she was to marry a divorcé, and aristocrats were so short of old money that they had to sell their crumbling country houses to celebrities and entrepreneurs. Against such social revolution the Cloud was a resplendent anachronism.

Each Cloud took three months to build, weighed over two tons, and had 12 coats of paint. The body sat on a mighty chassis and drum brakes were preferred because discs made a vulgar squealing noise. Beneath the hood slumbered straight six or V-8 engines, whose power output was never declared, but merely described as "sufficient." The Silver Cloud stands as a splendid monument to an old order of breeding and privilege.

OTHER MODELS

The Silver Cloud was replaced in 1966 by the more modern-looking, and monocoque-constructed, Silver Shadow — Rolls-Royce's most successful and profitable product.

R-R SILVER WRAITH II
Silver Wraith was meant to be a limo version of the Shadow with longer wheelbase and smaller rear window.

R-R SILVER SHADOW
The Shadow was more socially acceptable and technically superior, with disc brakes and hydraulic suspension.

GEAR SELECTOR

All Clouds were automatic, using a four-speed GM Hydramatic box which R-R used under license, but made itself.

DASHBOARD

A haven of peace in a troubled world, the Silver Cloud's magnificent interior was a veritable throne room, with only the finest walnut, leather, and Wilton carpeting.

WIDE REAR THREE-QUARTER PANEL WAS DESIGNED SO REAR OCCUPANTS COULD BE OBSCURED FROM PRYING EYES

ROLLS CLAIMED ITS CHROME PLATING WAS THICKER THAN ON ANY OTHER CAR IN THE WORLD

LEATHER COMFORT

The rear compartment might have looked accommodating, but Austin's little 1100 actually had more legroom.

QUALITY TOOLS

Every Cloud had a complete tool kit. So obsessed was Rolls-Royce with integrity that it tested every tool to destruction.

STANDARD WALNUT PICNIC TABLES WERE IDEAL FOR CHAMPAGNE AND CAVIAR PICNICS

EVERYTHING ABOUT THE CLOUD'S STYLING WAS ANTIQUE, LOOKING MORE LIKE A PIECE OF ARCHITECTURE THAN AN AUTOMOBILE

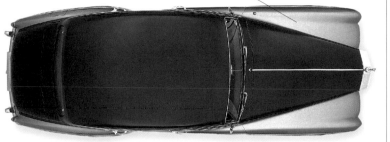

ENGINE

Cloud IIs and IIIs – aimed at the American market – had a 6230cc five-bearing V-8 power unit squeezed into a cramped engine bay. Cloud Is had a straight-six, 4.9-liter engine that could trace its origins back to before the Second World War.

BODYWORK

Standard steel bodies were made by the Pressed Steel Co. of Oxford, England, with the doors, hood, and trunk lid hand-finished in aluminum to save weight.

MASCOT

Perhaps the most famous car mascot in the world, the Spirit of Ecstasy graced a German silver patrician radiator shell that took several men five hours to polish.

THE FRONT FENDERS LOOKED AS IF THEY WERE SEPARATE FROM THE REST OF THE BODY

DEEPLY RESISTANT TO CHANGE, ROLLS-ROYCE MADE THE CLOUD'S HOOD OPEN SIDEWAYS IN THE BEST PREWAR TRADITION

MASCOT WAS ATTACHED BY A SPRING AND WIRE TO DETER SOUVENIR-HUNTERS

— THE NOUVEAU ROLLER —

Launched in 1955, styled like Big Ben, and with Stone Age mechanicals, the Silver Cloud was old before its time.

THE CLOUD I had a venerable straight-six 4.9-liter engine (conceived as early as 1938), heavy separate chassis, drum brakes, and no power steering. Its postwar engineering survived until the end of the decade, when Rolls was forced to pay lip service to modernity and exchange its ancient six for a V-8 and make power steering standard. Cloud IIs ran until 1962, when the car enjoyed its first major facelift – a lowered hood line and radiator shell,

with the addition of twin headlights as a concession to the all-important American market. But, for those who thought the Cloud's architecture was a bit flamboyant, there was the more discreet Bentley S-Series. At $250 less than the Cloud, it was identical, apart from the round-shouldered radiator, hubcaps, and labeling. But even the Bentley's self-conscious restraint could not protect it from a changing world.

ADVERTISEMENT FOR 1965 ROLLS-ROYCE SILVER CLOUD

ROLLS-ROYCE
Silver Cloud

MAX HEADROOM
The roofline was high in the best limousine tradition. Rear passengers had enough room to wear top hats.

DOORS WERE SECURED BY THE HIGHEST QUALITY YALE LOCKS

ROMAN NUMERALS WERE CHOSEN FOR THE CLOUD III SCRIPT TO LEND AN AIR OF DIGNITY

EEL 800C

GB

Previously, Royces had been driven by chauffeurs, but the Cloud was one of the first Rollers to be driven by owners. In the early '60s, a British film called *Man at the Top* was released, featuring a new breed of thrusting executive at the wheel of a Regal Red Cloud III. The film showed him driving the car himself, filling it up with gas, even breaking down and picking up hitchhikers. At roughly the same time, John Lennon decided to give his Phantom a psychedelic paint job. Both these events triggered a huge change in public perception of the Silver Cloud. It instantly slipped a social rung, and it was new rather than

JOHN LENNON AND HIS PSYCHEDELIC R-R PHANTOM

inherited money that now prized Rolls-Royces from showrooms.

By the late '60s the Cloud, looking like a prodigious antique, fell rapidly from grace and could be bought from downmarket car dealers for a few thousand dollars. In the '70s, many met with a low-rent end, stripped of

their haughty Edwardian dignity, whitewashed, ribboned, and harnessed into service as wedding workhorses.

NEW IMPROVED

When the Cloud II was unveiled in 1962, one magazine saw the changes as "more power, more passenger space, better lighting and easier steering."

ON THE VERY LAST CLOUDS, THE REAR-VIEW MIRROR MOUNTING WAS MOVED FROM THE DASHBOARD TO THE ROOF LINING

TURN SIGNALS WERE MOVED FROM THE FOGLIGHT TO THE FRONT FENDER ON THE CLOUD III

150-WATT 5.25-IN (14-CM) LUCAS DOUBLE HEADLIGHTS WERE NECESSITATED BY NORTH AMERICAN SAFETY REQUIREMENTS

SAAB 99 Turbo

EVERY DECADE OR SO, one car comes along that overhauls accepted wisdom. In 1978, the British motoring magazine *Autocar* wrote, "this car was so unpredictably thrilling that the adrenaline started to course again, even in our hardened arteries." They had just road-tested a Saab 99 Turbo. Saab took all other car manufacturers by surprise when it announced the world's first turbocharged family car, which promptly went on to be the first "blown" car to win a World Championship rally.

Developed from the fuel-injected EMS model, the Turbo had Bosh-K-Jetronic fuel injection, a strengthened gearbox, and a Garrett turbocharger. A hundred prototypes were built and between them they covered 2.9 million miles (4.8 million km) before Saab was happy with their prodigy. Priced at $9,998 it was expensive, but there was nothing to equal its urge. Rare, esoteric, and historically significant, the mold-breaking 99 Turbo is an undisputed card-carrying classic.

ENGINE
The five-bearing, chain-driven single overhead cam engine was an 1985cc eight-valve, water-cooled four cylinder unit, with low compression pistons and altered cam timing. The result was 145 bhp and 122 mph (196 km/h).

RALLY BREAKTHROUGH
Stig Blomqvist won the 1977 Swedish Rally and the next year gave the 99 Turbo some serious exposure. He made a thunderous run down Esgair Dafydd in Wales on the first televised rally sprint – with a punctured front tire.

RARE TWO-DOOR
Hatchback three-door versions are the most common 99 Turbo incarnation. The faster and lighter two-door cars are much rarer, with only 1,000 made.

BODYSHELL
Shell is stiff and light and a full four-seater. It is remarkably durable, too, with factory underseal and cavity wax injection.

INTERIOR

1970s interior looks tacky now, with red velour seats and imitation wood. Buyers did get a leather steering wheel and heated driver's seat.

SPECIFICATIONS

MODEL Saab 99 Turbo (1978–80)
PRODUCTION 10,607
BODY STYLES Two/three/five-door, four-seater sports sedan.
CONSTRUCTION Monocoque steel body shell.
ENGINE 1985cc four-cylinder turbo.
POWER OUTPUT 145 bhp at 5000 rpm.
TRANSMISSION Front-wheel drive four/five-speed manual with automatic option.
SUSPENSION Independent front double wishbone and coil springs, rear beam axle, coil springs, and Bilstein shock absorbers.
BRAKES Four-wheel power-assisted discs.
MAXIMUM SPEED 122 mph (196 km/h)
0–60 MPH (0–96 KM/H) 8.2 sec
0–100 MPH (0–161 KM/H) 19.8 sec
A.F.C. 26 mpg

STYLING

Never as visually threatening as the Audi Quattro (see pages 32–35), the 99 is pleasantly rounded but unremarkable.

SAAB 99 TURBO

The car appeared at the 1978 Frankfurt Show as a three-door EMS. The body has a certain business-like presence, helped by specially made Inca alloys designed to mimic the shape of turbocharger blades, standard front and rear spoilers, and a sliding steel sunroof. Colors were chosen to be deliberately assertive – only red and black. The chassis was a peach, with taut high-speed steering, four-wheel discs, minimal understeer, and incredible levels of grip. Between 40 mph (65 km/h) and 100 mph (161 km/h) it accelerated faster than any other four-seater of its day.

TURBOCHARGER

The turbo is reliable, but its Achilles heel is a couple of seconds lag on hard acceleration.

HANDLING

The 99 Turbos were poised. Crisp handling came from front-wheel drive, with prodigious adhesion courtesy of 195/60 Pirelli P6s.

COMMON PARTS

Turbo shared most parts with the Saab 99 EMS Sedan. But camshaft valves and pistons were uprated for performance and durability.

SUSPENSION

Independent front suspension was the usual wishbone and coil spring setup, with a dead beam axle at the rear.

SIMCA *Aronde Plein Ciel*

BY APING AMERICAN 1950s styling trends and regular face-lifts, Simca metamorphosed from a company building Fiats under license into France's top privately owned car maker. And the Aronde was the car that turned the tide. Brainchild of Henri-Théodore Pigozzi, the comely Aronde was the first popular French car to have postwar transatlantic style. Over a 12-year lifespan, 1.3 million Arondes were sold. By 1955 it had put Simca ahead of both Peugeot and Citroën.

With bodywork by Facel of Facel Vega fame *(see pages 94–97)*, the Aronde was an affordable *haute couture* confection based on run-of-the-mill components. 1958 saw a complete US-influenced redesign, with engine names such as "Flash Special." Even so, the Aronde is a quaint hybrid that stands as a testament to the penetrating influence of 1950s Detroit design.

(see pages 94–97)

OTHER MODELS

Plein Ciel Coupe and Ocean Convertible were rebodied Arondes, available up until 1963, when the range disappeared in favor of the 1300 and 1500 models.

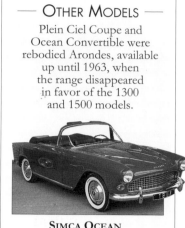

SIMCA OCEAN
The 1957 Ocean bears a deliberate resemblance to the Ford Thunderbird (see pages 116–17).

(see pages 116–17)

DASHBOARD
The interior is pure Pontiac pastiche, with no less than six different types of plastic – the Aronde's cabin is a riot of two-tone synthetic.

THE ARONDE NAME
A delicate birdlike thing, Aronde is French for swallow.

ENGINE
"Flash Special" had a four-cylinder, 57 bhp pushrod engine bored out to 1288cc, with a Solex carburetor. Four-speed manual gearbox had obligatory American-style column shifter.

WHEEL EMBELLISHMENT
Full-width polished chrome hub-caps and wheel trims were an American fad, embraced by European imitators.

WHAT'S IN A NAME?
Plein Ciel ("open air") motif accords with the airy cockpit and generous glass area.

SPECIFICATIONS

MODEL Simca Aronde Plein Ciel
(1957–62)
PRODUCTION 170,070 (Facel-bodied
Arondes)
BODY STYLES Cabriolet or hardtop
sports coupe.
CONSTRUCTION Steel body over
separate steel chassis frame.
ENGINE 1288cc four-cylinder pushrod.
POWER OUTPUT 57 bhp at 4800 rpm
("Flash Special").
TRANSMISSION Four-speed manual.
SUSPENSION *Front:* Independent by
coil springs and wishbones.
Rear: Semielliptic leaf springs.
BRAKES Four-wheel drums.
MAXIMUM SPEED 87 mph (140 km/h)
0–60 MPH (0–96 KM/H) 15.6 sec
A.F.C. 28 mpg

SIMCA ARONDE PLEIN CIEL

The Facel Vega connection is unmistakable,
especially in the steep wraparound windshield
and bubblelike cockpit. The finned rear,
flowing script on the front fenders, liberal
use of chrome, and raked rear lights would
not look out of place on a 1957 Chevrolet.
The moustachelike, eggcrate grille and
recessed parking lights lend the
Aronde an air of class and quality.

HANDLING
*The Aronde handled as well as it looked but, because it did
not have a smooth ride, the French motoring press disapproved.
Despite conventional underpinnings, it felt sporting with positive,
if unpowered, brakes, and a firmly tied-down chassis.*

COLOR
*The Aronde was
available in 22
different two-tone
color schemes.*

SEATING
*Despite a sloping
rear roof line, the
Aronde was just
about a four
seater.*

REFINEMENTS
*"Flash Special" engine had punchier
low-range torque, stronger crankshaft
and big-end journals, plus an improved
lubrication system.*

LUGGAGE CAPACITY
*The elongated rear meant that
the trunk was surprisingly ample,
even though the sill meant
loading baggage required some
serious lifting.*

MODERNISM
*Flush-fitting, lockable gas
cap-flap was surprisingly
avant garde for 1958.*

SUNBEAM *Tiger*

THERE WAS NOTHING NEW about placing an American V-8 into a pert English chassis. After all, that is exactly what Carroll Shelby did with the AC Ace to create the awesome Cobra *(see pages 22–23)*. When Rootes in Britain decided to do the same with its Sunbeam Alpine, it also commissioned Shelby to produce a prototype and although Rootes already had close links with Chrysler, the American once again opted for a Ford V-8. To cope with the 4.2-liter engine, the Alpine's chassis and suspension were beefed up to create the fearsome Tiger late in 1964. In 1967, the Tiger II arrived with an even bigger 4.7-liter Ford V-8, but this was a brief swan song as Chrysler took control of Rootes and was not going to sanction a car powered by a Ford engine. Often dubbed "the poor man's Cobra," the Tiger is still a lot of fun to grab by the tail.

SPECIFICATIONS

MODEL Sunbeam Tiger (1964–67)
PRODUCTION MkI, 1964–67, 6,496; MkII, 6,083
BODY STYLE Two-plus-two roadster.
CONSTRUCTION Steel monocoque.
ENGINE Ford V-8 4261cc or 4727cc.
POWER OUTPUT 164 bhp at 4400 rpm (4261cc), 200 bhp at 4400 rpm (4727cc).
TRANSMISSION Four-speed manual.
SUSPENSION Coil springs and wishbones at front, rigid axle on semielliptic leaf springs at rear.
BRAKES Power-assisted front discs, rear drums.
MAXIMUM SPEED 117 mph (188 km/h) (4261cc), 125 mph (201 km/h) (4727cc)
0–60 MPH (0-96 KM/H) 9 sec (4261cc), 7.5 sec (4727cc).
A.F.C. 20 mpg

SUNBEAM V8

Mk1 SCRIPT SAID 260 FOR CUBIC INCHES; FOR Mk2, V-8 SAID IT ALL

POWERED BY FORD
The first Tigers used 4.2-liter Ford V-8 engines, replaced later – as shown here – by a 4727cc version, the famous 289. It was not, however, in the same state of tune as those fitted to the Shelby Cobras.

SUNBEAM TIGER
MkII Tiger had an eggcrate grille to distinguish it from the Alpine. Earlier cars were less easy to tell apart: a chrome strip along the Tiger's side was the giveaway, plus discreet labeling.

ADAPTED ALPINE
Alpine chassis and suspension had to be beefed up to cope with the weight and power of the V-8. Modifications included heavy-duty rear axle, sturdier suspension, and chassis stiffening.

STEERING
The Tiger's steering system was rack-and-pinion, as the normal Alpine recirculating-ball gear would not fit with the V-8 engine. Wood-rim steering wheel was standard.

HOTHOUSE
Tigers often suffered overheating, which was not surprising as the Alpine engine bay originally accommodated a 1494cc four-cylinder engine.

RACE HOOD
Race and rally Tigers had improved air-flow with slightly raised hood.

Sunbeam

OPC 53E

TOYOTA *2000 GT*

TOYOTA'S 2000GT is more than a "might have been" – it is a "should have been." A pretty coupe with equipment and performance to match its good looks, it predated the rival Datsun 240Z *(see pages 84–87)*, which was a worldwide sales success. The Toyota failed to reach much more than 300 sales, partly because of low capacity at its Yamaha factory, but even more because the car was launched before Japan was geared to export. That left only a domestic market, largely uneducated in the finer qualities of sporting cars, to make what they could of the offering. As a design exercise, the 2000GT proved that the Japanese motor industry had reached the stage where its products rivaled the best in the world. It is just a pity that more people were not able to appreciate this fine car at first hand.

FASHIONABLE THREE-SPOKE WOOD-RIM WHEEL WAS LINKED TO PRECISE RACK-AND-PINION STEERING

SPEEDOMETER SHOWED AN OPTIMISTIC 160 MPH (257 KM/H)

SHORT-THROW WOODEN-TOP GEAR LEVER OPERATED A FIVE-SPEED, ALL-SYNCHROMESH BOX

ROLE MODEL
The 2000GT's snug cockpit featured a walnut veneer instrument panel, sporty wheel, stubby gear lever, form-fitting seats, and deep footwells. The eight-track stereo is a nice period touch.

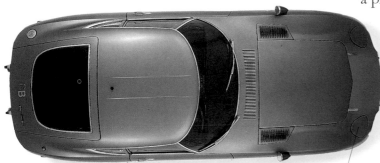

YAMAHA ENGINE
The engine was a triple-carburetor six-cylinder Yamaha, which provided 150 bhp. A competition version boosted output to 200 bhp.

TOYOTA 2000GT
The design of the Toyota 2000 GT is based on an earlier prototype penned by Albrecht Goertz, creator of the BMW 507 and Datsun 240Z. When Nissan rejected the design, it was offered to Toyota and evolved into the 2000 GT.

LIGHTING
Unusual combination of hightech pop-up and fixed headlights gives the front a fussy look.

TOPLESS STAR
A modified convertible starred with Sean Connery in the James Bond film, You Only Live Twice.

SIDE BOXES
Panel on the right conceals the battery; on the left is the air cleaner. This arrangement enabled the hood to be kept low.

SPECIFICATIONS
MODEL Toyota 2000GT (1965–68)
PRODUCTION 337
BODY STYLE Two-door sports coupe.
CONSTRUCTION Steel body on backbone frame.
ENGINE Yamaha inline DOHC six, 1988cc.
POWER OUTPUT 150 bhp at 6600 rpm.
TRANSMISSION Five-speed manual.
SUSPENSION Fully independent by coil springs and wishbones all around.
BRAKES Hydraulically operated discs all around.
MAXIMUM SPEED 128 mph (206 km/h)
0–60 MPH (0–96 KM/H) 10.5 sec
A.F.C. 31 mpg

TRIUMPH *TR2*

IF EVER THERE WAS A SPORTS CAR that epitomized the British bulldog spirit it must be the Triumph TR2. It is as true Brit as a car can be, born in the golden age of British sports cars, but aimed at the lucrative American market, where the Jaguar XK120 *(see pages 134–35)* had already scored a hit. At the 1952 Earl's Court Motor Show in London, the Healey 100 had been transformed overnight into the Austin-Healey, but the "Triumph Sports" prototype's debut at the same show was less auspicious. It was a brave attempt to create an inexpensive sports car from a company with no recent track record in this market segment.

With its dumpy *derriere*, the prototype was no oil painting; as for handling, incoming chief tester Ken Richardson described it as a "bloody deathtrap." An all-new chassis, revised rear, and other modifications saw Standard-Triumph's new TR2 emerge into a winner at the Geneva Motor Show in March 1953. No conventional beauty certainly, but a bluff-fronted car that was a worthy best-of-breed contender in the budget sports car arena, and the cornerstone of a stout sporting tradition.

— OTHER MODELS —
The TR2 began a fine tradition of sporting TRs that was only eventually let down by the controversially styled, wedge-shaped TR7 of the 1970s.

TRIUMPH TR3
The TR3 was the first development, with more power and front disc-brakes on later cars. External door handles and lift-off hardtop were options.

TRIUMPH TR3A
The most obvious difference from the TR3 was the full-width grille. The TR3A was produced from 1957–61.

ENGINE
Legend says that the TR2 engine came from a Ferguson tractor – in fact it and the tractor were developed from a Standard Vanguard engine. The twin-carburetor TR2 was reduced to just under two liters.

LIKE THE AUSTIN-HEALEY'S, THE TR CHASSIS RUNS UNDER THE AXLE AT THE REAR

STOCK DESIGN
There is nothing revolutionary in the design of the pressed-steel chassis; a simple ladder with X-shaped bracing. It was a transformation, though, from the prototype's original chassis.

SPORTING PROWESS
The car on these pages was a "factory built" competition car, pictured here with its driver, Ken Richardson.

THE TR2 CHASSIS WAS PRAISED FOR ITS TAUTNESS AND FINE ROAD MANNERS

FOR RACING
The TR2 came with small holes drilled in the cowl to fit racing windshields.

TRIUMPH TR2
The design, by Walter Belgrove, was a far cry from the razor-edged Triumph Renown and Mayflower sedans that he had previously styled. If not beautiful, the TR2 has chunky good looks with a bluff, honest demeanor. Unusual recessed grille presents a slightly grumpy disposition, but the low front helped the car to top 100 mph (161 km/h). Equipment was spartan – you did not even get external door handles.

INTERIOR
Stubby gear lever and full instrumentation gave TR a sports car feel. The steering wheel was large, but the low door accommodates vintage "elbows out" driving style.

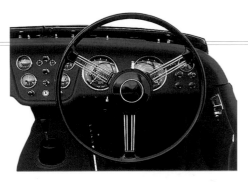

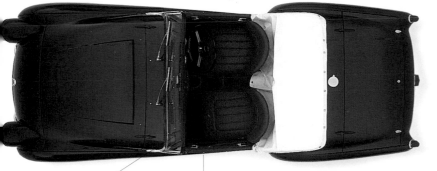

WINDSHIELD
It looks flat, but the windshield actually has a slight curve; this prevents it from bowing at speed, which is what the prototype's flat screen did.

LOW-CUT DOORS
You could reach out over the doors and touch the road. External door handles only arrived with the TR3A of 1957.

LUGGAGE SPACE
The prototype had a stubby tail with exposed spare wheel; the production model had a real opening trunk and locker below for spare wheel.

OVC 276

SPECIFICATIONS

MODEL Triumph TR2 (1953–55)
PRODUCTION 8,628
BODY STYLE Two-door, two-seater sports car.
CONSTRUCTION Pressed-steel chassis with separate steel body.
ENGINE Four-cylinder, overhead valve, 1991cc, twin SU carburetors.
POWER OUTPUT 90 bhp at 4800 rpm.
TRANSMISSION Four-speed manual with Laycock overdrive option, initially on top gear only, then on top three (1955).
SUSPENSION Coil spring and wishbone at front, live rear axle with semielliptic leaf springs.
BRAKES Lockheed hydraulic, drums.
MAXIMUM SPEED 105 mph (169 km/h)
0–60 MPH (0–96 KM/H) 12 sec
A.F.C. 30+mpg

SPORTY TRIUMPH
The Triumph sporting tradition was firmly established when TR2s came first and second in the 1954 RAC Rally.

WHEEL CHOICE
The first TR2s came with pressed-steel disc wheels, complete with chrome hubcaps, but most customers preferred the option of wire wheels, which were considered much sportier.

OVC 276

TRIUMPH *TR6*

TO MOST TR TRADITIONALISTS this is where the TR tale ended, the final flourishing of the theme before the TR7 betrayed an outstanding tradition. In the mid-1960s, the TR range was on a roll and the TR6 continued the upward momentum, outselling all earlier offerings. Crisply styled, with chiseled-chin good looks and carrying over the 2.5-liter six-cylinder engine of the TR5, the TR6 in early fuel-injected form heaved you along with 150 galloping horses. This was as hairy chested as the TR got. It was a handful, with some critics carping that, like the big Healeys, its power outstripped its poise. But that just made it more fun to drive.

OTHER MODELS

The TR6 was a natural progression from the original TR2; the body evolved from the TR4/5, the 2.5-liter six-cylinder engine from the TR5.

TRIUMPH TR4
The TR4 of 1961 was the first TR to carry all-new Michelotti-styled bodywork, updated by Karmann into the Triumph TR6.

TRIUMPH TR5
In 1967 the TR5 became the first of the six-cylinder TRs, its 2.5-liter engine going on to power the TR6.

ENGINE
The first engines, as on this 1972 car, produced 150 bhp, but public pressure for something more well-mannered resulted in a 125 bhp version in 1973.

AMERICAN VERSIONS HAD CARBURETORS RATHER THAN FUEL INJECTION AS HERE

INTERIOR
The interior is still traditional but more refined than earlier TRs. Yet with its big dials, wooden dash, and short-throw gear knob, its character is still truly sporting.

EASY ACCESS
Big, wide-opening doors gave easy access to the TR6, a long cry from the tiny doors of the TR2 and TR3.

FAT WHEELS
Wider wheels were a TR6 feature, as was the antiroll bar at the front.

POWER DROP
Revised injection metering and reprofiled camshaft reduced power from 1973; US carburetor versions were more sluggish (and thirstier) still, but sold many more.

SALES FIGURES
British sales stopped in February 1975, but continued in the US until July 1976. Ten times as many TR6s were exported as remained in Britain.

SPECIFICATIONS

MODEL Triumph TR6 (1969–76)
PRODUCTION 94,619
BODY STYLE Two-seat convertible.
CONSTRUCTION Ladder-type chassis with integral steel body.
ENGINE In-line six-cylinder, 2498CC, fuel-injection (carburetors in US).
POWER OUTPUT 152 bhp at 5500 rpm (1969–1973), 125 bhp at 5250 rpm (1973–1975), 104 bhp at 4500 rpm (US).
TRANSMISSION Manual four-speed with optional overdrive on third and top.
SUSPENSION Independent by coil springs all around; wishbones at front, swing-axles & semitrailing arms at rear.
BRAKES *Front:* discs; *Rear:* drums.
MAXIMUM SPEED 119 mph (191 km/h, 150 bhp), 107 mph (172 km/h, US)
0–60 MPH (0–96 KM/H) 8.2 sec (150 bhp); 9.0 sec (125 bhp); 10.6 sec (104 bhp).
0–100 MPH (0–161 KM/H) 29 sec
A.F.C. 25 mpg

TRIUMPH TR6

There is an obvious difference between the TR4/5 and the later TR6, restyled by Karmann; sharper, cleaner lines not only looked more modern, but also gave more luggage space. The chopped-off tail was an aerodynamic aid. One-piece hardtop was available as an option, and was more practical than the two-piece seen on earlier models. The TR6's good looks, and a long production run, made this model the biggest selling of all TR models.

ENGINE NOISE
Deep-throated burble is still a TR6 come-on.

ROOMY INTERIOR
The cockpit was more spacious than earlier TRs, providing excellent driving position from comfortable seats.

MERGER
The TR6 was launched just after the 1968 merger of Leyland and BMC.

BRITISH LEYLAND

VOLKSWAGEN *Beetle Karmann*

BEETLE PURISTS MAY WAX LYRICAL about the first-of-breed
purity of the original split rear-screen Bugs and the oval
window versions of 1953 to 1957, but there is one Beetle
that everybody wants – the Karmann-built Cabriolet.
Its development followed that of the sedans through
a bewildering series of modifications, but it always stood
apart. With its hood retracted into a bulging bustle, this Beetle
was not only cheerful, but chic too, a classless cruiser equally at home on
Beverly Hills boulevards, Cannes, and the Kings Road. The final incarnation of the
Karmann convertible represents the ultimate development of the Beetle theme,
with the peppiest engine and improved suspension and handling. This model is
from the final year of manufacture, the most refined Bug of all, but still true to its
original concept. It's strange to think that once, long ago, the disarming
unburstable Bug was a vehicle of fascist propaganda, branded with the slogan of the
Hitler Youth, "Strength through Joy." Today, its strength has given joy to millions
of motorists as the undisputed people's car.

OTHER MODELS

The Beetle was subjected to a
bewildering 78,000-plus
modifications through its
production life, but somehow
managed to retain its
essential character.

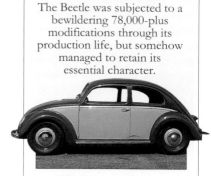

VW BEETLE SEDAN
*This 1131cc Beetle from
1947 shows how the myriad
modifications amount to
minor detailing only.*

DASHBOARD

The Beetle is still bare, its dash dominated
by the one minimal instrument; on this
model the speedometer incorporates a
fuel gauge. It also has a padded dash,
replacing the original metal version.

CURVED "PANORAMIC"
WINDSHIELD REPLACED
FLAT GLASS IN 1972

FOUR-SPOKE STEERING WHEEL
IS NOT AS CLASSIC AS EARLIER
THIN-RIMMED TWO- AND
THREE-SPOKED WHEELS

PRODUCTION PLANS

Before Karmann chopped the lid off the
Bug, there had been plans for a Beetle-
based roadster which in some ways
foreshadowed later custom
Bugs. The prototypes inspired
coachbuilders Joseph Hebmüller
& Sons to build a short-lived
roadster, but just 696 were built
before a factory fire ended
the project. That
opened the door for
the four-seater
Karmann
convertible.

ORIGINAL 16-IN (40-CM)
WHEELS WERE REDUCED
TO 15 IN (38 CM) IN 1952.
FRONT DISC BRAKES WERE
INTRODUCED IN 1966

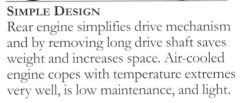

SIMPLE DESIGN

Rear engine simplifies drive mechanism and by removing long drive shaft saves weight and increases space. Air-cooled engine copes with temperature extremes very well, is low maintenance, and light.

THE WORLD RECORD FOR A BEETLE ENGINE SWAP IS JUST OVER THREE MINUTES

ENGINE

You can always tell that a Beetle is on its way before it comes into sight thanks to the distinctive buzzing of the air-cooled, horizontally opposed four-cylinder engine. Its capacity grew from 1131cc to 1584cc and the engines have a deserved reputation as robust, high-revving units.

FIRST CARS HAD FLAG TURN SIGNALS, THEN LIGHTS WERE FENDER-MOUNTED, AND IN SOME CASES PLACED WITHIN FRONT BUMPERS

SPECIFICATIONS

MODEL VW Beetle Karmann Cabriolet (1972–80)
PRODUCTION 331,847 (all Karmann Cabriolets from 1949 to 1980).
BODY STYLE Four-seater cabriolet.
CONSTRUCTION Steel-bodied, separate chassis/body.
ENGINE Rear-mounted, air-cooled flat four, 1584cc.
POWER OUTPUT 50 bhp at 4000 rpm.
TRANSMISSION Four-speed manual.
SUSPENSION *Front:* independent MacPherson strut; *Rear:* independent trailing arm and twin torsion bars.
BRAKES *Front:* disc; *Rear:* drums.
MAXIMUM SPEED 82.4 mph (133 km/h)
0–60 MPH (0–96 KM/H) 18 sec
A.F.C. 24–30 mpg

ONE-MODEL POLICY

The one-model policy that VW adopted in its early years was successful while Beetle sales soared, but by 1967 Fiat had overtaken VW as Europe's biggest car manufacturer. VW's new models had failed to displace the Beetle and it was not until 1974 that the Golf and Polo revived the company's fortunes.

ON ALL CABRIOLETS THE ENGINE BREATHES THROUGH SLOTS ON THE ENGINE COVER

THE WORLD BEATER

The VW Beetle is one bug they can't find a cure for. Hitler's vision of a "people's car" has become just that and more — the world car to beat all other contenders.

PRODUCED CONTINUOUSLY since 1945, every Beetle that rolls off the remaining Mexican and Brazilian production lines sets a new production record that is unlikely ever to be beaten. With production running as high as 1,000 a day, the Beetle is a 21-million-plus world beater.

But the Beetle had a long and painful birth. In the early 1930s, Hitler's vision for mass motoring began to take shape when he entrusted Dr. Ferdinand Porsche with the project.

1935 TATRA 77

Both Hitler and Porsche were influenced by the fabulous streamlined Czechoslovakian Tatras. Hitler, a keen automobile enthusiast, had ridden in Tatras on political tours of Czechoslovakia. He had often dined with Tatra designer Hans Ledwinka. After one of these dinner-table conversations Hitler is reported to have remarked to Porsche, "This is the car for my roads." Of Ledwinka, Porsche was reported as saying, "Well, sometimes I looked over his shoulder and

VOLKSWAGEN
Beetle Karmann

FRESH AIR
With the hood raised, the Karmann cabriolet is a bit claustrophobic, but it comes into its own as a timeless top down cruiser that is still a full four-seater.

CABRIOLETS LIKE THIS CALIFORNIA-REGISTERED CAR ARE A MAINSTAY OF SURFING CULTURE ALL OVER THE WORLD

KARMANN

COACHBUILDER
As well as the Beetle convertible, Karmann also built the Type 1 VW Karmann-Ghia, a two-seater based on Beetle running gear.

MANY LATER DESIGN CHANGES LIKE THESE "ELEPHANT FOOTPRINT" REAR LIGHT CLUSTERS WERE DRIVEN BY US REGULATIONS

CALIFORNIA
1RWL494

sometimes he looked over mine." There is also no doubt that the Beetle bore a marked resemblance to earlier Tatras, both in shape and concept. In fact, after the war a large out-of-court settlement was made to Tatra. Although the Tatra influenced the Beetle, it scrved as a departure point for a unique car, developed by Porsche and his team into a machine-age artifact. Some 630 or so Beetles had been made before hostilities disrupted production. Back then, Beetles were propaganda wagons, too, named KdF-Wagen, after the slogan of the Hitler Youth, "*Kraft durch Freude*," which

HITLER AND
FERDINAND PORSCHE

means strength through joy. When production resumed in 1945 the Beetle, now a more friendly Volkswagen, gathered an irresistible momentum, notching up 10,000 sales

in 1946, 100,000 by 1950 and a million by 1955. In 1972, it overtook the Model T Ford's production record of 15 million. Today, the amazing story of the world's most popular car is not yet over.

BEETLE PRODUCTION LINE

STATE OF PLAY
Although the Beetle is still in production, Karmann stopped making the elegant cabriolet in 1980. In 1994, combined daily Mexican-Brazilian Beetle production exceeded 1,000 on a good day.

REAR VISION WITH THE HOOD RAISED IS NOT MUCH BETTER THAN ON EARLY SPLIT-SCREEN AND OVAL-WINDOWED MODELS

FROM 1967, THICKER SO-CALLED EUROPA BUMPERS WERE FITTED

VOLKSWAGEN *GOLF GTi*

EVERY DECADE or so a really great car comes along. In the Seventies it was the Golf. Like the Beetle *(see pages 212–15)*, the Golf was a car designed to make deep inroads into world markets. Yet while the Beetle evolved into the perfect consumer product, the Golf was designed and planned to be one. The idea of a "hot" Golf was not part of the grand design. It came about almost accidentally, the brainchild of a group of enthusiastic VW engineers who worked weekends and evenings, impressing the management so much that it became an official project in May 1975.

Despite its extreme youth, the Golf GTi is as much a classic as any Ferrari. Its claim to fame is that it spawned a traffic jam of imitators and brought an affordable mix of performance, handling, and reliability to the mass-market buyer. Few other cars have penetrated the suburban psyche as deeply as the original VW Golf GTi.

INTERIOR
With its dark headlining and trim, the cockpit may be austere, but features like the golfball-shaped gear lever add a touch of humor.

ALUMINUM
Much admired cross-spoke BBS aluminum wheels were both factory and aftermarket options.

SIMPLE FRONT DESIGN
Factory spec Golfs were understated, with just a GTi label and a thin red stripe around the grille. Owners who wanted to show off would bolt on aftermarket front spoilers and twin headlight kits.

VOLKSWAGEN GOLF GTi
GTi suspension was lower and firmer than the standard Golf, with wider tires and wheels. Front disc brakes were ventilated along with a larger motor, but keeping standard drum brakes at the rear was a big mistake – early Golfs were very disinclined to stop.

REAR VIEW
The Giugiaro-designed Mk I Golf was neat, roomy, and compact, admirably predicting the then burgeoning 1970s craze for hatchbacks.

SPECIFICATIONS
MODEL Volkswagen Golf GTi MkI (1976–83)
PRODUCTION 400,000
BODY STYLE All steel sedan
CONSTRUCTION All steel/ monocoque body.
ENGINE Four-cylinder 1588cc/1781cc.
POWER OUTPUT 110–112 bhp at 6100 rpm.
TRANSMISSION Four- or five-speed manual.
SUSPENSION *Front:* Independent; *Rear:* Semi-independent trailing arm.
BRAKES *Front:* disc; *Rear:* drum.
MAXIMUM SPEED 111 mph (179 km/h)
0–60 MPH (0–96 KM/H) 8.7 sec
0–100 MPH (0–161 KM/H) 18.2 sec
A.F.C. 29 mpg

ENGINE
Easily capable of 150,000 miles (240,000 km) in its stride, the 1588cc four-cylinder power unit breathed through Bosch K-Jetronic fuel injection, pushing out 110 bhp. Later cars had five-speed gearbox and more willing 1781cc engines.

WIPERS
Driver's windshield wiper had a small aerodynamic wing. The faster you went, the more wind pressure pushed the wiper down onto the glass.

ENGINE SUCCESS
Initially, only 5,000 GTis were to be built for racing homologation, but the silky smooth engine and poised handling meant that sales went crazy.

SPOILER
Standard Golfs had a tiny front spoiler. This larger after-market BBS add-on makes the car look lower and meaner.

VOLVO *P1800*

THERE HAS NEVER BEEN a Volvo like the P1800, for this was a one-time flight of fancy by the sober Swedes, who already had a reputation for building sensible sedans. As a sports car the P1800 certainly looked stunning. Every sensuous curve and lean line suggests athletic prowess. But under that sharp exterior were most of the mechanicals of the Volvo Amazon, a worthy workhorse sedan. Consequently, the P1800 was no road-burner; it just about had the edge on the MGB *(see page 175)*, but only in a straight line. Another competitor, the E-Type Jag *(see pages 140–43)*, was launched in 1961, the same year as the P1800 and at almost the same price, but there the comparison ends. The P1800 did have style, though, and its other virtues were pure Volvo – strength, durability, and reliability. These combined to create something quite singular in the sporting idiom – a practical sports car.

LUGGAGE
As you would expect, the sensible sports car has a decent-sized trunk, although the spare wheel lies flat on the trunk floor and takes up space.

INTERIOR
The instrumentation has a real flight-deck feel; revs, oil pressure, and oil temperature are all displayed on a well laid-out dash. Although you are sitting low to the floor, the leather seats are comfortable.

SUPPORTING ROLE
The P1800 is eternally typecast as the "Saint Volvo" after appearing alongside Roger Moore in the long running television series, *The Saint*. The producers actually wanted to use the "sexiest car of 1961", the E-Type Jag; Jaguar declined and Volvo leapt at the chance. Roger Moore drove a P1800 off screen for many years.

JENSEN'S SIGNATURE
Early cars like this were built in Britain by Jensen, identified by Volvo label on rear pillar.

STEERING
Big, upright vertical wheel looks sporty, with twin spokes seemingly drilled for lightness.

COW HORNS
Attractive cow-horn bumpers became simpler, straight affairs in 1964.

TWO-PLUS-TWO COUPE
Space for two children only in the back, or one adult sitting sideways; rear seat folds down flat to increase load capacity.

SPECIFICATIONS

MODEL Volvo P1800 (1961–73)
PRODUCTION 47,707 (all models)
BODY STYLES Two-plus-two fixed-head coupe; sports wagon (P1800ES).
CONSTRUCTION Unit steel body/chassis.
ENGINE 1778cc straight four, overhead valves; 1985cc from 1968–73.
POWER OUTPUT 100 bhp at 5,500 rpm (P1800); 124 bhp at 6,000 rpm (P1800E, P1800 ES).
TRANSMISSION Four-speed manual with overdrive/optional automatic.
SUSPENSION *Front:* independent coil-sprung with wishbones. *Rear:* rigid axle, coil-sprung, Panhard rod.
BRAKES Front discs, rear drums.
MAXIMUM SPEED 105 mph (169 km/h, P1800); 115 mph (P1800 E/ES).
0–60 MPH (0–96 KM/H) 9.7–13.2 sec
0–100 MPH (0–161 KM/H) 31.4–53 sec
A.F.C. 20–25 mpg

VOLVO P1800

Official Volvo history credits the award-winning design of the P1800 to Frua of Italy, but it is not as simple as that. In 1957 Volvo approached Ghia to style a two-plus-two coupe and the assignment fell to chief designer Pietro Frua. However, he walked out halfway through, set up his own studio in Turin, and tendered his own proposals. The chosen design was actually created by young Swede Pelle Petterson, then a trainee at Ghia. The Italian influences are obvious in the final form.

ROBUST ENGINE
Early cars had 1778cc four-cylinder units with twin SU carburetors, as shown here; the 1985cc unit came later, followed by electronic fuel injection.

SHORT, STUBBY LEVER GAVE POSITIVE, SHARP CHANGES THAT FELT TRULY SPORTING

SAFETY MEASURES
The P1800 had a padded dash and seat belts of Volvo's own design.

WHEELS
Stylized fake spokes identify this as an early P1800.

SUPER-TOUGH GEARBOX WITH EXCELLENT SYNCHROMESH

THE INNOVATORS

From ground-breaking design to heroic failure, the following figures have all played their part in the development of some of the classic cars included in this book.

COLIN CHAPMAN *(1928–1982)*
Son of an innkeeper, engineering graduate Colin Chapman founded the Norfolk Lotus company which produced fiberglass pocket rockets like the trend-setting 1960s Elite and Elan. Lotus won the World Championship and Constructors Championship twice running.

ANDRÉ CITROËN *(1878–1935)*
Known as the French Mr. Ford, André Citroën started producing silent-meshing chevron-toothed gear wheels and went on to build the legendary 2CV, Traction Avant, and DS. An innovator rather than an accountant, his company was taken over by Michelin in 1934 and he died a year later.

JOHN DELOREAN *(1925–)*
John Zachary DeLorean headed a business empire funded by $500 million of other people's money. His Belfast-built gullwing stainless steel sports car failed along with his company, leaving a paper trail of skulduggery. He was indicted in a $24 million cocaine sting and, after a 63 day hearing, was acquitted.

HARLEY EARL *(1893–1969)*
Harley Earl designed the Cadillac Eldorado, Chevrolet Corvette and Buick Skylark and gave the American car its chrome pomp and ceremony. As General Motors' Chief of Design, he was responsible for the shape of 50 million cars. Few men have had such an influence on man-made objects.

HARRY FERGUSON *(1884–1960)*
Eccentric, irascible and rude, Ferguson built plows and tractors and sued Ford for $9.25 million for infringement of patents. His greatest achievement was the incorporation of his four-wheel drive system into the Jensen FF, the world's first successful production four-wheel drive car.

ENZO FERRARI *(1898–1988)*
Known as *Il Commendatore*, Enzo Ferrari gave his name to one of the most emotive cars in the world. As well as making extraordinary cars, he could pick skillful racing drivers, like Ascari,

Fangio and Lauda. A silver-haired recluse in dark glasses, Ferrari was as passionate and charismatic as the cars he made.

DANTE GIACOSA *(1905–)*
One of Italy's most outstanding designers, Giacosa helped establish Fiat as an Italian national institution. Obsessed with the economies of scale, he came up with the Topolino of 1936, the 600 of 1955, and the 500 of 1957, the first very small cars to really be refined and the first to be free of the savage compromises of size and usability.

DONALD HEALEY *(1898–1988)*
Donald Healey, a sharply dressed bon vivant, designed the rally-winning Austin Healey in his attic. The Healey-Austin alliance spawned one of the most successful and charismatic British sports cars of the 1950s and 1960s. After designing the Jensen-Healey, he went into retirement and died in the late 1980s.

LEE IACOCCA *(1924–)*
Originator of the Ford Thunderbird, Iacocca was a marketing genius. He saw a huge vacuum in the American youth market of the 1960s and promptly plugged it with one of the most perfectly conceived consumer products ever, the Pony Mustang.

SIR ALEC ISSIGONIS *(1906–1988)*
Alexander Issigonis, a charming, eloquent and artistic man, conceived the million-selling Morris Minor and that miracle of automotive packaging, the Mini. His basic design philosophy was always

stiff structure, independent suspension, low weight and high torque. He was knighted in 1969.

SIR WILLIAM LYONS *(1901–1985)*
An elder statesman of the British auto industry, Sir William Lyons was an inspirational engineer who single-handedly masterminded the Jaguar phenomenon. From SS100 through XK120, E-Type and XJ6, Lyons was the creator of one of the most admired marques in the world which won Le Mans five years in a row.

HEINZ NORDHOFF *(1899–1968)*
An ex-Opel executive, Nordhoff took over the war-ravaged Wolfsburg Volkswagen factory in 1948. Under his direction the Volkswagen Beetle became the largest-selling single car in the world with an estimated quarter of a million people earning their living directly from VW.

FERDINAND PORSCHE *(1875–1952)*
Son of a tinsmith, Porsche was the most versatile car engineer in history, working for Mercedes, Volkswagen, Auto Union and Cisitalia as well as designing the World War II Tiger tank. Despite creating the Beetle, one of the most famous cars in the world, his association with Hitler caused him to be imprisoned for two years by the Allies after the war.

CARROLL SHELBY *(1925–)*
A smooth-talking Texan chicken farmer and race driver, Shelby was responsible for the wild AC Cobra and Shelby Mustang. Firmly believing that there was no substitute for cubic inches, he was a seminal figure in the Sixties' American muscle car movement.

INDEX

ACKNOWLEDGMENTS

DORLING KINDERSLEY WOULD LIKE TO THANK THE FOLLOWING:
Helen Stallion for picture research; Mick Hurrell for setting the editorial ball in motion; Maryann Rogers of production for overseeing the book in its early stages; Colette Ho for additional design assistance; Ken McMahon of Pelican Graphics for a superb electronic retouching job; Gerard Maclaughlan, Cangy Venables, Tracie Lee, Sharon Lucas and Annabel Morgan for additional editorial assistance; Daniel McCarthy for additional DTP assistance; Clive Webster and Miriam Sharland for additional picture research; Kilian and Alistair Konig of Konig Car Transport for vehicle transportation and invaluable help in locating cars; Steve at Trident Recovery; Jenny Glanville at Plough Studios; Ashley Straw for assisting Matthew Ward; Garry Ombler, Andy Brown and Sarah Ashun for assisting Andy Crawford; George Solomonides for help with locating images; Antony Pozner at Hendon Way Motors for helpful advice and supply of nine cars; Phillip Bush at Readers Digest, Australia for supervising the supply of the Holden; Derek Fisher; Bill Medcalf; Terry Newbury; John Orsler; Paul Osborn; Ben Pardon; Derek Pearson; Peter Rutt; Ian Smith; John Stark; Richard Stephenson; Kevin O' Rourke of Moto-technique; Rob Wells; Colin Murphy; Bill McGarth; Ian Shipp; Jeff Moyes of AFN Ltd; Rosie Good of the TR Owners Club; Bob and Ricky from D.J. Motors; Acorn Studios PLC; Straight Eight Ltd; Action Vehicles of Shepperton Film Studios and John Weeks of Europlate for number plate assistance; and Peter Maloney for compiling the index. Ron Stobbart for jacket design.

DORLING KINDERSLEY WOULD LIKE TO THANK THE FOLLOWING FOR ALLOWING THEIR CARS TO BE PHOTOGRAPHED:

Page 20 courtesy of Anthony Morpeth; p. 22 A J Pozner (Hendon Way Motors); p. 24 Louis Davidson; p. 26 Richard Norris; p. 28 Brian Smail; p. 30 Desmond J Smail; p. 32 David and Jon Maughan; p. 36 restored and owned by Julian Aubanel; p. 38 courtesy of Austin-Healey Associates Ltd, Beech Cottage, North Looe, Reigate Road, Ewell, Surrey, KT17 3DH; p. 40 Tom Turkington (Hendon Way Motors); p. 42 courtesy of Mr Willem van Aalst; p. 46 A J Pozner (Hendon Way Motors); p. 50 Terence P J Halliday; p. 52 L & C BMW Tunbridge Wells; p. 54 "57th Heaven" Steve West's 1957 Buick Roadmaster; p. 56 Stewart Homan, Dream Cars; p. 58 Garry Darby, American 50's Car Hire; p. 62 Benjamin Pollard of the Classic Corvette Club UK (vehicle preparation courtesy of Corvette specialists D.A.R.T Services, Kent, UK); p. 66 car owned and restored by Bill Leonard; p. 68 on loan from Le Tout Petit Musée/Nick Thompson, director Sussex 2CV Ltd; p. 70, 72 courtesy Classic Restorations; p. 76 Derek E J Fisher; p. 78 Daimler SP 250 owned by Claude Kearley; p. 82 Steve Gamage; p. 84 Kevin Kay; p. 88 D Howarth; p. 90 Lewis Strong; p. 92 Neil Crozier; p. 94 owned and supplied by Straight Eight Ltd (London); p. 104, 106, 108 A J Pozner (Hendon Way Motors); p. 105 Dr Ismond Rosen; p. 110 by kind permission of J A M Meyer; p. 112 Janet & Roger Westcott; p. 114 Stu Segal; p. 116 Teddy Turner Collection; p. 118 Stewart Homan, Dream Cars; p. 120 Max & Beverly Floyd; p. 124 Bell & Colvill PLC, Epsom Road, West Horsley, Surrey KT24 6DG, UK; p. 128 Gordon Keeble by kind permission of Charles Giles; p. 132 David Selby; p. 134 Jeff Hine; p. 136 c/o Hendon Way Motors; p. 140 owner Phil Hester; p. 144 John F Edwins; p. 146 privately owned; p. 148 A R J Dyas; p. 150 courtesy of Ian Fraser, restoration Omicron Engineering, Norwich; p. 152 courtesy of Martin Cliff; p. 154 Geoff Tompkins; p. 158 owner Phillip Collier, rebuild by Daytune; p. 160 Alexander Fyshe; p. 162 Edwin J Faulkner; p. 164 Irene Turner; p. 170 Mrs Joan Williams; p. 172 courtesy of Chris Alderson; p. 174 John Venables; p. 175 John Watson, Abingdon-on-Thames; p. 176 Martin Garvey; p. 178 E.J. Warrilow saved this car from the scrapyard in 1974; restored by the owner in 1990, maintaining all original panels and mechanics; winner of many concourse trophies; p. 182 NSU Ro80 1972 David Hall; p. 183 Panhard PL17 owned by Anthony T C Bond, Oxfordshire, editor of "Panoramique" (Panhard Club newsletter); p. 184 Nick O'Hara; p. 186 Alan Tansley; p. 188 owner Roger Wait, Backwell, Bristol; p. 190 courtesy of Peter Rutt; p. 192 owner Mr P G K Lloyd; p. 194 c/o Hendon Way Motors; p. 196 Richard Tyzack's historic rally Alpine; p. 198 owned by Ian Shanks of Northamptonshire; p. 202 David C Baughan; p. 204 Julie A Lambert (formerly Julie A Goldbert); p. 206 Peter Matthews; p. 207 Lord Raynham of Norfolk; p. 208 E A W Holden; p. 210 Brian Burgess; p. 212 Nick Hughes & Tim Smith; p. 216 Roy E Craig; p. 218 Kevin Price, Volvo Enthusiasts' Club.

PHOTOGRAPHIC CREDITS

t= top b= bottom c= center l= left r= right a= above

All photography by Andy Crawford and Matthew Ward except:
Linton Gardiner: pp. 64–65, 114–115
National Motor Museum: pp. 11t, 13b, 167c, b
Nick Goodall: pp. 15br, 22cr, 38c, 79tl, tr, 118r, 128t, 132t, 135tc, 166tl, tr, 167t, cr, 168cr, 180t, 181tr, 185c, 190tr, 195cr, 206cr, 208cr, 222–23, 224
Clive Kane: 130–31

PICTURE CREDITS

AC Cars: 8t. Adams Picture Library: 56tr. Advertising Archives: 8b; 54cl; 118tr; 135tr; 200tr, b; 223t. Aerospace Publishing: 3; 48tl, tr, cl, cr; 48–49; 49t, cl, cr; 76tr, cr; 76–77; 77tl, tr, cl, crb; 90tl, tr, cl, cr; 90–91; 91t, cr, crb, 94cl, cr; 94–95; 95t, cl, cr, crb; 96c, b; 97b; 102t, cl, crb, 103tl, tr, c, b; 138t, 138tl, ca, cb; 138–139; 139tr, cl, cr; 145t, cra, clb, crb, b; 148c; 148tr; 148–149; 149tl, tr, cl, cr; 166cl; 167cla, crb; 168b; 169b; 207cl, cr, b. Allsport: 2; 123tr; Allsport/Mike Pavell: 192tr. Art Directors: 137cb. Autosport Photographic 35tr; Doug Baird: 40cl, b. Bell & Colvill 125tl; BMW : 50tr; 52tr. British Film Institute: *Back to the Future*/Copyright © by Universal City Studios, Inc. Courtesy of MCA Publishing Rights, a Division of MCA Inc. All Rights Reserved 88tr. Neill Bruce: 9t; 20bl; 26cr; 30tr; 44t; 66tr; 70tl; 79t; 106tr; 107crb; 110tr; 142tl; 176tr; 208t; 224b. Neill Bruce/Peter Roberts Collection 14t; 37br; 38cr; 45t; 60c; 61tl, c; 70tl; 80t; 86t; 87tl; 168tl; 169tl, tr; 215tr. *Classic and Sportscar*: 141clb; 155c. Ford Motor Company: 114cb; 127tr. General Motors/Pontiac Division: 190tr. Gordon Keeble Cars: 128t. Ronald Grant Archive: *The Living Daylights*/Danjaq 31cr; *Pink Cadillac*/Malpaso 59cl; *Bullit*/Warner Brothers Pictures 92tr; *Smokey and the Bandit*/Raspar 188tr. Haymarket Publishing: 12c; 28tr; 94tr. David Hendley: 177cr. Eddy Holden: 208clb. Hulton Deutsch Collection: 81t; 97t; 215tl; 220tr. Jaguar Cars: 143cr. LAT Photographic: 126tr. Ludvigsen Library: 42c; 85tr; 123tc; 140ct; 202c; 214t. Mathewson Bull: 213tr. Mercedes Benz: 166tl, tr; 167t, cr; 168cr; 222b. Don Morley: 35tl; 87tr; 162tr. National Motor Museum/Motoring Picture Library: 9b; 22tr; 26tr; 47c; 50cr; 58tr; 62bl; 64bl; 70tr; 73tl, crb; 79cl; 80c; 81c, 96t, 98tr, cr; 99cra; 101tl; 104cra; 113cr; 114bl; 121ct; 122tr; 123tl; 126c; 136cl; 139tl; 152tr; 156t; 166–167; 167cl; 181tl; 182cra; 184tr; 192cr; 194ca; 204tr; 210tr, cra. Peugeot: 185ca; 221b; Phillip Porter: 142tr. Popperfoto :124cl. Quadrant Picture Library: 10t; 11b; 12t; 17b; 18b; 26cl; 34t; 62tr; 74t; 75t; 76cl; 91cl; 112tr; 127c; 140tr; 143tl; 157tl, tr; 182 cla; 198tr, cr; 208cra; 212tl, tr. Readers Digest: 130tl, tr, ct, cl, cr; 131tl, tc, ca, cb, b. Rex Features: 100t; 101tr; 168tr; 201tr. Triumph: 15br; 208crb. Richard Tyzack: 196c. Volvo UK Ltd: 218cr; 219cb. Matthew Ward: 10b; 12b.

NOTE

Every effort has been made to trace the copyright holders. Dorling Kindersley apologizes for any unintentional omissions and would be pleased, in such cases, to add an acknowledgment in future editions.